Enhancing Personal, Social and Health Education

Enhancing Personal, Social and Health Education offers an accessible and thought-provoking approach to developing effective practice in PSHE. The book uses case study examples to offer insights and reflections that will support practitioners developing work in their own schools.

The authors begin by examining the national PSHE framework and guidelines and outlining the essential ingredients of effective practice. Subsequent chapters provide case study examples of PSHE practice in primary and secondary schools and broader whole school initiatives. The book offers many useful ideas for planning and teaching PSHE, but also raises fundamental questions about policy at national and local levels and the extent to which current guidance is helpful and supportive.

It will be essential reading for all teachers committed to nurturing the personal and social development of their students.

Sally Inman is Head of the Division of Education and Director of the Centre for Cross Curricular Initiatives at South Bank University.

Martin Buck is Headteacher of Lister Community School in the London Borough of Newham.

Miles Tandy is a Teacher Adviser for Creative and Cultural Education with Warwickshire Educational Development Service.

School Concerns Series
Edited by Peter Blatchford
Institute of Education, University of London

This topical new series addresses key issues that are causing concern in schools. Each book is based around a case study school which is used to illustrate and contextualise best practice whilst showing the real implications of current research on the everyday classroom.

The books provide an innovative and accessible approach to dealing with the inclusive classroom and are written by leading names in their respective fields. They will be essential reading for teachers, heads of department, headteachers and policy-makers determined to address the key concerns in education today.

Supporting Inclusive Education
Jenny Corbett

Educating Children with Emotional and Behavioural Difficulties
John Thacker, Dave Strudwick and Elly Babbedge

Bullying
David Thompson, Sonia Sharp and Tiny Arora

Enhancing Personal, Social and Health Education
Sally Inman, Martin Buck and Miles Tandy

Underachievement in Schools
Anne West

Enhancing Personal, Social and Health Education

Challenging Practice, Changing Worlds

Edited by
Sally Inman, Martin Buck
and Miles Tandy

RoutledgeFalmer
Taylor & Francis Group

LONDON AND NEW YORK

First published 2003
by RoutledgeFalmer
11 New Fetter Lane, London EC4P 4EE

Simultaneously published in the USA and Canada
by RoutledgeFalmer
29 West 35th Street, New York, NY 10001

RoutledgeFalmer is an imprint of the Taylor & Francis Group

© 2003 Sally Inman, Martin Buck and Miles Tandy

Typeset in Goudy by
Keystroke, Jacaranda Lodge, Wolverhampton
Printed and bound in Great Britain by
TJ International Ltd, Padstow, Cornwall

British Library Cataloguing in Publication Data
A catalogue record for this book is available from the British Library

Library of Congress Cataloging in Publication Data
Enhancing personal, social, and health education : challenging
practice, changing worlds / [edited by] Sally Inman, Martin Buck,
and Miles Tandy.
 p. cm. – (School concerns series)
 Includes bibliographical references and index.
 1. Life skills–Study and teaching. 2. Moral education.
3. Health education. 4. Interdisciplinary approach in education.
I. Inman, Sally. II. Buck, Martin. III. Tandy, Miles. IV. Series.

LC268 .E63 2003
370.11v5v0941–dc21   2002031751

ISBN 0–415–25042–0 (pbk)
ISBN 0–415–25041–2 (hbk)

Contents

Figures and tables

Figures

Tables

The authors

Martin Buck is Headteacher of Lister Community School in the London Borough of Newham. He was previously Headteacher of Harrow High School and has been an LEA inspector for Humanities. He has worked in London schools for over 25 years. He is co-author (with Sally Inman) of *Adding Value*, Trentham Books, 1995, and (with Sally Inman and Helena Burke) *Assessing Personal and Social Development*, Falmer Press, 1998. He has worked closely with the Centre for Cross Curricular Initiatives since 1991 and is a member of the management committee for the centre.

Sally Inman is Head of the Division of Education and Director of the Centre for Cross Curricular Initiatives at South Bank University. Her publications include *Adding Value*, Trentham Books, 1995 (with Martin Buck), *Shaping a Better Future – Development Education within Initial Teacher Training*, Oxfam Publications, 1997 (with Ros Wade), *Assessing Personal and Social Development*, Falmer Press, 1998 (with Martin Buck and Helena Burke), *School Councils: an apprenticeship in democracy?* Association of Teachers and Lecturers, 2002.

Miles Tandy is currently Teacher Adviser for Creative and Cultural Education with Warwickshire Educational Development Service. He was previously a Deputy Headteacher in Nottingham. Miles has wide experience in arts education, particularly in the fields of drama and story telling. His publications include 'Value Development in the Early Years' in Inman, S. and Buck, M. *Assessing Personal and Social Development*, Falmer Press, 1998 and (with Joe Winston) *Beginning Drama 4–11*, David Fulton, 1998.

The contributors

Andrew Bell is the Project Officer for Global Footprints, a project involving eight Development Education Centres across the UK. He was previously a Key Stage 2 teacher for eight years in an inner city, multicultural school, in London. He is also a freelance writer and his publications include travel articles on visits to countries of the South including Malawi and Bangladesh and reviews of citizenship resources for the Times Educational Supplement. He is currently commissioned by the Development Education Association to update and develop their global citizenship education website.

Anna Douglas is a Lecturer in Citizenship Education at the Institute of Education. She was previously the Social Science PGCE tutor at Goldsmiths College. She is currently involved in research exploring the way in which the political literacy strand within Citizenship Education is being delivered. Her publications include: (2000) 'Constraints on the teaching of social and ethical issues arising from biomedical research: a view across the curriculum in England and Wales', jointly written with Ralph Levinson *et al.*, Melbourne Studies in Education Year 2000, Volume (2000) *Learning as participation in social practices: interpreting student perspectives on learning, Changing English* Vol. 7, No. 2 (1999), 'They know more than they think: developing political thinking through negotiating concepts', *Talking Politics* Vol. 12, No. 1. reprinted in Teaching Citizenship Issue 1, Summer 2001

Mick Goodfellow is Deputy Headteacher of Park Lane Primary School, Nuneaton.

Jan Hamilton is Headteacher of Park Lane Primary School, Nuneaton.

Anne Hudson is Assistant Headteacher and Citizenship Coordinator at Deptford Green School. She has previously taught in a number of

London secondary schools and before that worked as a volunteer in Namibia. She is currently undertaking research into indicators for citizenship education.

Gill Pooley is Senior Teacher and Head of Faculty at Sydenham School. Her publications include *Moving Images in the Classroom* for BGI and Film Education and 'Researching Assessment Practice in PSE' in Inman, S., Buck, M. and Burke, H. (1998) *Assessing Personal and Social Development*, Falmer Press.

Nola Turner taught on the PGCE Secondary course at Goldsmiths College for many years. Recently she has worked on the Hackney Anti-Bullying Project and (with Sally Inman) on the evaluation of the Tower Hamlets 'Confronting Conflict' Project. She has a long-standing interest in behaviour management.

Gill Winston is in her third year of headship at Stockton Primary School, Warwickshire. She has been deputy of two infant schools and spent many years before that teaching throughout the primary age range. In September 2002 Gill became headteacher of a large primary school in Devon.

Jenny Wood is in her third year of teaching. She is Curriculum Area Leader for PSHE and Work Related Learning at Eltham Green School.

Acknowledgements

We should like to acknowledge all those teachers and young people who have been involved in developing the curriculum practice described in this book. They are too many to name here, but their contribution has been central to the shaping of our ideas.

Thanks to the Association of Teachers and Lecturers for allowing a shortened and amended version of 'School councils: an apprenticeship in democracy' to be used in the book. Also to Tower Hamlets Education for giving us permission to use the evaluation study as a basis for the chapter on conflict resolution.

Thanks to those teachers, advisers and NGOs who have given support to the Centre for Cross Curricular Initiatives over many years. Their continuing commitment to our work has proved invaluable. Thanks also to Alison Hatt for her able administration during the writing of the book.

Finally, thanks to the Toddington Service Station on the M1 for unknowingly providing the space for us to meet to put this book together. Countless hours were spent there without our cars being towed away.

Series Editor's preface

This is a stimulating and timely book. There is a current unease, shared by many, that the overriding concern with academic targets and school improvement, risks missing out an important pat of children's education. The future health of the country obviously depends on skilled and knowledgeable people, but it also depends on citizens who are able to engage productively at personal, local and national levels. The authors are successful in showing just how important is the personal and social development of children, and how it should be central to the work of all schools.

The chapters in this book cover a number of topics: sexual relations, global citizenship, conflict resolution, school councils, emotional literacy, use of drama, whole school approaches. It is relevant to both primary and secondary schools, and deserves a wide readership. The book works well at several levels. It is seeped in the experiences and practicalities of school life – it is written by authors with first hand experience of school practice. The authors have a keen eye for the rights and the voices of young people. One of the central and, for me, exciting themes is personal change: a concern with changing attitudes of pupils and developing understanding of relationships. But the book also explores issues involved in the successful teaching of PSHE and Citizenship, and the links between this and involvement in communities and more global issues. The book is also successful in showing how school improvement and governance can be informed by a commitment to personal and social development and citizenship. As the editors say in their preface, the book is about PSHE but also about the kinds of schools we want for our young people. At a time of civic disengagement and personal insecurities the authors' concerns have never been more relevant.

Peter Blatchford

Preface

This book is concerned with Personal, Social and Health Education practice in primary and secondary schools. Developing effective practice in current contexts is challenging for practitioners. Although the revised English National Curriculum (Curriculum 2000) gives a greater and more explicit place to PSHE and Citizenship, for school leaders and classroom teachers this can seem like yet another thing to add to their long list of jobs to be done and expectations to be met. Against a background of central government policy and rhetoric that is primarily concerned with standards and school improvement, the need to develop effective practice in PSHE and Citizenship could all too easily slide down the agenda. Yet the contributors to this book share a belief that the personal and social development of young people should be central to the purpose of schools, and that effective practice in PSHE plays a critical role in fulfilling that purpose.

In current education rhetoric, 'challenging' is too often used as a euphemism for the downright difficult. But the word need not have such negative connotations. Much of the practice described in this book is deliberately challenging for the teachers and young people concerned. It is practice that expects young people and their teachers to confront issues in ways that enable them to question the taken for granted, to make connections between the personal and the social and political, to understand and explore their own emotions, and to locate themselves in changing worlds at personal, local, national and global levels.

Challenging practice may mean challenging policy. Much of the practice described in this book raises fundamental questions about policy at national and local levels and the extent to which current guidance is helpful and supportive. Our intention is to provide a book that describes effective practice and uses that practice to explore theoretical and policy issues. In common with our previous work we are attempting to situate contributions to the book at a theory/ practice interface. Whilst we are confident that the reader will find many useful ideas for planning and teaching PSHE, the book is quite deliberately not a handbook for PSHE and citizenship co-ordinators.

The book relies heavily on the voices of young people and the adults with whom they work. This is intentional and reflects our belief that we have much to learn from voices of young people, especially in relation to their own learning. In addition, we make a strong argument throughout the book for the rights of young people to be heard, and we are attempting to model that practice in the writing of the book. In setting up the case studies we have attempted to enable people to tell a story of practice, unfinished and sometimes problematic. The contributors represent a range of practice, experience and interests but share a common commitment to the personal and social development of all young people.

In Chapter 1 we set a context for the case studies of practice that follow. We distinguish between PSHE and personal and social development (PSD) and provide a rationale for this distinction. We examine the national PSHE framework and guidelines and raise some issues about intellectual rigour, separation of PSHE and citizenship, the usefulness of the framework as a planning tool. We then set out some of the essential ingredients of effective PSHE practice. Finally we explore some of the elements of whole school approaches to PSD raising issues around coherence across the many initiatives; the links schools have with their communities and the centrality of ethos to effective practice.

Chapters 2, 3 and 4 provide case studies of PSHE curriculum practice in primary and secondary schools. In Chapter 2 Jenny Wood describes the planning and teaching of a course in sex and relationships for Year 8 pupils as part of the PSHE curriculum. She describes how the views of the young people in the school were taken into account in the planning and teaching of the course. She points to the continuing importance of making relationships, or what the young people call 'the stuff around it', central to all sex education. In Chapter 3 Andrew Bell describes Global Footprints, a European Union and Department for International Development funded project involving primary schools across the UK and European and Southern partners. The project is concerned with promoting global citizenship and sustainable development in primary schools. Andrew Bell explores how, through cross-curricular work and whole school initiatives we can help to challenge attitudes and raise young people's awareness and understanding of global issues.

In Chapter 4 Gill Pooley describes a PSHE scheme of work on rights and responsibilities for Year 10 students. The work forms part of the new

GCSE Citizenship Studies and provided an opportunity for the teachers to strengthen the connections between the personal, social and the political. The case study demonstrates a pedagogy that is engaging and demanding of students. The young people talk eloquently about what they have learned from the work, their voices reveal a sophisticated understanding of how they have been challenged to review their attitudes and reconsider their views of the world.

Chapters 5, 6, 7 and 8 provide case studies of broader whole school initiatives around personal and social development. In Chapter 5 Sally Inman and Nola Turner provide an account of conflict resolution projects in a number of secondary schools in the London Borough of Tower Hamlets. They use the understandings and voices of the young people and adults involved in the work to make a strong case for the potential of conflict resolution to contribute to the personal and social development of young people. However, they also point to the need to embed this kind of work firmly in routine school practice, in particular the need for conflict resolution skills and attitudes to be fostered through the PSHE curriculum.

Chapter 6 focuses on the contribution that school councils can make to broad citizenship and PSD. Drawing on a research study of school councils Sally Inman provides some case studies of effective practice in primary and secondary schools. She argues that there are some important defining characteristics of effective school councils, largely to do with their structure, form and scope. She also makes a case for making schools more democratic institutions, arguing that school councils can only be truly effective in contexts where the student voice is routinely respected and listened to. The focus of Chapter 7 is emotional literacy. Martin Buck describes a collaboration between Lister Community School and Antidote in which the latter is used as a 'critical friend' in a whole school initiative concerned with using the development of emotional literacy of staff and students to strengthen the role of personal and social development within learning and achievement across the school.

In Chapter 8 Miles Tandy outlines two projects in which the devising and performance of drama were central to deepening children's understanding of issues and raising their self-esteem. Miles uses these examples to explore the complex relationship between drama and self-esteem, challenging some common assumptions.

Chapters 9, 10 and 11 take the theme of whole school approaches to PSD, including PSHE and citizenship. In Chapter 9, Mick Goodfellow and Jan Hamilton explore the complexities of developing an ethos in their large primary school. Chapter 10 is the story of a small village primary school which OFSTED placed in Special Measures in 1999. In charting how dramatically the school improved, Gill Winston stresses the centrality of attending to children's personal and social development. In particular, she explores the specific interventions which were needed to listen to the views of the children, the need to demonstrate that those views counted, and the need to attend to the self-esteem of everyone involved with the school. In Chapter 11 Anne Hudson and Anna Douglas discuss the interrelated elements of developing a school for citizenship. Using the term 'community of practice' they describe how Deptford Green School has tried to create a sustained collaborative dialogue between all members of the school and community in moving forward. They explore curriculum and whole school initiatives that engage young people in important questions of local, national and global citizenship.

Chapters 12 and 13 are concerned with pulling things together and providing some coherence for schools, teachers and young people. Chapter 12 looks at the issues involved in leading and managing a school that is committed to PSHE and personal and social development. Martin Buck explores some different models of curriculum management and organisation for PSHE and PSD in primary and secondary schools and then discusses how Fullan's notions of effective school leadership might be usefully applied to the leadership of PSHE and PSD in schools. In the final chapter we consider some of the implications for future practice and policy. Drawing together a number of threads from the case studies, we explore some principles for developing effective practice at school level in the current climate. We also outline some contributions to the debate about the future shape and content of the school curriculum, indicating how many of these place children's personal and social development as a central purpose.

This book seeks to make a contribution to the discourse around PSHE and citizenship at a time of significant national developments in these areas. We believe that the descriptions of current practice offer insights and reflections that will support practitioners to develop work in their own schools. Of equal significance, the book raises questions about the relationship between PSHE, citizenship and the broader personal and social development of young people and in doing so poses some important issues around the nature of schooling, relationships and pedagogy. Thus the book is both about PSHE and the kinds of schools we want for our young people.

Sally Inman, Martin Buck and Miles Tandy

Chapter 1

Personal, social and health education: challenging practice

Sally Inman, Martin Buck and Miles Tandy

It is a warm afternoon in June. A two-day project, which involves all the Key Stage 2 (7–11) children from a small Warwickshire primary school, culminates in a performance. Teachers, teaching assistants, a midday supervisor and a governor all come to watch, but the performance is not public: the real audience is the children themselves. They represent, explore and celebrate what they have made, achieved and learned.

The work began by exploring what the children knew of the story of Tutankhamun: his life, death and burial; the discovery of his tomb by Howard Carter; stories of the 'curse'. They discussed the events surrounding the death of Lord Carnarvon and made still images to represent photographs that might have appeared on the front page of the papers at the time. To these images they added 'headlines' – sensational representations of the story – all of which alluded to 'the curse'.

Discussion then moved on to thinking about how and when Tutankhamun's mummified body and the treasures which accompanied it were first placed in the tomb. The children speculated that it was likely the events were accompanied by some kind of ceremony: they began by experimenting with carrying a PE bench from one end of their hall to another, first as if they were just moving it, then approaching and carrying it as if they were Ancient Egyptians and the bench contained the Pharaoh's body. Though few of them had ever been to a funeral, they brought their collective knowledge of ceremony and how it functions to bear on their work. They then developed their ideas further by small groups of children miming the bringing and offering of 'gifts' for the Pharaoh's afterlife. Their carefully choreographed movement culminated in a spoken tribute which took the form 'Oh mighty Pharaoh, we bring you this . . . (gift) that you might . . . (some reference to the gift's value and purpose) in the afterlife'. All the groups then brought their work to assemble the ceremony: as each group moved towards the Pharaoh's tomb another group played music to accompany them. Once their offering had been made, children took up a still shape around the sarcophagus to represent statues 'guarding' the Pharaoh. Once the last gift had been offered and the last statues were in place, the 'curse' could be spoken. The room was then plunged into darkness as the tomb was 'sealed up'.

The teacher then narrated that, 'The statues had stood guard over the Pharaoh for over three thousand years until one day there was a scratching and a scraping sound; then came a light; and behind the light came the figure of a man.' The teacher had negotiated that as she came into the space with a torch, the statutes would whisper to her as the light fell on them. The whispers ranged from 'You're going to die!' to 'Beware the curse!' to a simple 'Get out!'.

Next the group developed the idea that Carter had a dream in which he dreamt himself lying where the Pharaoh's body had, surrounded by the statues. The dream was enacted by the teacher taking the role of Carter and lying in place of the sarcophagus. The 'statues' talked to him and tried to convince him that he should leave the tomb undisturbed. Using the unlikely idea that Carter was convinced by the dream, a meeting was enacted where Carter went to Lord Carnarvon to try to convince him of the need to leave the tomb alone. The meeting was enacted using the drama device of 'forum theatre' in which the teacher took the role of Carnarvon and one of the children played Carter. As the meeting develops the child playing Carter could stop the action and seek help from her classmates – she either continued with the role and took note of their advice or offered the role to another child to continue the action. The positions the two men took were irreconcilable: rather than be asked to choose between them, the children were invited to stand along a line which represented the two extremes of removing all the treasures and leaving the tomb undisturbed. From these positions they made statements about their thoughts and feelings.

The children also used ICT to create a representation of Carter's dream. They planned and captured images using a digital camera, manipulated them using photo-editing software, recorded and manipulated sound files, and assembled the sounds and pictures using Microsoft PowerPoint. The result was a powerful, frightening evocation of the dream.

So on that June afternoon the work all comes together. The children stand in two lines down the sides of their darkened school hall. One by one groups run into the space and take up their stills representing the newspaper front pages; they shout their headlines over and over again until the sound is like a room full of competing street newspaper sellers. The sound reaches a crescendo and stops. The children return to their places and enact their burial ceremony. Rather than walk into the space, the teachers shine torches into the tomb from the four corners of the hall with an effect reminiscent of searchlights penetrating the darkness of the tomb. The whispers begin. Then comes the PowerPoint dream: as the work was developing the projector had accidentally projected the image onto the ceiling, the extreme 'keystone' effect leaving an almost coffin shaped image. The children decided to keep that for their performance. When the dream is over the children move out of their statue shapes and take up positions to make statements about the rights and wrongs of disturbing the tomb. These final statements are a moving tribute to the depth of thought that the children brought to their work and the understanding they took from it.

But where in the curriculum does such work belong? Was it history? There can be no doubt that considerable liberties were taken with historical accuracy both in the enactment of the ceremony and the events surrounding the discovery of the tomb. Drama, then? Performance was certainly the key to the way in which these children were affected by the issues that surround archaeology. ICT perhaps? The children's skills developed markedly as they made their representations of the dream, but it was not part of a planned ICT curriculum.

The work took an unashamedly cross-curricular approach. But this approach not only exploited links between subjects; the personal and social development of those children was a core purpose of the teachers who planned it. These young people were invited to engage with 'big questions' surrounding the rights and wrongs of disturbing the Pharaoh's tomb, and given the chance to be affected by these issues through a multiplicity of media and modes of expression. Throughout they needed to work collaboratively and put their work into a collective 'whole'. Their comments during and after the performance indicated that many of them were deeply affected not only by the issues that the work had raised, but also by the high quality and power of their own work.

This example of primary practice raises some important pedagogical issues that have implications, not just for how we might teach lessons as part of a Personal, Social, Health Education (PSHE) curriculum, but for how a school committed to the personal and social development (PSD) of young people might approach any teaching and learning. The approach is essentially collaborative. There is a strong sense of teacher and learners engaged in a common endeavour to explore and understand something of importance to them all. The views and contributions of all are welcomed and valued and teacher and learners feel safe to make them. The learners are subtly yet deliberately engaged with the subject matter, then encouraged to enquire further and more deeply. The learners are given time to reflect on their learning, not only through talk, but by having access to a range of other media. They use Information and Communication Technology (ICT) (and develop their ICT skills considerably) in context to support and deepen their learning. The work has a question of deep human significance – a moral question, at its heart, and the teacher uses a number of devices to make that question relevant, accessible and discussible for the young people involved. The teacher does not set out to teach the children that archaeology is right or wrong, rather to explore some questions that surround it. There are abstract concepts such as respect and justice at the heart of the work, but they are explored within contexts that are meaningful and relevant for the learners, even though those contexts are well beyond their daily experiences. The work is carefully designed to allow for a range of abilities and learning styles, allowing all the learners to begin to access the ideas at its heart. The teacher has expertise: specific skills and knowledge are needed at different times to inform and extend the learning. But she also goes through a learning process herself. She expects to be part of the learning process and recognises the complexities of the issues she raises, enjoying the experience of having her own understandings challenged and extended. We would contend that such pedagogy is essential for the effective teaching of a PSHE curriculum. But should pedagogy belong to the PSHE curriculum alone? If a school puts the personal and social development of young people at the heart of its purpose, should not all teaching and learning have these ingredients?

How do we describe the work? Is it PSHE? Is it cross-curricular work that is used to promote the children's personal and social development? Why does the question matter? You might say that as long as young people get opportunities to engage in work like this, it doesn't matter what we call it and how we place it in the curriculum. But the reality may be that many young people get few, if any, such opportunities. What we call it, how teachers understand and teach it, how it is planned for within the curriculum, what resources are directed towards it – all these matters will have a profound effect on the extent and quality of such work.

National Curriculum 2000

The revised National Curriculum (NC 2000) marks an important change for schools and teachers that are committed to making the personal and social development of their young people central to the educational purpose. For the first time in England we have, at a national level, an explicit rationale and aims for the school curriculum; moreover one in which the personal and social development of young people would seem to have the centre stage. The section in the National Curriculum handbook that describes the values, aims and purposes of the curriculum would suggest an explicit recognition by the government that the proper purpose of education is very centrally to do with the PSD of young people.

> Foremost is a belief in education, at home and at school, as a route to spiritual, moral, social, cultural, physical and mental development, and thus the well-being of the individual. Education is also a route to equality of opportunity for all, a healthy and just democracy, a productive economy, and sustainable development.
>
> (NC 2000)

> The school curriculum should promote pupils' spiritual, moral, social and cultural development and, in particular, develop principles for distinguishing between right and wrong. It should develop their knowledge, understanding and appreciation of their own and different beliefs and cultures, and how these influence individuals and societies. The school curriculum should pass on enduring values, develop pupils' integrity and autonomy and help them to be responsible and caring citizens capable of contributing to the development of a just society. It should promote equal opportunities and enable pupils to challenge discrimination and stereotyping. It should develop their awareness and understanding of, and respect for the environments in which they live, and secure their commitment to sustainable development at a personal, local, national and global level.
>
> (NC 2000)

These are bold and complex aims and purposes; to realise them in practice will be challenging for all schools. The fact that the basic structure of NC 2000 was not underpinned by such aims and purposes but added later have made this challenge more difficult, even for those schools with a central commitment to the personal and social development of the young people in their care.

The National Curriculum 2000 includes two 'new' elements or subjects in the curriculum: Personal, Social and Health Education

(PSHE) and Citizenship. There is, for the first time, a national framework for PSHE Key Stages 1–4, albeit non-statutory. Citizenship is made a statutory subject from Key Stage 3. This potentially gives PSHE a status and role within the curriculum that it has not achieved before. As the reader will be aware, the history of PSHE has largely been one of low status, especially in secondary schools, with occasional moments of prominence due largely to prevailing moral panics at any one time. We must ensure that the current prominence does not turn out to be once again a temporary response to current moral panics to do with, for example, the level of teenage pregnancies, the lack of interest in mainstream politics amongst young people, or their levels of drug use. The current national importance given to PSHE makes it critical that we, as it were, 'seize the moment' and develop a curriculum and practice that makes a real and lasting contribution to the PSD of young people.

PSHE and PSD

This book is concerned with the theory and practice of Personal, Social and Health Education (PSHE) in primary and secondary schools. However, it is not just concerned with the practice of PSHE as constituted within the taught curriculum but how such practice supports and contributes to the overall personal and social development (PSD) of young people. We believe that it is important to distinguish between PSHE and PSD. In our view the term PSHE is best used to describe that element of explicit and often discrete curriculum provision that schools construct as a specific contribution to PSD; the latter is essentially whole school and therefore the responsibility of all members of the school community. Why is the distinction so important? For us it is not just a question of terminology but is to do with how we most effectively conceptualise and organise schools so as to make young people's personal and social development central to our purpose. For us, PSHE is a necessary but not sufficient ingredient in a school's provision for PSD.

The distinction between PSHE and PSD has been often blurred in national policy and guidelines. There is a history of confusion and mixed messages around the terms. As a result national policy and guidance has often been less than helpful to schools and teachers as the terms are used with varying meanings and often as if they were interchangeable. For example, in the late 1980s during the development of the first National Curriculum HMI produced a document as part of their series Curriculum Matters (HMI 1989). This was entitled Personal and Social Education from 5 to 16. The paper set out a definition of what HMI called PSE.

> In this paper personal and social education refers to those aspects of a school's thinking, planning, teaching and organisation explicitly designed to promote the personal and social development of pupils. . . Personal and social education is concerned with qualities and attitudes, knowledge and understanding, and abilities and skills in relation to oneself and others, social responsibilities and morality. It helps pupils be considerate and enterprising in the present, while it prepares them for an informed and active involvement in family, social, economic, and civic life. It plays an important part in bringing relevance, breadth and balance to the curriculum.

More recently the same confusion of terms can be seen in some of the QCA guidance on PSHE and citizenship. For example, in 'Personal, social, health education and citizenship at Key Stages 1 and 2' (QCA 2000) we are given a definition of PSHE, derived from the report of the National Advisory Group on PSHE (National Advisory Group on PSHE 1999). The definition states that, 'PSHE comprises all aspects of schools' planned provision to promote their children's personal and social development, including wellbeing.'

Surely all aspects of schooling should be explicitly designed to promote the personal and social development of pupils? Isn't this what education is about? Should PSHE then *be* the school curriculum?

The confusion can have some unfortunate unintended consequences. On the one hand, it can lead to schools reviewing their PSHE curriculum programmes in line with the new requirements in the belief that these programmes will in themselves take care of the personal and social development of their young people. In secondary schools this has long been a danger where too often PSD has been the responsibility of PSHE rather than the responsibility of all. On the other hand, in primary schools there has been a danger of a different kind, where PSD is sometimes 'everywhere and nowhere' in that although PSD is apparently central to everything, there is a lack of explicitness about precisely when and where it happens in a planned and systematic fashion. For primary schools there is an important and different discussion to be had about the place of PSHE within the curriculum. Should it be added into the already crowded timetable as an extra 'subject'? Should individual teachers be expected to make explicit 'PSHE links' in all their curriculum planning?

The PSHE framework

One of the difficulties that schools and teachers face in planning their PSHE within a broad provision for PSD is the nature of the framework for PSHE. The framework contains both what are essentially broad PSD learning outcomes alongside more narrowly defined learning outcomes that can clearly be met within the PSHE curriculum. For example, the Key Stage 3 PSHE guidelines contains both precise areas of knowledge and skills such as 'basic emergency first aid procedures and where to get help and support' and 'basic facts and laws' alongside broad areas of learning such as 'how to empathise with people different from themselves'.

In essence, some of the learning outcomes outlined in the framework cannot be achieved through PSHE in itself but require a whole school approach in which PSHE plays a vital but clearly defined role alongside other subjects and broader school practices and structures. The guidance for PSHE and citizenship does acknowledge this and suggests that both will be best 'delivered' through a combination of discrete curriculum provision, whole school activities and through other subjects. However, it is not PSHE that is best provided through this combination of provision but PSD.

Despite these confusions we should be hopeful that more high quality and effective PSHE will become more central to the work of schools and to the experience of the young people in their care. However, there are some serious pitfalls in the current configuration of PSHE. The pitfalls revolve both around the nature of the framework and guidance for PSHE and in the separation of PSHE from citizenship from Key Stage 3 onwards. The issues are not unrelated, as we shall see.

The PSHE framework outlines the knowledge, skills and understandings to be taught (there is no explicit mention of values and attitudes though they underpin many of the statements). It describes the opportunities that young people need to develop these attributes and a summary of what young people should learn in each key stage, including subject links. The problems revolve around what is to be taught both in relation to the nature of the 'content' and in relation to curriculum planning. Whilst the non-statutory status of the framework means that, in theory, schools and teachers have the freedom to do things differently, there is a danger that, for example, the pressures of time, overcrowding of the curriculum and Ofsted inspections will encourage schools to stick largely to what is suggested in the framework. The QCA schemes of work and the flurry of handbooks and guides coming from commercial publishers, especially for citizenship, are perhaps unintentionally encouraging this.

Rigour

For us one of the significant weaknesses is the lack of rigour and critical edge in the PSHE framework. Complex and difficult issues and problems are too often reduced to simplistic, unproblematic statements, which too easily end up sounding like exaltations. As a group of PGCE students remarked when looking at the framework, 'It feels at times as if it is implying that as long as young people are taught these things they will somehow develop into "good, healthy citizens"'. For example, some of the statements within the section 'Developing a healthy, safer lifestyle' reduce complex and often fraught areas of our lives to somewhat simplistic statements about being healthier and safer.

> What makes a healthy lifestyle, including the benefits of exercise and healthy eating, what affects mental health, and how to make informed choices.
> (PSHE and citizenship framework Key Stage 2)

What is a healthy lifestyle? What exactly *does* affect mental health? These are immensely complex questions which need to be explored in ways that acknowledge the range of economic, political, social as well as personal issues that affect our health. Of course young people must be made aware of the importance of a healthy lifestyle. However, knowing what makes a healthy lifestyle is one thing, being in the economic, social or personal position to act is another. We cannot always make informed choices if we haven't the material or social means to do so. The framework has a tendency to individualise health in a way that suggests that we can stay healthy if we know certain things and practise particular skills.

In the Key Stage 1 section of the PSHE framework we are told that children should be taught 'To recognise, name and deal with their feelings in a positive way'. If only it were that simple! Naming and dealing with our feelings is a complex and lifelong struggle for most of us. Maybe the implication here is that if children are taught it before they are seven, then they will avoid this struggle in later life – one doubts this. Lived reality sometimes has a nasty way of making things more rather than less difficult.

Essentially, the framework lacks a conceptual base; the tools of analysis and critical thinking are strikingly absent from it. This leads to guidance around critical areas being presented in ways that obfuscate the complexity of the issues involved. This doesn't help young people come to terms with the issues in the context of their own lives. For example, there are many references to stereotyping, prejudice, bullying and racism. This is welcome. However, it is difficult to see how young people can understand these critical areas of oppression and learn to challenge them without developing the conceptual tools to do so. Concepts such as power, equality and justice are essential tools in understanding such issues. It is by exploring these concepts and applying them to real life situations that young people develop the knowledge and skills to challenge such thinking and behaviour.

In contrast, the national guidance for education for sustainable development (ESD) (QCA 2002), and developing a global dimension in the curriculum (DfES 2000), place importance on conceptual development. Ironically, many of the concepts provided in the guidance for these areas are central to PSHE and their inclusion would strengthen the existing PSHE framework. Table 1.1 shows the concepts for a global dimension and Table 1.2 shows the concepts for sustainable development education.

Table 1.1 Developing a global dimension in the curriculum

• Citizenship
• sustainable development
• social justice
• values and perceptions
• diversity
• interdependence
• conflict resolution
• human rights

Source: DfES (2000)

Table 1.2 ESD

• interdependence
• uncertainty and precaution
• citizenship and stewardship
• sustainable change
• quality of life
• needs and rights of future generations
• diversity

Source: DETR (1998)

The guidelines for global citizenship produced by Oxfam provide a further very useful example of a more conceptually based approach (Oxfam 1997)

A planning tool?

The framework is not a useful planning tool for PSHE. Teachers have already discovered that it does not easily lend itself to planning topics or themes in any meaningful way. In order to plan coherent PSHE provision teachers are required to take the framework apart and develop themes and topics that pick up aspects of the different areas. Teachers are well practised in these kinds of exercises and there is now some very helpful planning material emerging from NGOs, LEAs and commercial publishers. *The PSHCE Co-ordinator's Handbook*, by Noble and Hofmann, for example, is a particularly useful resource for planning (Noble and Hofmann 2002). However, it remains a matter of regret that the framework has not been designed in ways that make it more immediately usable as a curriculum-planning tool for PSHE.

PSHE and citizenship

In our view the separation of PSHE from citizenship from Key Stage 3 is a major weakness. What is PSHE if it is not about citizenship in its broadest and most meaningful sense? The separation, put together with the problematic nature of the PSHE framework, would seem once more to suggest that PSHE deals most effectively with the personal whilst citizenship deals more effectively with the public and political. With this goes another message which is that citizenship is more intellectually challenging and deals with 'hard' things whilst PSHE remains 'soft', thus replicating the long held view of many teachers and young people that PSHE is easy and can be taught by anyone. The fact that citizenship at Key Stage 3 is statutory and has attainment targets further underlines the difference in status.

We see this separation as reproducing a false and unhelpful distinction between PSHE and citizenship. As we have long argued, effective PSD provision, including PSHE and citizenship, must engage pupils at the interface of the personal and social, there must be a constant interplay between the two for effective development to take place.

> Personal and social development involves engaging pupils in thinking about, inquiring into, discussing and confronting issues

that have simultaneously, profound importance both at a deep personal level and at a societal and global level.

(Buck and Inman 1991)

The words of Mark Smith remain compelling:

> Helping people to meet developmental needs must involve education in politics and in making plain the values and assumptions that underpin their work. Personal problems and experiences can only be fully understood and acted upon when they are seen as both private troubles and public issues.
>
> (Smith 1981)

The fact that many schools are integrating citizenship within the PSHE curriculum is a hopeful sign. However, where this isn't happening there is a worrying possibility that young people will have less opportunities than they might to engage in issues in ways that enable them to see their relevance both for their personal lives and for the wider, including the global, society.

The separation has given rise to other, perhaps unintended consequences. Citizenship, with its new statutory status and assessment requirements has understandably become the focus of attention for national guidance, professional development and publishers. The flurry of activity around citizenship has not yet been seen around PSHE. Perhaps that will change as citizenship 'beds down' but if not this will give a further message to teachers about the lower status and priority to be given to PSHE.

Effective Practice in PSHE

We have been critical of aspects of the ways in which PSHE is described in the NC 2000. We have discussed the lack of rigour and critical edge and the separation of the personal from the social and political. How then would we define effective practice in PSHE? For us there are some defining characteristics of effective PSHE practice:

1   PSHE should confront, challenge and affect young people at both an intellectual and a personal and emotional level. PSHE should confront young people in a powerful way, at all these levels, enabling them to question their own and others' attitudes, views and understandings. It should have the capacity to help young people to

question, and sometimes change their worldviews. It should develop the tools whereby young people are better able to shape their own lives and 'make a difference for the better'. PSHE should foster the development of an interconnected set of knowledge and understandings, skills, values and emotional growth.

Integrating the personal and the social – 11 September 2001

The need for a balanced and integrated approach between the personal and social can be well understood by the events of 11 September 2001. This event was dramatically brought into the homes of many millions of households throughout the world. The sophisticated communication link between the USA and Europe meant that the immediacy of the event thrust schools in the front line of supporting, interpreting and making sense of the damage and loss of life. There were questions about what had happened, who was responsible and why. Schools were immediately caught up in the feelings of anger, loss, and fear. The magnitude and immediacy of the feelings of both students and staff was overwhelming. Many schools nevertheless understood their responsibility to contain the emotional response, whilst attempting to create opportunities for pupils to reflect on their own feelings and responses inside a rational framework of explanation. Schools dealt with this event in different ways. Emergency staff meetings were called in some schools to digest what was known and to gauge immediate student and staff responses. Senior staff worked with their colleagues and developed advice papers and guidance over the remaining days of that week. Numerous assemblies were held, and opportunities were provided for students to share feelings and thoughts. Many lessons were given over to making sense of what had occurred. By the second week many students had been given the opportunity to analyse media coverage of the events and their aftermath.

In many inner city multicultural schools the response was far from straightforward. This was especially the case in schools attended by a majority or large minority of Muslim pupils and staff. It became clear that there was no simple 'one world' view on the events. Emotional responses were automatically combined with social and cultural responses that were often being shaped from another continent with again the power and immediacy which satellite broadcasting brings. Muslim students in particular were being offered at the very least other versions of where responsibility lay and who might have carried out the actions in

Washington and New York. These versions encapsulated a more sceptical view and, from some quarters, hostility towards United States hegemony.

These schools were faced with an immense challenge. The challenge concerned how to establish a moral framework, including an abhorrence to the loss of life, in which to discuss the event whilst, at the same time, acknowledging the complexity of the personal, social and political motives and actions of those directly involved. Many schools in London, Birmingham, Bradford and other large diverse multicultural cities struggled to keep emotional responses and political judgements from overspilling into acts of verbal aggression and occasional violence in corridors and playgrounds. Many schools were aware of the need to work tirelessly to keep talking to their pupils and listen to them, as well as taking advice from, and working with, community groups.

Our experience of 11 September both directly, and as reported to us by friends and colleagues, was that schools played a significant role in supporting, guiding and containing emotional responses to the events and their aftermath. But they also offered a moral and political framework for individuals and groups of students to reflect upon their own feeling, attitudes and opinions around this significant world event. Inevitably some schools had a more significant impact than others, depending on the willingness of staff to engage in complex matters, and the degree of positive liaison with parents and the community which were afforded to those involved, often in different social and cultural community contexts.

There is one thing of which we are certain, no school could 'manage' this significant piece of learning by dividing the personal from the social. In our judgement this was neither possible nor desirable. This meant that the focus was sometimes on exploring the links between al Qaida and the Taliban; the different media images in newspapers and TV news coverage in Karachi and London; or with older secondary students US foreign policy in the Middle East and Afghanistan. Time was also given to dealing with anger and loss through talk, prayer and various modes of writing in support of containing what appeared at first was as the uncontainable. But at significant points this spectrum of the personal and social had to be brought together, not just for those pupils in primary schools but for older students, secondary schools and colleges. For this act, however terrible, was a human act, carried out by human beings in the name of a belief and vision of a different world. It had to be understood by other human beings, young and old, from diverse cultures and social settings and in doing so it had to be 'felt' however differently and partially.

2   Effective PSHE should be intellectually rigorous as well as personally challenging. Young people need to be able to understand and use concepts such as power, interdependence, equality, and justice as ways of making sense of the issues and problems that they explore. Issue based PSHE without such rigour is not helpful to young people as it makes it difficult for them to analyse the issues, draw comparisons and conclusions. As a result they may be more knowledgeable about the issue, but unable to locate it in historical, social and political arenas. Concepts are essential elements of the intellectual tools young people need to make sense of particular issues and to translate their understandings to other issues.

3   Effective PSHE demands a pedagogy in which young people actively participate in their own learning and experience a range of teaching and learning styles. Readers will be familiar with many of the approaches we can use to promote such pedagogy. There is also much useful current guidance for teachers on effective PSHE pedagogy. For example, the Teacher's Guide for Citizenship for Key Stages 1 and 2, 3 and 4 contains many useful ideas on how to engage young people in active learning in and out of the classroom (QCA 2002).

An effective pedagogy in which active learning is central and the teacher is also a learner will embrace a range of learning activities. These include circle time, collaborative group work; enquiry based activities including investigative research; simulation and role-play; media analysis; and community involvement of various forms. The case studies in this book provide examples of such learning activities in operation.

4   Effective PSHE is predicated on the quality of the relationships between young people and adults and between young people themselves.

At the heart of education is the relationship between teachers and learners and by extension the relationship between learners – young people themselves.

(Robinson 2001)

The way that adults behave and communicate with each other, with students and with parents send important and telling messages.

(SCC 1995)

The quality of the relationships between adults and young people within PSHE lessons is central to effective practice. The kind of PSHE we will be describing can only take place in a relationship of trust and mutual respect, and in a learning environment that enables young people to feel good about themselves (McBer 2000). If young people are to feel able to express their ideas and emotions then they must feel that the adults take what they say and feel seriously (Fielding 2001).

There are implications here for the attributes required of teachers to work in this way with young people. What kinds of knowledge, understandings and skills best enable teachers to relate to young people in the ways described above? Are these the attributes that are currently at the heart of the training process or continuing professional development? What role does the personal and social development of teachers play in enabling or hindering effective PSHE? How can teachers help young people to confront important personal and social issues if they are not confident or experienced in doing this for themselves?

PSHE and whole school PSD

Coherence

As the reader will be aware, in the lead up to NC 2000 a number of advisory groups were set up to produce recommendations around aspects of personal and social development. Thus we saw the publication of the advisory group on citizenship's report (Crick Report 1998), the advisory group for PSHE (National Advisory Group for PSHE 1999), the report of the panel on sustainable development education (The Panel for Education for Sustainable Development 1998) and All Our Futures, the report of the advisory group on creative and cultural education (DfEE / DCMS 1999).[1] In addition, a working group at the Department for International Development (DfID) was set up to work on development awareness within formal education. During this same period there was further pilot work on spiritual, moral, social and cultural development and the work on school and community values through the National Forum for Values in Education and the Community continued.[2] The range of different working groups and advisory bodies is significant in that it meant that, from the start the curriculum revision in relation to PSD was likely to reflect the political lobbying power of the various groups. Things might have been different had the ill-named Preparation for Adult Life group (PAL) been formed first to draft some overall framework to which the various aspects of PSD would contribute.

We have also seen the rise of other allied national initiatives; for example, the Healthy School Standard (Healthy School Standard

2000), thinking skills (DfEE 2000), global dimensions (QCA/DfEE 2000), sustainable development education (QCA 2002). There is a renewed concern with emotional literacy in schools (Antidote 2001) and a welcome increase of interest in a range of wider curriculum projects and strategies aimed at fostering aspects of pupils' personal and social development. We ourselves have been involved in work around school councils, peer mentoring programmes, and conflict resolution projects. Significant work is going on in schools around, for example, peer education, extra-curricular activities, and community involvement.

At one level this is exciting; PSD, including PSHE and citizenship, are central to a whole range of current national and local initiatives. However, the reality for schools is complex and contradictory. Schools are being asked to implement a range of PSD initiatives at local and national level. Some of these initiatives would seem to make claims to be *the* appropriate overall framework on which to hang other developments around PSHE and citizenship. So senior managers of schools are sometimes in a position where they feel as if they have to make choices between being predominately a healthy school, an Eco-school, an emotionally literate school, or a school committed to global citizenship, or a community school.

So whilst this is a time of high profile for PSD, PSHE and citizenship, the situation for schools is not straightforward. Schools are often left to make the decisions about what kind of whole school framework might best enable them to hang a range of what can seem quite disparate and competing initiatives. The decisions that schools make have critical implications for a whole range of school matters including curriculum organisation, time allocation, use of specialist staff, and extra curricular activities.

How can schools best respond to this situation? How can they develop more coherent whole school provision? First and foremost, schools will need to have developed an explicit curriculum direction in which PSD is central. The strength of this direction will need to be such that the school can remain 'on course' in the face of the many other initiatives that come each day. This will require commitment and collective responsibility at the highest level. Schools will need to identify some generic whole school PSD learning outcomes for their young people. This will involve identifying the knowledge, understanding, skills and attitudes that underpin a range of initiatives, including those within the PSHE framework and citizenship. There will also need to be mechanisms by which to identify and distinguish the contributions of various aspects of school provision to the overall PSD of their pupils. For example, schools will need to decide which areas of knowledge, skills and attitudes are best promoted through the taught PSHE/citizenship curriculum and which are most effectively promoted through whole school schemes such as school councils, peer mentoring, or conflict resolution programmes. These two elements are clearly not mutually exclusive approaches and will need to reinforce and complement each other in an explicit whole school approach.

The school and its communities

Effective PSD and PSHE require schools that have strong links with their communities. The PSHE framework, guidance and the citizenship programmes of study and schemes of work stress the importance of young people having opportunities to actively engage in a range of community activities. However, developing and sustaining effective community links is not unproblematic for many schools. For example, any urban school is likely to be working with a number of differing local communities, whose interests may sometimes be in conflict. The school's priorities may be perceived differently by its business community, by its religious faith communities, and by the various political groupings which surround it. Schools frequently are sites of educational and cultural conflict, in which competing demands are expressed within the broader political, local, regional, and national arena. Furthermore, some schools operate in communities that are characterised by deprivation and increased inequality. Racism and racial harassment is a regular experience for some young people and their families both in their own homes and for young people in travelling to and from school. The increased hostility towards refugees; heightened negative relationships between different groups in the community are all, in part, symptoms of this inequality as much as they are part of the daily lived experiences of many school students and teachers.

There is a danger in painting a dispiriting and negative picture of the experience of many working-class families, including those from minority ethnic backgrounds. In practice, many of these communities are involved in active work towards social change and improvement and are supported by their local schools. Nevertheless the point remains that many schools operate in difficult circumstances within communities under pressure. In these contexts active involvement within the community requires sensitive planning.

Ethos

Much has been written about the importance of school ethos both in providing coherence for PSD and in facilitating effective PSHE (SCCC 1995; Eisner 1994). Later chapters of this book have much to say about the centrality of ethos to effective practice. However, we should remind ourselves that ethos is about the lived experience of teachers as well as pupils. An ethos that reflects and promotes PSD will take the PSD of teachers as seriously as that of pupils. For example, if we seek to stress the importance of co-operation and collaboration we have to design school organisations so as to make it possible for teachers as well as pupils to collaborate with each other. If we take the student voice seriously then we must also listen to the voices of teachers and other adults within the school community. Otherwise we talk about what we cannot accomplish (Fielding 2001). Schools have discovered these complexities as they have attempted to realise their stated aims and ethos.

Conclusion

This chapter has attempted to set a context for the case studies that follow. We have argued for a PSHE practice that is emotionally and intellectually challenging, integrates the personal and the social, and is set within a whole school context in which the PSD of young people is central. The case studies explore the nature of that practice and the whole school contexts in which it can best operate.

Notes

1   It is worth noting that All our Futures was a more radical document than the others in that it suggested a complete rethink about the school curriculum.
2   The values for education and the community from the National Forum are reprinted in the NC 2000.

References

Antidote (2001) *Developing an Emotionally Literate Society*, London: Antidote.

Buck, M. and Inman, S. (1991) *Curriculum Guidance No. 1: Whole School Provision for Personal and Social Development*, Centre for Cross Curricular Initiatives, Goldsmiths College.

Crick Report (1998) *Education for Citizenship and the Teaching of Democracy in Schools*: Final Report of the Advisory Group on Citizenship, London: HMSO.

Curriculum Matters 14 (1989) *Personal and Social Education from 5–16*, London: DES/HMSO.

Department for Education and Skills (2000) *Developing a Global Dimension in the School Curriculum*, London: DfES.

DfEE / DCMS (1999) *All Our Futures: Creativity, Culture and Education*. Report of the National Advisory Committee on Creative and Cultural Education.

Eisner, E. (1994) *Ethos and Education*, Scottish Consultative Council on the Curriculum: Dundee.

Fielding, M. (2001) 'Beyond the rhetoric of student voice: new departures or new constraints in the transformation of 21st century schooling?' *Forum* Vol. 43, No. 2.

Inman, S. and Buck, M. (1995) *Adding Value*, Stoke on Trent: Trentham Books.

Inman, S., Buck, M., Burke, H. (1998) *Assessing Personal and Social Development*, London: Falmer.

McBer, H. (2000) *Research into Teacher Effectiveness*, London: DfEE.

National Advisory Group on Personal, Social and Health Education (1999) *Preparing Young People for Adult Life*, London: DfEE.

The National Curriculum (2000) London: DfEE.

National Healthy School Standard (2000) London: DfEE.

Noble, C. and Hofmann, G. (2002) *The PSHCE Co-ordinator's Handbook*, London: RoutledgeFalmer.

Oxfam (1997) *A Curriculum for Global Citizenship*, Oxford: Oxfam

The Panel for Education for Sustainable Development (1998) *Sustainable Development Education Panel Report*, Department for the Environment, Transport and the Regions, London DETR

Qualifications and Curriculum Council (2002) *Education for Sustainable Development*, London: QCA.

Qualifications and Curriculum Council (2000) *Personal, Social and Health Education and Citizenship at Key Stages 1 and 2*, London: QCA.

Qualifications and Curriculum Council (2000) *Personal, Social and Health Education at Key Stages 3 and 4*, London: QCA.

Qualifications and Curriculum Council/ Department for Education and Skills (2001) *Citizenship – a Scheme of Work for Key Stage 3*, London: QCA/DfES.

Qualifications and Curriculum Council/ Department for Education and Skills (2001) *Citizenship – a Scheme of Work for Key Stage 4*, London: QCA/DfES.

Robinson, K. (2001) *Out of Our Minds. Learning to be Creative*, Oxford: Capstone.

Scottish Consultative Council for the Curriculum (1995) *The Heart of the Matter*, SCCC.

Smith, M (1981) *Creators Not Consumers*, National Youth Bureau.

Teacher Training Agency (2002) *Qualifying to Teach, Professional Standards for Qualified Teacher Status and Requirements for Initial Teacher Training*, London: TTA.

Part I

Case studies of PSHE curriculum practice

Chapter 2

'The stuff around it': Sex and relationships education within PSHE

Jenny Wood

The national context

In June 1999 the government published a report on teenage pregnancy. The report outlined a national teenage pregnancy strategy. The government's aim is to halve conceptions to people aged under 18 by 2010 and to reduce the social exclusion of people who do become young parents.[1] The government took this step because every year there are nearly 90,000 conceptions to teenagers in England and the effects for the 56,000 young women who give birth can include poverty, unemployment, poor health and isolation.[2] In addition, the daughters born to these young women are more likely to become teenage parents themselves[3] and a cycle of social exclusion can begin. These figures are the highest in western Europe. Teenage birth rates in the UK are twice as high as in Germany, three times as high as in France and six times as high as in the Netherlands.[4]

There has been a lot of media attention about teenage pregnancy, which has put forward a range of groups that are to 'blame' for this situation, including schools, parents, health authorities, the government, young people and even the media itself. There have also been a number of conflicting arguments about the role of Sex and Relationships Education in combating the problem, with some people thinking that there is too much and others not enough. Young people themselves say that the Sex and Relationships Education they have received is too little, too late and is too focused on biology.[5] The problem is that there are many complex reasons why young people become parents.

The government acknowledges this complexity and it sets out four key problems in its report.

The report's analysis has also shown the complex set of problems that contribute to the UK's high rates of teenage conceptions and exacerbate the poor outcomes for those who do go on to give birth:

- sex education here often does not equip teenagers with the facts or with the ability to resist pressures;
- access to and knowledge of contraception is patchy;
- there are too many British teenagers who look at their prospects and see no reason not to become parents; and
- not enough is done to get those who become parents back into education and on the road to a job.[6]

The government goes on to say that 'no one group can achieve by itself a reduction in teenage pregnancy rates' and sets out a strategy to include both local and national government; health and education and housing; and a national publicity campaign.[7]

As part of this strategy funding has been given to education authorities to tackle the issue and in the borough where I work some of this funding has been passed on to schools to develop their own projects.

The local context

I teach in a borough in South East London. Schools were invited to bid for funding for specific projects. Five secondary schools made successful bids. One school decided to focus on specialist support for parents. Another decided to use parenting simulation dolls. At my school we decided to focus on sex and relationships education for Year 8 students and to design a scheme of work that would involve young people and would develop self-esteem. Funding was used to appoint a co-ordinator and to provide time and resources that would not otherwise be available. The Pregnancy Prevention Project has lasted for just over a year and has included the development, implementation and evaluation of the scheme of work.

To understand the project it is important to know something of the context of the school. I work in an 11–16 comprehensive school that is classed as 'facing challenging circumstances'. It has around 750 students, more boys than girls. More than half of the students are eligible for free school meals and a higher proportion than that are on the register of special needs.[8] Many students come from communities that have high levels of social and economic deprivation. The aspirations of our students are often low. Within the area there is a strong community feeling and many families have stayed and plan to stay in the community for years. Many students come from families where teenage pregnancies are the norm.

There is a relatively new senior management team and over the last three years the school has gone through rapid development. Many initiatives have been introduced to improve the school and it has gone from being in special measures to now being classed as low priority by HMI (March 2001). I mention this because it is directly relevant to the 'mood' of the school and therefore has relevance for anything that is part of the school. It is a very exciting place to be and everyone (staff and students alike) feel that they are contributing to something that is getting better and there is a keenness to be involved in new projects.

The project was directly linked to the aims of the school, which has raising self-esteem and involving students at its heart. This meant that it supported and was supported by a range of other initiatives in the school. One of the most significant developments within the school is the move to involve all students and staff more directly in decision-making processes. In particular, older students have been given respon-sibilities as monitors around the school; the role of the school council is being developed; and a peer supporter's scheme has been introduced. Some of these students became involved in the Pregnancy Prevention Project.

PSE is timetabled as a discreet subject and students have one 50-minute lesson per week throughout years 7–11. It has traditionally been designed and taught by the senior management team. This has a number of effects: PSE is highly regarded by senior management and students and is used as an important way of teaching and reinforcing the school ethos; there are rarely discipline issues; students enjoy the close contact they have with the senior management team; and new initiatives to establish good practice are often implemented through PSE. These factors are relevant to the outcome of the Pregnancy Prevention Project.

Students are banded according to academic achievement right across the curriculum. This is a new structure and its effects are not yet fully understood. Banding means that PSE is taught in ability groups and I have found that this affects discussions within lessons. Later on I describe how banding affected the Pregnancy Prevention Project and this is clearly an area that is worth further research.

The Pregnancy Prevention Project

The school submitted a bid to the local authority in July 2000 to develop the project. It set out the aims and objectives of the project.

Aims

- To develop awareness of the ways in which teenage pregnancy can be reduced.
- To work with outside agencies in developing assertiveness among male and female students in relation to their sexual choices.
- To build upon existing practice in the school in relation to peer supporting developing a focus on sex and relationships education.
- To develop research skills through involvement in action research.

Objectives

- To work with appropriate outside agencies and peer mentors to devise a programme of assertiveness training with a particular focus on sex and relationships education.
- To deliver the programme in tandem with peer supporters.
- To monitor, evaluate and write up the project through an action research based approach to ensure the work is sustainable for future years.
- To evaluate the project in relation to new guidance for PSHE and citizenship education.

The project started in October 2000 with my appointment as co-ordinator. Initial discussions led to further aims that I believe characterise the values of the project. These were:

- To directly involve students in the planning and development of the curriculum.
- To promote the knowledge, skills and understanding to enable students to challenge stereotypes both explicitly and implicitly. In particular, cultural differences, gender and sexuality.
- To develop the relationship skills of students including self-esteem, assertiveness, listening and negotiation.
- To incorporate a range of teaching and learning styles, using resources and materials for students of all abilities, and to incorporate literacy, numeracy and ICT.

The starting point for our Pregnancy Prevention Project was to talk to our young people about what they thought were the causes of teenage pregnancy and about their experiences of sex and relationships education. We then used this to inform the scheme of work. I welcomed the opportunity to get students directly involved in making decisions about the curriculum and they enjoyed being listened to and seeing that their opinions were noted at the beginning and end of the course.

The first step was to give questionnaires to the peer supporters. These students were very mature and had a developed understanding of the issues around sex and relationships education. They were asked at what age they thought it was appropriate for young men and women to start sexual relationships. The vast majority of students thought that it was appropriate for young people to start sexual relationships at 16 years and above. However, they thought that it was normal for young people to start sexual relationships one to two years earlier than the age they thought was appropriate. As the students were completing the questionnaires it was apparent that these students had benefited from training and time and space to develop their views about issues facing young people. I was concerned that they were not representative of students' opinions as a whole. Therefore, I gave questionnaires to the whole school through form tutors [Appendix 2.1]. This had the added benefit of giving a focus to registration time and involved form tutors in the project.

The results were very similar to those I received from the peer supporters. I looked at a range of responses from students of different ages, abilities, and responses from boys and girls. There were no significant differences in responses from these different groups.

When asked about the appropriate age for sexual activity they again said 16 and above and again put the normal age for sexual activity at one to two years earlier.

Students were also asked about why they thought that young people started sexual relationships and why young people got involved in teenage pregnancy. The response was very varied. However, few students thought that 'to get benefits' was an important reason for teenage pregnancy. Their responses would seem to demonstrate that young people are not necessarily influenced by tabloid headlines and that they thought carefully about a range of reasons.

Students were asked about their knowledge of a range of contraceptive choices. Most students had at least heard of the range of contraceptives available but few felt that they understood them. Students across the board knew more about condoms and the pill than other choices, which confirms what I would expect.

Perhaps the most interesting results came from the section where they were asked what they thought they should be taught in sex and relationships education and at what age. They were given a wide range of options and the space to add their own. Most students thought that everything should be covered at some point and were thoughtful about the age at which each topic should be taught. Many thought that sex and relationships education should start in primary school. Most students, however, thought that Year 8 was the most appropriate time for most topics. I was surprised with the awareness of students and the wide range of opinions that they held.

I then interviewed a mixture of students [Appendix 2.2]. I hoped to get qualitative rather than quantitative results and to get a feel of the attitudes held by young people and what they wanted from their sex and relationships education. Some of the students were peer supporters who were experienced speakers and listeners and some were Year 8 students who were going to be taught the course.

The students were able to describe the attitudes young people had about sex and sex and relationships education. It was these attitudes that were informative, fascinating and, at times, alarming. They were clear about what they wanted out of their relationships but were pessimistic about what actually happened.

> I think people want that lovey dovey thing where you go to each other's houses and your parents are alright with it and you like each other, you both love each other the right amount and you take each other out. I think that's what people want these days but they don't usually get it so they go for sex.

> There's peer pressure, pressure from friends. People say I've had sex and its good or whatever and you should go and do it with your boyfriend but it shouldn't work that way. It should depend on whether you want to or not.

> The first time you have sex should be special because once you lose your virginity you're never gonna get it again. It should be right 'cos it's not like the adverts 'Oh, I've lost my virginity again'.

This particular comment led to a discussion about the role of the media in young people's attitudes. One student was disappointed by the image of young mothers that soap operas give and felt that these images influenced young people.

> I think that that situation made things worse with teenage pregnancy because Sonia [Eastenders] was like 'oh, I've got a baby, I'll put it up for adoption' and some girls think 'oh, if I get pregnant I can put it up for adoption' and Sarah in Coronation Street she had a kid but it's all alright, she goes to school, she goes out 'cos her mum looks after it. My mum wouldn't look after it.

The students spoke a lot about the differences between young men and young women.

> From the boys' point of view, I've got five brothers and they say I'm gonna go out and feel a girl up. The boys just want one thing. The girls are like 'I love you so much' but my brother isn't really interested.

> With a boy it would be like yeh, go on there, but with a girl it would be like you're a slag.

> It's very hard for girls because they get pressured into doing it by their friends when their friends are lying and saying that they've done it with their boyfriend. They've got to get the time just right because if everyone else hasn't done it and they do it they become different from everyone else and if they haven't done it when everyone else has they're still different.

> Relationships are very important. If you haven't got a boyfriend it's like you're ugly, you can't get one and if you go from boyfriend to boyfriend then again, you're a slag. You can't win.

These comments on gender were particularly interesting because they didn't reflect the views shown in the quantitative results I got from the questionnaires. When talking to the young people about their experiences I found that they still felt that there were different expectations for young men and young women. However, when looking at their responses to the questionnaires these views were less apparent. When asked at what age they felt it was appropriate for young men and young women to be sexually active and at what age they felt that young men and young women were actually sexually active, students, regardless of age, gender or ability said the same ages for young men and young women. It seemed that the students wanted the attitudes towards young men and young women to be the same but that they felt that there was nothing they could do to make this happen.

The attitudes that the students outlined supported the already existing aims of the project. They brought it home to me that it was important to continually challenge gender stereotypes and to make young people feel that they can make a difference to prevalent attitudes. The interviews also confirmed that young people need training in how to get the relationships they know they want. It frightened me that the young people I spoke to seemed to be resigned to accepting the reverse of this.

The students were able to give some details about the changes they would like to see in sex and relationships education.

> They should give you more detail about sexually transmitted diseases, not just say there's this one and this one.
>
> They should tell you more about babies 'cos I've got a baby sister and it's a lot different than what you think.
>
> They should show you what a condom looks like and how to put it on.
>
> They should tell you stuff at a younger age 'cos people are having sex at a younger age so we should be taught younger.
>
> Another thing is the teacher, they shouldn't be embarrassed.
>
> In science it should be the nuts and bolts but in PSE it should be all the stuff around it.

I then got the opportunity to interview one of our young mothers who had given birth to her son six months previously and had returned to school to complete her GCSEs. Her eloquent and open account gave me a real insight into the issue of teenage pregnancy and I am sure that her account would have surprised a lot of young people who thought that it was difficult to get pregnant.

> For me I was unlucky 'cos I only ever done it once and I was caught out straightaway. Some people think you don't get pregnant just like that. For me it was harder because I'd never slept with anyone, I'd never done anything before. It was my first proper boyfriend and I was with him for a year and a half before anything happened. I slept with him once and then I fell pregnant . . . I thought I was mature enough to have sex but I wasn't mature enough to talk about it first.

She had interesting comments about her own sex and relationships education and suggestions for changes.

> I don't think they gave us enough information about actual pregnancy, they mainly focused on disease and stuff like that. I think they should have spoken to us individually, girls and boys, that's what I think they should've done because boys, they just muck around, whereas girls they take it much more seriously than the boys do. There should be more detail about children and what it would be like for children to have children . . . If I was at a young age and I was thinking, yeh, kids are easy and if someone said to me what it was really like it would change my mind.

She really wanted the opportunity to tell younger students about her situation and felt very strongly that she didn't want others to end up in a similar situation.

> I don't want to see kids going through what I'm going through now because everything I do boils down to my kid now. I would tell kids what it is really like, it's not something you can just put down, it's a lot harder. You get all emotional. You know that things are gonna change, that your friends will go out and you'll wanna go out. My mum would let me do that but I don't feel that I wanna do that now but I know that I've got a kid and I've got responsibilities now. I think I'd tell the kids that it ties you down and just messes your head up . . . When the baby came along everything changed. I got all emotional and was thinking that I didn't want the baby . . . When your friends are all going out you think I'm missing out on a lot and I'm gonna miss out on a lot . . . I think if I could've done things differently I believe I wouldn't have done it in the first place because life isn't all about sex, it's about having a life . . . Me and my boyfriend, we were getting on okay before the baby was born, we were really close and everything, but as soon as the baby came along there was arguments and we just broke up. I didn't keep the baby because I thought he'd stay with me, I kept the baby because it was my mistake. But if I knew what I knew now I wouldn't have kept the baby.

This young woman told me how she had been alarmed by the numbers of other young women who had approached her when she was pregnant, and who had been excited about the prospect. She had also been approached by a number of young women who feared they were in the same situation. They had chosen to talk to her rather than anyone else in the school. She made the issue real and there was nothing glamorous about her story.

We planned for her to talk to groups of students as part of the curriculum. In the end her situation became more complicated and she was unable to do this. I have no doubt that this sort of peer contact would be very valuable and perhaps the most effective way of reducing teenage pregnancies. However, it is very likely that there will be practical problems with this sort of peer contact, which makes it very difficult for PSE teachers to incorporate real life examples into the curriculum. In the end, I used published, written accounts of young people. These were useful but lacked the impact of having a local teenage mother who could answer students' questions.

The Lessons

The voices of these students informed both the values and the content of the scheme of work. The scheme of work aimed to develop relationship skills, such as assertiveness, listening and negotiation and to develop knowledge and understanding of puberty, sexual organs, self-esteem, motivations for sexual activity, relationships, contraception, the effects of early sexual relationships and in particular teenage pregnancy. See Table 2.1 for scheme of work.

The first two lessons were designed to equip students with the tools they would need for the rest of the course. Lesson 1 established ground rules for the group and revised knowledge of sexual organs and terminology. Lesson 2 looked at self-esteem, with the aim of providing a core message about how to ensure we are able to make positive choices.

The next two lessons were designed to get students to think about the relationships they wanted and the choices they wanted to make within those relationships. Lesson 3 examined why young people embark on sexual relationships and reinforced the message about positive choices. The lesson looked at pressures surrounding sexual activity and set up alternative choices for young people. Lesson 4 examined what makes a good relationship and emphasised that students should choose a good relationship and not end up in a bad one.

The next three lessons were designed to empower students to put into practice the choices they wanted to make. Lesson 5 gave students the space to practice, through role play, different relationships skills. Lesson 6 and 7 gave students information about contraception and how to access sexual health services.

The next two lessons looked at the possible effects of a sexual relationship and the effects that not making positive choices can have. Lesson 8 asked students to think about the choices that come out of different situations. Lesson 9 focused on teenage pregnancy and the experiences of young parents. The final lesson allowed students to reflect on what they had learnt and gave them space to get any unanswered questions answered.

The lessons were designed in a way in which students would first learn about and discuss issues as a whole class or in small groups. They then got the chance to reflect on the issue in terms of their own lives. This was accomplished through a student diary that contained worksheets to guide them through thinking about the issues.

All the lessons and the materials produced were designed to tackle stereotypes and to develop students' understanding of equal opportunities issues. This was done explicitly through discussions. For example, in Lesson 3 students discussed gender stereotypes and double standards when looking at young people's motivations for sexual activity.

Stereotypes were also challenged implicitly, particularly through the examples used in scenarios. In Lesson 2, when looking at the issue of self-esteem students were given five scenarios about different stages of a relationship (Figure 2.1). They were asked to discuss possible outcomes and to think about which outcomes would enhance self-esteem and which would undermine self-esteem.

In the third scenario when one young person wants a relationship to become more sexual, it is 'Ellie' who wants the relationship to progress and 'John' who does not. I think that this implicit challenge of gender stereotypes is important in encouraging young men and women to feel more comfortable about their own experiences and challenges the impression that the students had that it is okay for young men to be sexually active and not okay for young women.

I think it is important to explore why young people still feel that there are double standards imposed on them when they don't agree with those double standards themselves. It is also important that teacher responses to questions asked by young people continually challenge stereotypes by giving answers that are relevant to all students.

The examples used in scenarios were also important in challenging students' attitudes about sexuality. In the second and fourth scenarios non-gender specific names were used so that students could make their own conclusions about the sexuality of the couples. I had expected students to assume that the couples were heterosexual but they asked immediately whether they were boys or girls. I responded by asking them

Table 2.1 Sex and relationships education scheme of work Year 8

Underlying objectives: To provide factual information to enable positive relationships; to give students the opportunity to reflect on skills to negotiate positive relationships

Topic	Objectives	Activities	Citizenship knowledge and skills	PSHE guidelines
Revision of puberty and sexual organs	To establish groundrules for Sex and Relationships Education. To develop their understanding of what is required for a safe atmosphere and group cohesiveness. To revise their knowledge from Year 7 on sexual organs. To know and understand the language that will be used throughout the unit.	*Lesson 1* Circle time. Teambuilding game. Something they have learnt/ something they would like to learn. Labelling giant diagrams of sexual organs and functions. List alternative language and establish terminology. *Student diary worksheet* 'Talking about sex'	Students should be taught: To contribute to group and exploratory class discussions, and take part in debates (2c). To reflect on the process of participating (3c).	Students should be taught: To recognise the physical and emotional changes that take place at puberty and how to manage these changes in a positive way (2a). To communicate confidently with their peers and adults (3k). Students should be given the opportunity: To develop relationships (4f).
Self-esteem	To understand the meaning of self-esteem. To identify factors that enhance and undermine self-esteem.	*Lesson 2* Group discussion on what self-esteem is, what affects it and what effects it has.	Students should be taught: To contribute to group and exploratory class discussions, and take part in debates (2c).	Students should be taught: To recognise how others see them, and be able to give and receive constructive feedback and praise (1c).

	Learning objectives	Activities		Teaching content
	To consider how self-esteem affects our behaviour. To think about how different responses enhance and undermine self-esteem in relationships.	Group work on Relationship Scenarios what outcomes enhance/undermine self-esteem. Reinforcement of self-esteem from teacher and peers. *Student diary worksheet* 'My self-esteem'.	To reflect on the process of participating (3c).	How to deal positively with the strength of their feelings in different situations (1d). To recognise that goodwill is essential to positive and constructive relationships (3h). To communicate confidently with their peers and adults (3k). Students should be given the opportunity: To feel positive about themselves (4b). To develop relationships (4f).
Why do young people have sex?	To identify and evaluate different motives teenagers have for sexual relationships. To understand gender stereotypes in relation to sexuality and the influence they have on behaviour. To reflect on personal views of stages of stages in a relationship.	*Lesson 3* Brainstorm of motives for early sexual activity. Class discussion of positive and negative motivations and alternatives to early sexual activity. Discussion about gender stereotyping in sexual activity. Completion of Double Standards Sheet. *Student diary worksheet* 'Which floor do you want to stop at?'	Students should be taught: about the diversity of identities in the UK and the need for mutual respect and understanding (1b). To think about topical moral, social and cultural issues and problems (2a).	Students should be taught: about the effects of stereotyping and prejudice and how to challenge them assertively (3a). To recognise the stages of emotions and how to deal positively with their feelings in the context of the importance of relationships, about human reproduction, contraception, STDs, HIV and high risk behaviours including early sexual activity (1d, 2e). To recognise some of the cultural norms in society, including the range of lifestyles and relationships (3d).

continued

Table 2.1 continued

Topic	Objectives	Activities	Citizenship knowledge and skills	PSHE guidelines
Relationships	To identify elements of a good relationship. To develop listening skills. To revise concepts and practise skills of negotiation and assertiveness in relationships. To practise how to say 'no'.	*Lesson 4* Class consensus exercise on the elements of a good relationship/partner. *Student diary worksheet* 'My Ideal Partner'. *Lesson 5* Role Play using what has been learnt about assertiveness, self-esteem and the elements of a good relationship. *Student diary worksheet* 'My body, my feelings, my choice'.	Students should be taught: To reflect on the process of participating (3c)	Students should be taught: How to negotiate within relationships, recognising that actions have consequences, and when and how to make compromises (3i). To recognise the stages of emotions and how to deal positively with their feelings in the context of the importance of relationships, about human reproduction, contraception, STDs, HIV and high risk behaviours including early sexual activity (1d, 2e). To recognise when pressure from others threatens their personal safety and well-being and to develop effective ways of resisting pressure (2g).

		Students should be taught	Students should be taught
Contraception	To understand where to get, how to use and the advantages and disadvantages of the main contraceptives available to young people. To receive information on sexual support services. To practise negotiating safe sex.	*Lesson 6* Visit from school nurse to show different methods of contraception and sexual health services. *Lesson 7* Consolidate understanding of contraception through 'Contraception Reaction Sheet'. Role play. *Student diary worksheet* 'Who's out there?'	Students should be taught: about the diversity of identities in the UK and the need for mutual respect and understanding (1b).	Students should be taught: To recognise and manage risk and make safer choices about healthy lifestyles (2f). To recognise the stages of emotions and how to deal positively with their feelings in the context of the importance of relationships, about human reproduction, contraception, STDs, HIV and high risk behaviours including early sexual activity (1d, 2e).
Effects of a sexual relationship	To identify some of the problems with having a sexual relationship. To examine images of teenage parents. To understand the impact of being involved with a teenage pregnancy.	*Lesson 8* Brainstorm effects of a sexual relationship. Completion of 'Life Choices' diagram to think about possible choices if a sexual relationship goes wrong. *Student diary worksheet* Images of teenage parents.	Students should be taught: To think about topical moral, social and cultural issues and problems (2a).	Students should be taught: To recognise the stages of emotions and how to deal positively with their feelings in the context of the importance of relationships, about human reproduction, contraception, STDs, HIV and high risk behaviours including early sexual activity (1d, 2e).

continued

Table 2.1 continued

Topic	Objectives	Activities	Citizenship knowledge and skills	PSHE guidelines
		Lesson 9 Circle time on attitudes about parenthood. Reading accounts of being involved in a teenage pregnancy and list effects on everyone concerned. *Student diary worksheet* 'Teenage parents'		
Evaluation	To reflect on learning throughout the term.	*Lesson 10* Evaluation *Student diary worksheet* 'Dear Exxo Xtra Terrestrial'	Students should be taught: To reflect on the process of participating (3c).	

Julie has fancied a boy in the year above her for a while; she has decided to ask him out.

Sam and David have been seeing each other for a few weeks. David is describing Sam to his mates but he doesn't realise that Sam can hear him.

Ellie and John have been going out for a while and Ellie wants the relationship to be more sexual. She isn't sure why they haven't gone further than they have. She decides to talk to John about it.

Louise and Jamie have just had sex for the first time.

Nathan is listening to his friends talking about their relationships. He has never kissed anyone and wants to ask them what it is like.

Figure 2.1 Scenarios about relationships

whether it made a difference to the task and they were happy that it didn't and made their own conclusions about the gender of the characters. Some groups chose to make the couples heterosexual and some chose to make the couples homosexual. Their reaction to the issue of sexuality arising in the lesson was different to that I had experienced before. Usually, some students would be very vocal and negative about the issue but in this instance where the reference to sexuality was more low key they seemed more able to think about the situation and come to rational conclusions.

Care was taken to ensure that pictures and examples reflected a range of cultures but not to reinforce assumptions made about different cultural attitudes about sexual activity. It is important to allow space for difference in the classroom but not to impose difference on students from different cultural backgrounds.

There were two underlying principles to the scheme of work. These were to provide factual information to enable positive relationships and to give students the opportunity to reflect on skills to negotiate positive relationships. Early on in the course students learnt about self-esteem and thought about the effects of low and high self-esteem. They then put this in the context of relationships using the above scenarios. Some students were unable to identify why self-esteem was relevant to Sex and Relationships Education but the lesson did encourage positive relationships within the classroom, which enabled more constructive discussions later on in the course. Students were then taught explicitly about what makes a good relationship and assertiveness skills. They then used what they had learnt to role-play difficult relationship situations. These skills were reinforced two weeks later when students used role-play to think about how they would negotiate the use of contraception. Students responded very positively to this opportunity to practise what they had learnt.

Teaching and learning styles

We employed a wide range of teaching and learning styles in the unit. Our aim was to use learning activities that could engage all students in the course. Circle time was used to establish ground rules in Lesson 1 and students were able to set out their own learning objectives for the course. Using circle time early on in the course established a non-threatening environment for discussions. This method was revisited in Lesson 9 when students discussed their attitudes towards pregnancy and parenting. They were given statements Figure 2.2 and were asked to discuss whether they agreed with the statement or not.

Contraception should be the responsibility of women

A father is someone who brings up children, not someone who makes them

Men need to know about contraception

It's very important for a man to have a job

If you get pregnant you should have the baby

It is a woman's choice whether to have an abortion or not

Women should always get custody of the children

If a woman gets pregnant she is a slag

Men don't have to be responsible until they have a family

Being a parent is fun

To be a good parent, all you need is love

Figure 2.2 Statements for discussion

Students were more confident in expressing their opinions and had developed their speaking and listening skills.

Students were able to experience some of the emotions they were learning about. For example, when students entered the room for Lesson 2 about self-esteem they were greeted with a compliment and then asked to reflect on how that had made them feel. At the end of the lesson they were invited to compliment anther student before they left the room.

Kinaesthetic learning was used in a variety of ways. In the first lesson students attached labels to large diagrams to learn about sexual organs. In Lesson 6 the School Nurse was invited into the lesson to talk to students about contraception and students got the opportunity to see and touch the different methods available.

Students practised their discussion skills on a number of occasions. In Lesson 4 they practised negotiation skills by having to reach a whole class consensus on what makes a good relationship. They started by thinking of three ideas individually and then had to explain their examples and listen to others to come up with a short list. This activity also used kinaesthetic learning, as students were able to move around the room if they agreed or disagreed with one of the statements.

Students used brainstorms to examine their ideas about the motivations that young people have for sexual activity (Lesson 3). They also used this method to think about difficult situations that arise in relationships and to think about the effects of early sexual activity (Lesson 8).

Students were given the opportunity to manipulate the information they were given. After brainstorms, students were asked to categorise the examples they had come up with. After learning about the different methods of contraception students were asked to think about which methods were suitable for young people (Lesson 7). By asking students to think further about information their learning was reinforced.

Students were able to think about real life examples. In Lesson 9 students read accounts written by young parents and used the information to think about the consequences of teenage pregnancy.

In each lesson students were given the opportunity to work in a range of groups, sometimes as a whole class, then in small groups or in pairs, and they finished the lesson by working individually. In the groups they practised what they had learnt in role-plays. In pairs students thought about the comments that parents make to their children about sex and thought about the effect that double standards can have. During every lesson students had to contribute to whole class discussions.

At the end of the lesson students reflected on what they had learnt by completing a diary. This consisted of an evaluation sheet that encouraged them to review the lesson. They then completed a worksheet on the theme of the lesson and asked them to think about the topic in relation to their own experience.

To support the lessons a wide range of books and leaflets were made available to students. They were able to access these from the peer supporters rather than having to ask an adult. This also had the effect of encouraging literacy, and many students who were reluctant to read chose to borrow books.

Student views on the course

After the course I interviewed a range of students of different abilities, some peer supporters, some not; some had been interviewed before, some hadn't. I happened to interview them in banding groups because of the timetable. This proved interesting. The group of low-banded students was incredibly hungry for any information and knew clearly what they wanted from sex and relationships education. The group of high-banded students were much more laid back and identified no needs regarding sex and relationships education. They also commented that it didn't really matter because they 'didn't have a test in it'.

This issue would need much more research but it seemed to me that the high-banded students were 'younger' in terms of sexual development and did the activity that the teacher set without demanding that their needs were met. They were more focused on facts and wanted information.

The low-banded students, on the other hand, knew what they needed and felt more strongly about demanding it. They wanted biological information 'got out of the way' in Year 7 with just a reminder in following years. They repeatedly asked for 'more stuff about feelings' and what came out most clearly was that they wanted a forum to discuss relationships and how to have a good relationship.

> 'I kept saying that we should do stuff about relationships but we just kept doing stuff about the body.'

The students' wants for the course matched closely the aims of the course but it appeared that they still felt dissatisfied. It seems that there is a real conflict between making sure students understand how everything works so that they have the knowledge to discuss sex and relationships and making sure that there is still time to have the discussion.

All of the students thought that role-plays were good.

> 'The role-plays were cool 'cos when you get older you're gonna have to talk about stuff and it's good to practise it now.'

They had clearly enjoyed taking part in role-plays about relationships and wanted more of these so that they could practise how to conduct themselves in different situations.

I was surprised that they wanted to be put off having sexual relationships. I had carefully avoided the dictatorial, 'don't do it' approach and instead had gone for encouraging students to make positive choices and to avoid sexual activity until it was right. They agreed that they didn't want a teacher telling them not to have sex but said that they did want to be 'put off' and wanted more discussion about why young people shouldn't have sex.

> 'We should have discussed it as a class and said the reasons why we shouldn't, then it might have got through to people. I think that if we should have done relationships a bit more 'cos obviously we're growing up and people have boyfriends and girlfriends and that but we weren't really influenced. I'm not saying they should have said don't do it but a bit more on how not to do it.'

These comments pose a dilemma for teachers. How can you influence young people away from sexual relationships without saying 'don't do it'. The students themselves gave a good solution. They enjoyed using role-plays to explore their feelings about issues and wanted to be empowered to come up with their own reasons. This again shows how mature and eloquent the young people were in knowing what they wanted from sex and relationships education.

The students made useful comments about grouping. They wanted the opportunity to discuss some things in single sex groups.

> 'I wanted to be in little groups of about 10 and only with girls. Especially for personal stuff. Then, other things, that everyone needs to know, come back together.'

They were also frustrated by students who made inappropriate comments and students 'who were bragging when it's nothing to brag about'. They wanted to be grouped according to behaviour but realised that it wasn't possible to exclude students who weren't behaving appropriately. They also understood that people were being silly because they were embarrassed. This again needs looking at more closely by educators. Somehow we need to be able to expose young people to sex and relationships education when they are mature enough for it but before it is too late.

I was particularly interested in their views about the student diaries. I had hoped that these would be a way to get young people to really think about the information they were getting in terms of their own lives. I was disappointed by the outcome. Too often, there was not enough time for this reflection and the diaries demanded too much of the students. The students I interviewed did not like them at all. However, their responses did give me ideas on how to develop them in the future.

> 'I think it was a good idea to think about things but even though miss said that it wouldn't go out of the lesson people were looking. I would like a blank diary to take home or to talk to someone that you want to talk to.'

'Less able' students needed the worksheets to guide their thinking, but the 'more able' students commented that they liked the opportunity to reflect. They found that the worksheets were too restrictive and they wanted the opportunity just to write what they thought generally. I still believe that it is important to encourage students to reflect on what they have learnt in relation to their own lives and this provided an opportunity for them to plan for the future to some extent. However, the format of these diaries was too restrictive and time consuming.

The variety of learning styles used enabled students of all abilities to become engaged and students commented that they found that the course was at the right level. 'Less able' students were given support through worksheets, which reinforced the examples they had been given orally. 'More able' students were expected to demonstrate their learning through extension role-plays and written explanations. Whole class discussion enabled the teacher to support and challenge where necessary.

Conclusion

Students overwhelmingly commented that they had enjoyed the course. I too, enjoyed the opportunity to put extra time and resources into developing and evaluating a scheme of work.

I feel that in this scheme of work we tried hard to empower students with the knowledge and skills to make positive choices about their relationships. However, at the end there were still issues about whether individual students had had access to what they needed, when they needed it. I think that there needs to be more work done on making sure that young people have flexible access to the information and support that they need.

I am left with many questions about the effect that 'ability' has on the needs of young people with regards to sex and relationships education. I would like to look more deeply into issues around banding and PSE.

The key to this scheme of work was the core values that it tried to encourage. These were established with the students at the beginning. This meant that all the content and skills that were then 'taught' had meaning and focus.

For me, the most important thing I have learnt in doing this project is that it is young people themselves who need to guide Sex and Relationships Education. They are very clear and responsible about what they want to know and incredibly inventive about how they can learn. I am looking forward to working with them in this way more in the future.

Notes

1. Teenage pregnancy: Report by the Social Exclusion Unit (1999: 91).
2. Teenage pregnancy: Report by the Social Exclusion Unit (1999: 6).
3. Teenage pregnancy: Report by the Social Exclusion Unit (1999: 6).
4. Teenage pregnancy: Report by the Social Exclusion Unit (1999: 6).
5. FPA (2000)
6. Teenage pregnancy: Report by the Social Exclusion Unit (1999: 90).
7. Teenage pregnancy: Report by the Social Exclusion Unit (1999: 91).
8. Data from 2000–2001 as documented in an HMI report, March 2001.

Acknowledgements

Thanks to my colleagues at Eltham Green School for collaborating on this scheme of work. A special thanks to the students for their engagement, enthusiasm and wisdom.

Appendix 2.1: Sex and young people questionnaire

Please answer the questions as fully as you can. If you don't understand a question move on to the next. All responses will remain confidential. Hand back to your tutor or Ms Wood.

Form_____

Are you   Male ☐   Female ☐

11 ☐   12 ☐   13 ☐   14 ☐   15 ☐   16 ☐

1) Why do you think young people have sex?
    Please number all answers you think are relevant starting with 1 for most important and so on.
    Pressure from other people   ☐
    Pressure from partners   ☐
    Fun   ☐
    They are curious   ☐
    As the next step in a relationship   ☐
    To hold on to a partner   ☐
    Other (please specify)   ☐

2) At what age do you think it is appropriate for young people to start having sexual intercourse?

	Young Men	Young Women
11	☐	☐
12	☐	☐
13	☐	☐
14	☐	☐
15	☐	☐
16	☐	☐
17	☐	☐
18	☐	☐

Other (please specify)   _____   _____

Depends (please explain)

3) Please circle above the age you think is young people normally start having sex.

4) Why do you think young people have babies?
   Please number all answers you think are relevant starting with 1 for most important and so on.

   Poor sex education   ☐
   They plan to   ☐
   Lack of contraception   ☐
   Contraception not working   ☐
   Pressure from friends/partners   ☐
   They don't have other plans for the future   ☐
   To get benefits or a flat   ☐
   Other (Please specify)   ☐

   _____

5) Think about what you already know about contraception and for each contraceptive say whether you have heard of it, know a little bit about it, or whether you know everything about it.

	Heard of	Know a little about	Understand
Male Condom	☐	☐	☐
Female Condom	☐	☐	☐
Combined Pill	☐	☐	☐
Progestorone only/Mini Pill	☐	☐	☐
Injection	☐	☐	☐
Implant	☐	☐	☐
Diaphragm/Cap	☐	☐	☐
IUD/Coil	☐	☐	☐
Spermicide	☐	☐	☐

6) Please circle the methods of contraception above that you would consider using.

7) Do you want to have children?   Yes ☐   No ☐
   If yes, at what age?   Under 18 ☐
   18–21
   21–25
   25–30
   30–35
   Over 35

8) Look at the topics listed below. Which do you think you should be taught as part of sex education (please tick) and at what age do you think they should be taught (5–16)?

Add any other topics that you think have been missed.

Topic	Yes, it should be taught	Age
Puberty		
Menstruation (periods)		
Masturbation		
Sexual organs		
Fertilisation		
Contraception		
Abortion		
Places to get support and health advice		
Sexually transmitted diseases		
Relationships		
Safer sex		
Discrimination		
Body image		
Assertiveness skills		
Negotiation skills		
Listening skills		
Families		
Sexuality		
Law affecting young people and sex		
Pregnancy and childcare		

9) What do you think are the most important things you have learnt in sex education so far?

10) Is there anything you think you should have been taught but you haven't been?

11) What could have been improved about the sex education you have had so far?

12) Please add any other comments about sex and sex education that you think would be useful.

Appendix 2.2: Questions for initial peer interviews

Sex and Relationships Education

What do you think of the Sex and Relationships Education you have had so far?
What improvements do you think should be made?

Teenage relationships

What makes a good relationship?
How important are relationships to young people?
At what age should young people have relationships?
Why do you think young people have sex?
Do some young people have sex when they don't want to?
Do young people plan to have sex?
Are there social rules about sexual relationships?
What do people think when the rules are broken?

Teenage pregnancy

Why do you think young people get pregnant?
If you were in charge of a project aimed at reducing teenage pregnancy, what would you do?

Chapter 3

The Global Footprints project: steps towards a global dimension in primary schools

Andrew Bell

> A footprint means pressing down and global means the world, so global footprints means pressing down on the world and we don't want to press down too hard.
>
> (Marina, aged 9)

This chapter explores the contribution of a global citizenship education project to curriculum provision and enhancement and school development in primary schools. The chapter draws on information, experiences and case study material provided by the project's participants.

The implications of incorporating global citizenship into core curriculum areas such as numeracy is investigated and the impact of such projects in influencing or directing school policy and practices as well as their effect on wider national initiatives is also examined.

Global Footprints: background information

As the quote above demonstrates, sometimes we rely on children themselves to define concepts that may seem to teachers and educationalists as hard to get across. This definition from a 9-year-old girl is one of the most succinct definitions of Global Footprints (GF) to have emerged.

This three-year project funded by the European Union and the UK government's Department for International Development (DfID) has been a groundbreaking collaboration between eight Development Education Centres (DECs) around the UK.[1] Each DEC has worked with one or more primary schools in their region. GF has also involved European partners in Ireland, Portugal, Netherlands and Greece, and Southern partners in Bangladesh, India, Peru and Kenya.

The development and promotion of the GF website (www.global footprints.org) has been an important emphasis during the project. The site has focused on global citizenship activities and lesson plans, particularly for numeracy and literacy: activities that have been developed and trialled by DECs and participating primary schools.

Measuring footprints

Naturally, a key element of the project is the use of the footprint. GF took the 'Ecological Footprint' model developed by Rees and Wackernagel (1996) as its starting point. The Ecological Footprint is defined as 'the biologically productive area needed to produce the resources used and absorb the waste generated by [a given] population' (Redefining Progress 2002). In short, it seeks to provide a mathematical measure of human impact on the environment. The Global Footprint seeks to extend this ecological impact assessment to include the social and global effects of human activity. A later section in this chapter explores how the concept of the Global Footprint has been used in schools.

The aims of the GF project are:

- To provide children with the essential knowledge and skills to challenge and tackle poverty, injustice and environmental destruction both locally and globally and understand the links between the countries of the North and those of the South.
- To use the concept of the *Global Footprint* as a means of developing an understanding of the social, economic and ecological impact of human activity and to explore this impact in the school context.
- To explore with children and the wider school community how sustainability indicators and methods of measuring footprints can provide a clearer understanding of how human social or environmental impact may be reduced or improved.
- To develop and trial in schools activities which incorporate issues of global citizenship and sustainable development into the delivery of the national/regional curriculum, particularly literacy and numeracy initiatives.
- To encourage and enable all those involved in the project, but particularly the young, to become involved in decision making within their schools and local community through such processes as School Councils and Local Agenda 21.
- To share information, activity ideas and best practice in global citizenship education and Education for Sustainable Development (ESD) through the GF web site.

The delivery of the GF project in schools

The implementation of the GF project has occurred in diverse ways and to differing degrees within the different participating DECs, the schools they have worked with and other partners such as Local Education Authorities or the Earth Centre in Doncaster.

In some schools work has focused on ensuring a global dimension to the curriculum. In others the concept of the footprint has been explored and this has been used as a starting point for discussion and debate on how to reduce or improve the social, global or ecological impact of pupils' or the whole school community. In a few schools the project has impacted on school ethos and influenced the School Development Plan. Below are some examples of the diverse extent to which such a project can influence the various participating partners.

The concept of the Global Footprint

An important aspect of the GF project has been the development and application of indicators to assess and evaluate a school community's impact, locally and globally; North and South. This section examines how messages on sustainable development and global citizenship can be delivered through using such indicators.

Two quizzes providing schools and students the opportunity to 'measure' their Global Footprint have been developed through the project. Both can be completed on line and provide 'footprint ratings' (www.globalfootprints.org/issues/kidsquiz/kidsquiz1.htm and www.global footprints.org/issues/footprint/councquiz1.htm). The two sets of indicators were based on quantitative and qualitative factors – ecological, social and global – and were finalised after extensive debates among the participating DECs. The indicators relate to a series of issues selected because of their impact, both at a school-based level and a wider community level both locally and globally.

It is important to realise that the indicators selected are subjective and incomplete and the quizzes do not attempt to provide a mathematical measurement of the footprint in the way that the Ecological Footprint model does. However, the quizzes do provide children and the school community with an opportunity to learn about and reflect on their impact on the community.

The quizzes aim to:

• raise important issues of global citizenship in an interactive and engaging way;

- provide a starting point or vehicle for encouraging discussion and debate on important global, social and environmental issues;
- stimulate the school community into actions that will help reduce their impact;
- bring about if not a change in attitudes and behaviour, at least a degree of questioning and critical thinking.

Before children use the quiz, teachers are encouraged to use an introductory activity on the concept of the footprint. One method of doing this is to link together two ideas: different sizes of footprint and different levels of impact. This has been done as part of a whole process examining footprints at a school in Tower Hamlets. Year 5/6 children were given the dictionary definition of the word *impact* (a forcible striking upon or against; effect, influence) and a visual demonstration using a drum. They were then shown a globe with different size feet on it. Combining these two images demonstrates that we all have an impact on the earth which leaves a footprint, and this footprint can vary in size depending on the extent of our impact.

The next stage is to explain to children that our footprint relates to the effect we have on other people or the environment. Having grasped this basic concept, children can be divided into groups and given various scenarios, e.g. driving a car through a city centre, eating a take-away burger from a fast food restaurant and vandalising a young tree in the park; in essence any scenario that has clear social or environmental impacts.

For each scenario, groups are asked to think of all the possible impacts of that scenario on people or the environment, both locally and globally, i.e. what footprint/mark it leaves. Once feedback is obtained from each group, the main impacts identified can be written on to paper feet and stuck on a map of the globe. This produces a good display and identifies with the children some of the main issues affecting our footprint on the earth, e.g. loss of local/traditional businesses, damage to cultures (as a result of fast food restaurants setting up in communities), destroying wildlife, air pollution, irresponsible behaviour, farming, etc.

This type of activity provides a good introduction to the Global Footprint and prepares children for the on-line quiz. It is also important that the quiz is not completed in isolation and that some of the issues raised by the quiz are addressed/investigated further.

Each on-line question/issue in the quiz has an information box which provides quirky, alarming or informative facts and figures to back up the issue. They also present a slightly provocative discussion starter, inviting children to express their views on the issue. These have been used to engage children in written responses via the website, or in a group discussion. The choice of issue for further debate or research may reflect whatever is currently topical, be issues or subjects currently being studied, or be selected on the basis that particular observed behaviours or attitudes may need confronting and challenging. Such discussions will invariably address one or more of the requirements identified in the citizenship/PSHE curriculum for KS2, in particular 'preparing to play an active role as citizens' and the requirement that, 'pupils should be taught to talk and write about their opinions, and explain their views, on issues that affect themselves and society' (National Curriculum 2000).

Work with secondary students on the Ecological Footprint has indicated that footprints provide students with 'a method of visualising and quantifying their global impacts so that they [can] work towards a deeper understanding of the links between the causes and effects of their actions' (Heath 2002: 7). Similarly, a group of eighteen 12-year-old boys at a school in Galway, Ireland, who tried the GF quiz 'were very impressed with the concept of a "footprint" and found it a great tool for visualising their impact on the planet' (Bradley 2002). This trial and evaluation for the children's quiz also concluded that, 'the teacher felt the quiz was very well pitched for this age group, with relevant and pertinent questions that could act as an excellent launch pad for further work in these areas' (ibid.).

Providing starting points was always the intention of the quizzes. They provide an interesting and interactive way into a debate on issues of sustainable development and global citizenship. They help the school community to consider the level of impact they are having as individuals, as an institution and on the wider community and to consider how this impact might be reduced or improved.

Incorporating global citizenship and Education for Sustainable Development into numeracy

One of the principal aims of the GF project was to develop activities that could be incorporated into numeracy and literacy lessons in primary schools. This section is based on action research carried out by the GF Project Officer for a dissertation as part of the South Bank University MSc in Environment and Development Education.

The research/dissertation involved an 'evaluation of the feasibility and effectiveness of incorporating global citizenship education into the

KS2 numeracy lesson' (Bell 1999). The research was carried out with a Year 5 multicultural, mixed ability class at Sir John Cass Foundation School in the City of London, one of the GF schools.

The National Numeracy Strategy (NNS), introduced in 1999, presents a 'top-down' model of education: policy makers producing a national framework which teachers deliver in the classroom. The strategy represents a knowledge and skills based curriculum, advancing 'legitimate and official knowledge' (Apple 1996) as defined by the 'dominant economic and political elite intent on "modernising" the economy' (ibid.). It aims at uniformity and conformity in teaching practice, ensuring all schools adhere to the same prescriptive methods of curriculum delivery.

With its call for 'dedicated mathematics lessons every day' (NNS 1999), it has effectively segregated maths from the rest of the curriculum. While there is 'time in other subjects for pupils to develop and apply their mathematics skills' (ibid.) the new strategy contrasts deeply with the ideology witnessed in the 1980s. The then Inner London Education Authority (ILEA), for example, suggested, 'there are no prescribed routes to success in mathematics' (ILEA 1988) and argued for 'using children's own interests and ideas as a starting point for mathematical work'. It could equally be argued that the educational ideology underpinning the NNS conflicts dramatically with the holistic, cross-curricular ideology behind global citizenship and ESD.

However, the National Curriculum (NC) review of 2000 demonstrates that there are also interesting conflicts, contradictions and tensions between different educational 'stakeholders', between government departments and even within them. This is particularly evident with the more holistic aims and values presented in the new NC which states that the school curriculum 'should develop [children's] awareness and understanding of, and respect for, the environments in which they live, and secure their commitment to sustainable development at a personal, local, national and global level' (NC 2000). Indeed there are numerous mentions to sustainable development in the new NC, particularly in geography. Furthermore, the Advisory Group on Citizenship recommended that the concepts, values, skills, knowledge and understanding which underpin citizenship education 'are neither inclusive to citizenship education nor mutually exclusive. They can be adopted and applied within other subjects and parts of the curriculum' (QCA 1998).

The citizenship/PSHE curriculum for KS2 calls for pupils to 'develop their sense of social justice and moral responsibility and begin to understand that their own choices and behaviour can affect local, national or global issues . . .'. Even the NC for maths calls for the need to 'use and apply maths in practical tasks, in real life problems . . .'

With numeracy severed and segregated from a previously more holistic primary curriculum, the incorporation of global citizenship and ESD can provide an opportunity for delivering numeracy that encourages children to make links with other areas of the curriculum and address some of the aims of the citizenship/PSHE curriculum. It also provides global perspectives and meaningful contexts to a knowledge and skills based agenda.

Because the action research took place before the launch of the citizenship/PSHE curriculum, the Oxfam curriculum for Global Citizenship was used as a reference point. This provided assistance in planning or adapting activities to include key elements of global citizenship and ESD.

One of the difficulties of incorporating global citizenship or ESD into teaching is that some of the issues addressed are often controversial and 'involve a critique of society' (Cross 1998). Tackling issues which may both confront and contradict teacher's own lifestyles and challenge society at large may prove uncomfortable for some teachers. However, in recognition that education for citizenship necessarily involves teaching controversial issues, the Advisory Group on Citizenship concluded that, 'education should not attempt to shelter our nation's children from even the harsher controversies of adult life' (QCA 1998). Further, they suggested that, 'to be completely unbiased is simply not possible, and on some issues, such as those concerning human rights, it is not desirable' (ibid.).

The activities delivered to the Year 5 class during the research deliberately contained 'issues of controversy' such as infant mortality and global gender inequality. This was on the basis that by avoiding controversial issues, 'we reinforce the predominant values in our society, which are not leading to a sustainable future and may be perpetuating inequality and injustice' (Symons 1996).

It was essential for the justification and validation of the activities that learning of numeracy concepts as identified by the NNP was taking place. Using a 'before and after' assessment test, which focussed exclusively on the mathematics content, it was clear that a significant increase in knowledge and understanding of the numeracy concepts occurred.

Several activities were trialled with the Year 5 children in the autumn term. (See appendix 1 and www.globalfootprints. org/teachers/matrix. htm#20 for examples)

In a 'numeracy diary' completed by the children following each activity, most children mentioned both the numeracy and the global citizenship elements to the activity. This demonstrated that they were able to make the link between numeracy and global issues. They were able to gain an insight into what numeracy could reveal about the real world and its application beyond the trivial.

Some children also displayed the further questioning which any citizenship programme would hope to encourage, though this did mainly come from the more able children. One boy asked, 'Why do some countries have so little when some have so much'? Clearly such activities can serve as a starting point to developing further study, discussion and debate.

The majority of children recognised that the lessons were different from other numeracy lessons (70%). This suggested children have a perception of what they think a numeracy lesson should be like, based, in this case, on two years' experience of the numeracy hour structure.

A questionnaire at the end of the programme sought to elucidate from children three 'things you remember doing or learning' and asked them to describe how they thought the lessons were different from 'normal' numeracy lessons. The result showed a far greater reference to the global citizenship elements of the lessons than the numeracy. This was true of both boys and girls.

The girls tended to be more reflective in their comments, e.g. 'lessons weren't just about maths they were also about the world and I think geography' and, 'we don't normally have a source of geography in maths'.

Perhaps most encouragingly, many children made mention of the opportunities the activities provided for developing group work and discussion skills. Both boys and girls highlighted the participative, democratic and reflective nature of the activities. One girl commented that, 'the lessons gave everyone a chance to speak and say what they think', and a boy commented that they were different because '[the researcher] lets us express our feelings about things in the lesson'.

The practical activities were by far the most referred to, e.g. the trading game (see Appendix 3.1) which involves a simulated role-play. Plant and Firth (1995) note that effective use of role play has the potential to promote critical thinking and 'facilitate the delivery of a range of attitudes, skills and knowledge which a knowledge-bound, discipline-based curriculum might be hard pressed to do'. With the boys mentioning the practical aspects of the programme more than the girls, it suggests that such methods while successfully delivering global citizenship and ESD into activities might also be more effective at engaging boys in numeracy.

The less able, and consequently often the least confident children, in maths were very positive about the activities. This could be because they find the subject more enjoyable and less threatening when it is 'disguised', i.e. when it incorporates other issues which they feel they can relate to, and confidently contribute to.

An inspector carrying out an observation/assessment of numeracy teaching at Sir John Cass School and who observed one of the global citizenship/numeracy lessons (on gender inequality) commented:

> A particular feature of the work in Year 5 was the class's involvement in an innovative project, which focused on global citizenship and numeracy. This work involved them in estimating and interpreting tables, drawing conclusions, expressing simple ratios and checking their findings. The worksheets provided the pupils with the opportunity to discuss and form opinions on equality and bias in world issues.

Her informal feedback at the end of the lesson indicated that such work was essential to broaden the curriculum and that the content was such that it 'engaged children in feeling for the task', increasing their motivation towards the maths. She reflected on the comments of one girl who was quite indignant about the injustice of the inequality between men and women.

The action research carried out at Sir John Cass School successfully demonstrated the feasibility of incorporating global and sustainable development issues into numeracy teaching and effected the future direction and development of activities for the GF project. The activities were positively received by pupils, teachers and inspectors, and high levels of enthusiasm and motivation among pupils were observed and demonstrated.

Of course, how effective the programme was in raising awareness and understanding of global citizenship issues and to what extent it challenged attitudes remains highly questionable. Certainly the activities provided an excellent starting point and stimulus for discussion and debate on global, social and environmental issues. However, addressing these issues entirely within the regimented confines of the numeracy lesson was inadequate and there was little evidence that the issues were discussed again or revisited after the numeracy activity.

The best that can be hoped for perhaps is that children will make links with other areas of the curriculum and ask critical questions in the future, either inside or outside school, when confronted with issues in the media for example.

In summary, the main conclusions to emerge from the research were:

1   There is a concern among educationalists that children find it increasingly difficult to make links between what they learn through the NNS and its application outside the classroom. Incorporating global and environmental issues can provide a valuable opportunity for children to experience how numeracy can apply to the real world, and reveal information about how the world is and how it functions: it can demonstrate numeracy as an important tool in 'informed citizenship' and 'political literacy'.

2   There are clearly emergent conflicts and contradictions in ideology between different aspects of the curriculum and how it should be delivered. Educationalists expressed some reservations about the activities due to a perceived tension between the required numeracy focus and the global citizenship content. There were concerns raised about the effects on numeracy coverage and pace, undoubtedly reflecting the prevailing macro political climate of targets, results and performance tables which are currently the driving force in education.

3   Such a programme which in a sense 'disguises numeracy' or presents it in a more relevant and 'real world' way may increase levels of confidence, interest, enthusiasm and motivation amongst children particularly among boys and less able children, though with such a small sample and limited time frame it is impossible to draw firm conclusions on this.

4   The activities were delivered by a research-practitioner operating outside the day-to-day pressures of 'the system'. The programme was clearly appropriate to the researcher-practitioner's knowledge and understanding of global citizenship issues. It was also delivered in a class where the class teacher had a particular interest in including a global perspective in teaching and learning. How successfully such a programme could be delivered by a practitioner working within 'the system', faced with all its hegemonic, ideological and political pressures and who perhaps does not have the same knowledge and experience of or motivation or commitment towards global citizenship, remains highly questionable.

What underpins all the conclusions of the research is that, to be effective, global citizenship/ESD requires a 'whole school approach' where the teaching and learning of global, social and environmental issues is central to the school ethos and included in the school development plan and curriculum planning across the whole curriculum.

A whole school approach to Education for Sustainable Development

This section examines how involvement in a project such as GF can help promote ESD across the primary school curriculum and impact on the school development plan. Information provided by Lancashire Global Education Centre (LGEC) and a case study written by Beech Hill Primary School for the QCA provide the basis of this section.

Beech Hill Primary School (http://www.beechill.wigan.sch.uk) in Wigan is a school with 500 pupils from nursery to Year 6.

The school has developed ESD work with various partners over several years, integrating ESD into the ethos, management and curriculum of the school. ESD is planned and delivered across the curriculum, ensuring all classes and year groups are involved. Teachers have developed units of work in different subjects and have built these into long-term curriculum planning, with progression in ESD as pupils move through the school. The curriculum is delivered using a variety of learning styles, with work in one curriculum area supported by activities in other subjects.

The activities have been developed from the school's participation in the GF project and with the help of the GF project worker from LGEC. The activities aim to develop skills and knowledge of global citizenship in order to help pupils challenge poverty, inequality and environmental change, both locally and globally, and to understand social, economic and environmental connections between more and less economically developed countries.

Many of these Global Footprint activities combine ESD objectives with subject-specific objectives. The ESD objectives of the activities include:

- raising awareness and exploring action to reduce individuals' impact on the environment;
- developing indicators to measure the school's progress towards reducing its environmental impact;
- encouraging children to devise their own solutions to problems;
- encouraging pupils to become involved in decision-making processes.

ESD spans the curriculum and is linked to QCA Schemes of Work. Examples include science (scientific enquiry and materials and their properties), art and design (developing work to reflect views and ideas) and geography (improving the local environment). Some specific examples of ESD work include:

1   **Song of the world, an art and design unit of work for Year 5**. The activities enabled pupils to communicate ideas by making a collaborative textile, and are adapted from the QCA Art Scheme of Work Unit 5C 'Talking Textiles'. Pupils explored how textiles from different places and times represent events and stories. They used photographs of a modern tapestry, 'The Song of the World', displayed in Wigan's 'twin town' in France. This ensured a European dimension/link to the work. Pupils discussed different elements of the tapestry before developing their own. The theme of 'The Joy of Living' was selected, and using information and ideas from various sources, including the Internet, pupils worked in groups to assemble items and complete a 'collaborative tapestry'. The school intends to develop this work in future, using e-mail to communicate and share ideas with French pupils at a school in their 'twin town'.

2   **A science activity on babies' nappies for pupils in Year 3**. This aimed to develop an understanding of the impact of human activity and how people's individual choices can affect the environment. Over a number of lessons pupils investigated the properties of materials by observing, measuring and investigating the absorbency of different types of disposable and re-usable nappies. The environmental and economic impacts of different nappies were then considered (e.g. use of energy and water by washing nappies and landfill from disposable nappies, etc). This work was extended to consider local, national and global implications (e.g. cost, amount of waste, etc).

3   **What do we throw away?** This Year 4 activity built on work in geography, and developed ideas on 'handling data' from the QCA Geography Scheme of Work Unit 25: 'Geography and Numbers'. Over half a term, pupils collected and weighed classroom rubbish and were encouraged to think about and discuss its effects (e.g. smell and hygiene) and implications (e.g. where does rubbish get moved to?). Pupils looked into the issue at school and home and considered the people involved, linking with work in geography on how to improve the local area. Another purpose of the activity was to develop indicators to help measure the school's progress in reducing its impact and thereby reflect the aims of the school's ESD policy. It is important that work in the classroom feeds into and links with school policy on ESD as it is clearly vital that taught values are reflected in school practice.

The school has adapted other units from the QCA Geography Scheme of Work as part of their work on ESD, including Unit 8 on improving the environment, Unit 12 on traffic, and Units 10 and 18 on how people connect with other parts of the world.

The activities are part of a whole-school approach to ESD. This is consistent with the approach adopted by the Panel for Sustainable Development Education which argued that, 'ESD must be integrated throughout the curriculum as a whole, not treated as a separate subject' (DETR 1998). The school considers that this approach has motivated pupils and helped them begin to make connections between their role as members of the school to a role as citizens in the local and global community. Evidence of this seems to come from the School Council where discussions and decisions seem to reflect a greater emphasis on a sustainable development agenda than might otherwise be expected. A letter from the chairperson on the School Council to the Local Council Waste Officer requests 'a paper and card recycling box for every classroom and the office'. The letter concluded, 'I hope you will be in agreement with us as I am sure it will be of benefit to the environment to put all the waste in school to good use'.

The establishment of School Councils has been one of the un-anticipated positive outcomes of the GF project. This may simply reflect the fact that as part of PSHE, schools are realising the importance of democratic processes involving pupils. The QCA suggests that, '[the] involvement [of pupils] in the running of the school or class councils and other decision-making . . . promotes responsibility and learning about democracy' (QCA 2000).

The introduction of School Councils could also reflect a realisation that sustainable development cannot be achieved without the representative and active participation of the community. Either way, GF seems to have encouraged emerging and established School Councils to consider policy and practice issues which have environmental or social effects at a local or global level, as the above example demonstrates.

As if to reinforce the view that ESD contributes to more democratic structures in schools and more informed and participative citizenship, an OFSTED inspection report on Beech Hill noted that the GF/ESD work had helped pupils apply their understanding to new contexts, and encouraged discussion and exchanging of opinions which demonstrated justifications of points of view.

The project also appeared to encourage teacher collaboration and improve teaching and learning through combining skills and knowledge from different curriculum areas.

The schools consider that the key ingredients for success have been:

- developing and sharing a commitment to ESD at the school;
- identifying opportunities for developing ESD skills and concepts in different subject areas;
- planning for progression of knowledge and understanding of ESD;
- encouraging colleagues to share ideas and develop their understanding of ESD in the curriculum;
- reviewing successful activities from the school's schemes of work to give them an ESD emphasis, and not planning to deliver completely new content.

The headteacher believes the success of ESD in the school is due to resisting 'on-off' glamour projects and ensuring that all the activities fit into existing timetabled subjects. He also believes it is down to, 'a shared understanding of sustainable development . . . the availability of external models and the regular support of [the GF project worker] from LGEC' (Coulsan 2002).

Healthy school initiative

This section demonstrates how a global citizenship/ESD project can impact on national initiatives, influencing the direction and delivery of that initiative at a local level.

In Tower Hamlets, the Humanities Education Centre (HEC) GF project worker became involved in the Healthy Schools (HS) Programme. This national initiative has been part of the government's drive to improve standards of health and education and to tackle health inequalities. It has been designed to 'support and complement the new PSHE framework' (DfEE 1999).

Reflecting the principles of global citizenship/ESD, 'healthy school activities are intended to be holistic in the truest sense – embraced and emphasised across every curriculum area and actively backed by every section of the school community' (ibid.). To find a programme advocating so unequivocally a holistic approach 'in the truest sense' stands in sharp contradiction with the prevailing pedagogy of 'limited learning styles and didactic teaching, marginalisation of the arts and humanities subjects and valuing what can be measured rather than measuring what is valued' (Sterling 2001). The initiative therefore provided an ideal opportunity for incorporating a global/sustainability agenda.

The GF project was regarded by the Tower Hamlets Healthy Schools Co-ordinator as being able to provide an extra dimension to the HS agenda. The GF project worker was therefore invited to become part of the HS Steering Group, which included dieticians, drugs education agencies, sports initiative representatives, and citizenship co-ordinators.

Specifically, involvement in the HS programme resulted in:

1   GF providing a global/sustainability perspective to the setting up of Fruit Tuck Shops, an important element of the HS programme. This was achieved through teacher INSET on Fruit Tuck Shops and 'pupil days' in schools where issues of trade and composting were addressed alongside health issues.
2   Global Citizenship workshops and INSET sessions. A practical workshop was offered to teachers attending a regional HS conference examining how to incorporate issues of global citizenship, PSHE and health education into numeracy and literacy.
3   INSET to schools setting up School Councils, another important aspect of the HS programme which calls for 'pupils' needs and views [to] inform planning and teaching and learning in PSHE and citizenship' and 'two way mechanisms [to be] established for involving pupils in school development' (Denning et al. 2000). The project worker also worked with School Councils in Tower Hamlets schools involved in GF to help them become involved in planning, establishing, and running Fruit Tuck Shops.

Learning points from the project

As a project model, GF has been highly experimental. This chapter has focused on the positive outcomes of the project and how it has contributed to curriculum development and enhancement and how the project has successfully impacted on school development. However, such a groundbreaking project has also revealed some important learning points for DECs working jointly on a project and the effectiveness of delivering such projects in schools.

Towards the end of the project an evaluation was carried out by an external evaluator (McKenzie 2002).[2] Unless otherwise stated, all quotes in this section are from the End of Project Evaluation.

The report acknowledges:

> GF is an important and timely project in the development education world, providing lessons for development educators planning projects

across several DECs, offering insights into ways of structuring complex curriculum initiatives and contributing, from a development
education vantage point, toward both education for sustainability
and education for citizenship.

However, for a project involving such geographically and contextually
diverse DECs, 'the purpose behind the collaboration of organisationally
different and geographically disparate DECs needs to be made *explicit*
in project aims and objectives'. The end of project evaluation has highlighted that without such an explicitly stated purpose to such diversity,
'it may be more productive to involve DECs from only one jurisdiction'.

With schools also, there were clear differences in the impact GF had
in terms of influencing curriculum and school development within
different DECs and regions. 'Local implementation problems were often
associated with the DEC's relationship with their school or schools, some
having established cordial and productive relations, while others were
unable, despite their best efforts, to attain the working relations that
were hoped for.'

Clearer expectations and stated minimum requirements in terms
of 'commitment of head/several teachers to involving DEC in planning'
could have resulted in the project having greater impact and improved
the performance of schools. As it was, 'some schools seemed to be very
much more part of an active DEC–school partnership' than others.

'Contractual agreements' between DECs and schools could also have
helped clarify goals and expectations especially as 'schools have particular
needs and interests, which may not coincide with a project's agenda'.

One project worker believed the difficulties involved in getting
commitment from schools was part of a wider issue to do with the
prevailing educational hegemony: 'There is still no central "push" to
encourage primary schools to do this kind of [global citizenship/
education for sustainability] work.

The different commitments and roles of project workers also help
explain the different results from different DECs and schools. 'Some
workers were full-time while at least one was part-time, and some
workers clearly had more time for project work than others.' This meant
that 'project workers did not . . . have much of a project "script"' to work
to. One project worker commented that a full-time commitment to
the project would have resulted in 'more support on policy and whole
school ethos as well as the curriculum development'.

The website was generally regarded as an excellent resource for DECs
and schools alike. As well as providing an ideal medium for disseminat-

ing the aims of the project, case studies of work in schools and a range of global citizenship classroom activity ideas, it has provided consonance and convergence to a project which clearly has demonstrated much difference and diversity. In recognition of the quality of the website and the activities and resources it contains the site has received National Grid for Learning status.[3]

Generally, with a few exceptions, links with Southern partners have been unproductive. 'International partnerships are a complex matter' (ibid.) often fraught with communication difficulties and lack of clarity over purpose. So often with projects such as GF, 'grant applicants often submit over-ambitious projects to make their applications appear distinctive and innovative', something 'funders, either wittingly or un-wittingly, tend to abet . . . by expecting a greater return from grants than is reasonable and possible'.

In interviews with teachers in GF schools, all indicated that they 'enjoyed working on the project and felt that both they and their pupils had learned from the experience'. Teachers said they were 'applying the concept of GF across the curriculum and were increasingly making use of GF in their PSHE/citizenship teaching'. Teachers from schools where GF had been incorporated into their school development and curriculum plans considered the project 'had achieved sustainable impact in their schools'.

One of the positive, but largely unforeseen impacts of the project was that schools involved in GF had prompted many to establish School Councils. This has demonstrated the impact such a project can have not only on PSHE in schools but also on school ethos and management. One headteacher remarked on how she felt the project had, 'had a significant impact on both teaching practices and children's classroom behaviour in terms of listening skills and group co-operation'.

The external evaluator concluded:

> The GF Project has been an informative and positive experience for most, if not all, of the actors involved. What remains now, is not only how much can be learnt from the experience but also how much can be disseminated and transferred into future DEC work.

Notes

1. Development Education Centres (DECs) are independent local centres that support teachers, youth workers, community educators, higher education institutions and students in learning about global and sustainable

development issues and how to 'think globally and act locally'. Further details are available from the Development Education Association (www. dea.org.uk/dec/index.html).

The eight DECs taking part in the GF project are: Belfast One World Centre, Development Education in Dorset (DEED), Global Connections (Pembrokeshire), Gloucestershire DEC, Tower Hamlets Humanities Education Centre (HEC), Highlands One World Centre, Lancashire Global Education Centre and Leeds DEC. In addition, the Earth Centre in Doncaster worked in partnership with Leeds DEC. The project has been co-ordinated by HEC.

2. The GF Final Evaluation methodology involved: questionnaire surveying of HEC and DEC representatives, leading to the production of a discussion document; four, semi-structured interview samplings of HEC and DEC representatives and teachers from participating schools, culminating in the production of a final report.

3. The National Grid for Learning 'provides a network of selected links to web sites that offer high quality content and information' (www.ngfl.gov.uk).

Appendix 3.1 Global citizenship numeracy programme activity examples

Activity: Gender inequality

Topic: Examining percentages of men and women in different roles (global figures)
Introduce at a basic level that percentage means 'out of every 100'. Children are presented with a bar chart showing the percentage of men and women occupied in different roles.

Activity: (Sheet with 0–100, but no intervals marked on). By examining the bar chart, estimate the percentage of men and women for each category;

For each category round up or down the number of women in each category to the nearest 10. Use this information to convert the number of women from out of 100 to 'out of 10'.

SEN/less able: (sheet with intervals of 10 on). Estimate number of women 'out of 100' for each category. Round up or down each to the nearest 10.

Curriculum for Global Citizenship	Activity reference to Global Citizenship curriculum	Numeracy reference based on pages 22–23 of NNS
Knowledge and Understanding • Social justice and equity • Diversity • Globalisation and interdependence • Sustainable development • Peace and conflict	**Causes and effects of inequality** Enabling children to explore their views and understandings on gender inequality. **Nature of prejudice and ways to combat it.** Enabling children to voice their feelings (and prejudices) about the differences they believe exist between men and women and why they hold those views	Estimate the position of a point on an undivided line: for example the whole number on a line from 0–100 (Y4 p10) Use the vocabulary of estimation and approximation Estimate by approximating (round to the nearest 10 or 100) then check result.

Appendix 3.1 continued

Curriculum for Global Citizenship	Activity reference to *Global Citizenship* curriculum	Numeracy reference based on pages 22–23 of NNS
	Impact of conflict. Enabling children to critically examine why it is that men often cause and fight wars, but women and children are often the greatest casualties – refugee figures	Begin to understand percentage as the number of parts in every 100, and find simple percentages of small whole-number quantities Derive quickly: two-digit pairs that total 100 (Y5 p39)
Skills • Critical thinking • Ability to argue effectively • Ability to challenge injustice & inequalities • Respect for people and things • Co-operation and conflict resolution	*Detecting bias, opinion and stereotypes.* Enabling children to explore, and acknowledge that women and men are stereotyped and that their own views may reflect these stereotypical images *Recognising and starting to challenge unfairness.* To understand that power largely rests with men, but women do the majority of work and acknowledge the injustice of this.	

Values and attitudes	Sense of justice
• Sense of identity & self-esteem • Empathy and sense of common humanity • Commitment to social justice and equity • Valuing and respecting diversity • Concern for the environment & commitment to sustainable development • Belief that people can make a difference	To acknowledge the injustice of gender inequality.

continued

Appendix 3.1 continued

Activity: The trade game (a more detailed description of this activity can be found on the Global Footprints website: www.globalfootprints.org/teachers/matrix.htm#20)

Topic: Trading relations and Fair trade

Children divided into 5 preferably mixed ability groups to represent 5 different countries. In their teams they must draw birds-eye view mahogany tables with an area of 24cm² and also calculate the corresponding perimeter. As most will not have the necessary resources at the beginning of the game, namely pencils, rulers and 'mahogany logs' (paper) to produce the tables, countries will need to trade with each other to obtain the necessary resources. Talk to the children briefly about the idea of trading and the rules of the game.

Curriculum for Global Citizenship – key elements	Activity reference to Global Citizenship curriculum KS2	Numeracy reference based on pages 22–23 of NNS
Knowledge and Understanding	*Fairness between groups; Causes and effects of inequality* Active demonstration and experience of unfairness and inequality through role playing	Know by heart all multiplication facts up to 10 × 10
Social justice and equity		Derive quickly … doubles of all whole numbers 1 to 100
Diversity	*Trade between countries; Fair trade* Through actively engaging in trading, children gain an understanding of how world trading relationships work and the inequalities between rich and poor countries.	Understand, measure and calculate perimeters of rectangles
Globalisation and interdependence		Understand area measured in square centimetres (cm²)
Sustainable development		
Peace and conflict		

Use the activity to provide children with information about fair trade and how this promotes greater fairness and social justice **Relationship between people and environment;** The game demonstrates how countries are often forced to exploit and damage their environments in order to engage in trade **Awareness of finite resources;** Opportunity to discuss where mahogany comes from and the importance of rainforest eco-systems; make children aware that current practices make mahogany trees and other rainforest timbers essentially finite **Our potential to change things** Through the activity provide children with a chance to consider ideas for creating a fairer world and what part they can play in achieving this; provide information on fair trade	Understand and use the formula in words 'length × breadth' for the area of a rectangle Choose and use appropriate number operations to solve problems, and appropriate ways of calculating: mental, mental with jottings, written methods Explain methods of reasoning, orally and in writing Solve mathematical problems or puzzles, recognise and explain patterns and relationship, generalise and predict. Explain a generalised relationship (formula) in words

Appendix 3.1 continued

Curriculum for Global Citizenship – key elements	Activity reference to Global Citizenship curriculum KS2	Numeracy reference based on pages 22–23 of NNS
Skills Critical thinking Ability to argue effectively Ability to challenge injustice & inequalities Respect for people and things Co-operation and conflict resolution	**Recognising and starting to challenge unfairness** Through playing the game, recognise the unfairness of trading relations **Making choices and recognising the consequences of choices** Enable children to learn about the consequences of buying rainforest timber and the positive benefits of buying fair trade products **Accepting and acting on group decisions;** **Compromising** The game essentially involves team work skills	
Values and Attitudes Sense of identity and self-esteem Empathy and sense of common humanity Commitment to social justice and equity Valuing and respecting diversity Concern for the environment and commitment to sustainable development Belief that people can make a difference	**Sense of justice** Enabling children to understand the injustice of world trade and the greater social justice that results from fair trade **Sense of responsibility for the environment and the use of resources** Understand the consequences of purchasing products which damage the environment and be aware that alternative choices can be made	

References

Apple, M. (1996) *Cultural Politics and Education*, Milton Keynes, Open University Press.

Bell, A. (2000) *Evaluation of the Feasibility and Effectiveness of Incorporating Global Citizenship Education into the KS2 Numeracy Lesson*, South Bank University.

Bradley, S. (2002) *Report on the Trial of the Global Footprints Quiz*, Galway, One World Centre.

Coulsan, P. (2002) *Education for Sustainable Development Case Study – Information Sheet* – completed for the QCA.

Cross, R. (1998) Teachers views about what to do about sustainable development, *Environmental Education Research* 4(2).

Dennin, S., Jowett, K. and Power, P. (2000) *East London Healthy Schools Scheme Handbook*, Newham, Hackney, Tower Hamlets and Corporation of London Education Authorities.

DETR (1998) *Sustainable Development Education Panel – First Annual Report 1998*, Department of Environment, Transport and the Regions.

DfEE (1999) *National Healthy School Standard: Getting started – a guide to schools*, Department for Education and Employment.

Heath, R. (2002) 'Putting your foot in it', *Teaching Geography* 27(2): 7.

ILEA (1988) *Mathematics in ILEA Primary Schools: Children and mathematics, Part 1*, Inner London Education Authority.

McKenzie, A. (2002) *Global Footprints Final Evaluation*.

National Curriculum (2000) Online (www.nc.uk.net).

NNS (1999) *The National Numeracy Strategy*, Department for Education and Employment.

Plant, M. and Firth, R. (1995) Quoted in *Theory into Practice – Global Citizenship Education*, Helen Walkington (1999), The Geographical Association.

QCA (1998) *Education for Citizenship and the Teaching of Democracy in Schools*, Qualifications and Curriculum Authority.

QCA (2000) *Personal, Social and Health Education and Citizenship at Key Stages 1 and 2*, Qualifications and Curriculum Authority.

Redefining Progress (2002) Paper *Ecological Footprint Accounts*: (www.rprogress.org).

Rees, W. and Wackernagel, M. (1996) *The Ecological Footprint: Reducing Human Impact on the Earth*. The New Catalyst Bioregional Series, New Society Publishers.

Sterling, S. (2001) *Sustainable Education: Re-visioning learning and change*, Green Books for the Schumacher Society.

Symons, G. (1996) Chapter 4 'The Primary Years', in J. Huckle and S. Sterling, *Education for Sustainability*, Earthscan.

Developing students' rights and responsibilities through the PSHE curriculum

Gill Pooley

'I understand that it doesn't matter where you come from, ethnicity, religion or skin colour, what matters is what is inside your character.'

(Student)

'The unfairness of employment and cheap labour in appalling conditions really shocked me because it makes me realise how awful life can be for children my age.'

(Student)

Context

Sydenham School is a large girls' comprehensive school in Lewisham in Inner London. There is a wide ethnic mix in the school, reflecting the rich ethnic diversity of the local area. Just under half the pupils are white. With 138 refugee pupils, there is a much larger proportion than nationally (26.8 per cent) of pupils for whom English is an additional language, which reflects the local area.

PSE at Sydenham School has been taught as a discrete subject by a specialist team for eight years. At Key Stage 4 we felt that there was a need for a form of accreditation as students value their work and PSE is seen as a strength of the school. Consequently from September 2001 we became part of the GCSE short course Citizenship Studies pilot. The course suited us because there were close links between the specifications and the PSE course we were already offering. However, we are concerned to keep the best of our previous course and are aware of the danger that some aspects could be lost. The PSE programme as a whole is intended to be student centred. It aims to enable students to develop the knowledge, understanding and skills to become self-confident, critical, analytical and responsible young people who are able to make informed decisions about their lives and about their contribution to the community. The existing PSE programme has always had a strong focus on the personal and social, but the course had lacked a strong political strand. We aimed to provide opportunities for students to make the connections between the personal, social and the political and the new GCSE has reinforced this. This case study focuses on just one aspect of the GCSE Citizenship Studies, namely the first unit, 'Citizenship – Rights and Responsibilities' (see Appendix 4.1 for scheme of work).

Citizenship – Rights and Responsibilities

The aims of this unit are as follows:

Knowledge and understanding

- Understanding of what it means to be a citizen.
- Knowledge of the concepts of rights and responsibilities in local, national and global context (families, schools, cultures, international).
- Understanding of the differences between the concepts of moral and legal responsibilities.
- Knowledge of the law around rights and responsibilities.
- To increase awareness of international agreements around rights and responsibilities.
- To explore issues of ethnic, religious and national diversity in relation to the concept of rights and responsibilities.
- Understanding of the rights and responsibilities of the media.
- To explore the importance of mutual respect and understanding within and between communities, as well as the consequences of discrimination.

Skills

- Research
- Communication
- Participation
- Analysis
- Collaboration

Teaching and learning styles

The unit uses a range of active teaching and learning styles to meet the learning needs and preferences within the classroom and to encourage active participation. When planning this unit we were conscious of the tension between the need for written evidence as well as providing opportunities for thought and discussion.

Learning outcomes and assessment

The learning outcomes for this unit come out of the broader aims outlined above. While our aims are a general statement about what we are intending to teach, the learning outcomes are a more specific statement about what we expect students to know and understand by the end of this unit. To a large extent our learning outcomes for this unit were determined by the GCSE specifications, although we had also tailored these to the particular needs of our students. These are as follows:

Knowledge and understanding of:

- rights and responsibilities of children, parents, carers and schools (legal and moral);
- criminal and civil law;
- the nature of the diversity within and between communities;
- rights and responsibilities of the media.

Skills of:

- collaboration;
- discussion;
- research;
- presentation;
- analysis.

In planning our unit of work we specified an assessment focus for each lesson. This did not always involve any formal methods of assessment, but included observation of discussion, questions and answers, marking written work, group presentations, etc. We felt very strongly that we wanted to keep assessment methods broadly based and not to become too overly affected by the end exam. Having taught other GCSEs over the last fourteen years, I am very aware that assessment methods can become too concerned with practice questions and essays. We normally write an assessment task for each unit throughout our PSE course Years 7–11. The purpose of these is to enable students to practise applying their knowledge and understanding, to show students' progress against our intended learning outcomes and to allow students to reflect on their strengths and areas for improvement. Each assessment task includes an element of self and unit evaluation. For this unit we focused on racism and human rights and wrote a resource based assignment. This was to give students some experience of exam style questions and to use their knowledge and understanding and to formulate their opinions about the topic. The response to this assessment task was varied. Some found it very difficult but others responded well to the challenge and it gave students a realistic picture of the level of response required to be successful in the GCSE. As the course progresses we will need to build in a range of formal assessment opportunities as well as continuing to use the wider range of activities that PSE has been so good at in the past. Figures 4.1 and 4.2 show examples of the unit assignment and students' work.

Moral and legal rights within the school community

Moral and legal rights within the school community forms the third lesson in the unit. The aim of the lesson was to develop students' understanding of the idea that all members of the school community have moral and legal rights and responsibilities. The next two lessons focused on our rights and responsibilities within the wider society and the global community. We began the lesson by discussing five scenarios in groups. Each scenario was about the responsibilities of different groups within the school community for issues such as bullying, behaviour, truancy and drug use. Groups had to respond to each scenario using the prompt questions and record their ideas in writing. We then had feedback and discussed the different ideas raised around responsibilities. Many students made a distinction between what they thought someone should do in a situation and what they legally had to do. Most students felt, in the case of witnessing bullying, that they had no legal responsibility to intervene but that they did have a moral responsibility to at least tell someone about it. Examples of the scenarios are shown in Figure 4.3.

The same groups were then given some of our school policies on anti-bullying, behaviour and attendance. These can be seen in Figure 4.4.

Again, we asked students to discuss various aspects of these policies using prompt questions. We wanted students to understand the moral

GCSE CITIZENSHIP STUDIES: RIGHTS AND RESPONSIBILITIES
RESOURCE-BASED QUESTIONS ASSESSMENT – INSTRUCTIONS

AIMS
To assess your knowledge and understanding, as well as your use of
skills learnt during the unit on rights and responsibilities.

TASK
To read a book of source materials and answer five questions based
on these resources.

ASSESSMENT FOCUS
The five questions will assess your knowledge and understanding, and
your skills. In the syllabus, these are called ASSESSMENT OBJECTIVE
I (AOI) AND ASSESSMENT OBJECTIVE 2 (AO2)

AOI: KNOWLEDGE AND UNDERSTANDING of

- Rights and responsibilities (legally, morally, culturally, within school
  and within families)
- Interdependence – the need for mutual respect and understanding
- The legal and justice system – civil and criminal law
- The rights, responsibilities and influence of the media

AO2: SKILLS of

- Interpretation
- Analysis
- Explanation
- Written presentation

Figure 4.1 Unit assignment

Look at Source D. Explain how you think the legal system in this country should have dealt with this case and Stephen's murderers. How could the Lawrence family use the legal system in this country to deal with the 'police incompetence' mentioned in the MacPherson report?

Source D
Stephen Lawrence was 18 when he was set upon by a gang of youths and fatally stabbed in Eltham, South London in April 1993. He died only a few yards from where a 16-year-old Asian youth, Rohit Duggal, had been murdered in a racial attack the previous year.

The report of an enquiry into the police handling of the investigation into the murder of Stephen Lawrence, known as the Macpherson Report, stated that police incompetence and institutionalised racism had hindered the search for Stephen's killers who have never been brought to justice. The report also warned about complacency in other institutions.

Student A
'The legal system in England could have dealt with the Stephen Lawrence case by taking it more sternly and treat the case as important as other murder cases, which in respect do their best to find the suspects and bring them to justice. They could have set up a press conference so they could hope to gain the support from the public, which could have helped bring them closer to solving the case. However, the police didn't handle the case in a very fair and professional manner, they seemed to have a less concerned and uncaring approach. 'Everyone has the right to legal protection when the law of your country is not respected and your human rights are ignored.' Stephen Lawrence's family can use the legal system in this country by making an official complaint and sue the police of breaking the law of committing institutionalised racism because they gave up too easily and took it too effortlessly in the route of finding the killers of Stephen Lawrence.'

Student B
'The murder of Stephen Lawrence and its resulting investigation is perhaps one of the most infamous cases of police discrimination and incompetence of the last decade. The metropolitan police was criticised in its investigation for "a combination of professional incompetence, institutionalised racism and failure of leadership by senior officers.' To this day Stephen's murderers still have not been prosecuted for their crime and walk free despite having been named as the killers by a large number of informants, contrary to the police claims of a 'wall of silence'.

continued

Evidence proves that the legal system was at fault at every level of the investigation and highlights what needs to be done in order to ensure that cases like this never happens again. Here are some ways in which the case should have been dealt with:

- Police should have administered first aid to Stephen at the scene of the crime
- Investigation should have been more organised and directed during the vital hours after the murder and should have been led by more able and competent police officers
- Liaison with the Lawrence's and friends should have been dealt with with more sensitivity and openness
- All possible sources of information should have been utilised (Holmes police computer was not used because of lack of trained officers) and key witnesses to the murder – Duwayne Brooks – was 'side lined and ignored' due to prejudice on the polices behalf.
- Investigation and surveillance of suspects should have been more thorough, organised and documented
- Police officers involved in the investigation should have been un-tainted by outside influences. Unprejudiced, unbiased and sensitive
- The murder should have been recognised as a racial attack from the beginning
- More racial awareness training should have been given to police officers on every level of the investigation to prevent unappropriated and offensive language such as the terms 'negro' and 'coloured'.

The Lawrence family dealt with the police incompetence mentioned in the Macpherson report by fighting for an internal investigation, by campaigning and increasing public awareness. This forced the issue out into the open and made sure that reforms would be made and police negligence highlighted and condemned.'

Figure 4.2 Scenarios

framework of these policies, to be clear about how they are linked to the rights and responsibilities of members of the school community and to be able to challenge these ideas. The prompt questions can be seen in Figure 4.5.

For homework, we wanted students to move on from this activity to think more broadly about the rights and responsibilities of young people in relation to adults. For this we asked students to choose two statements and to come up with arguments both for and against each one. This was then used to feed in to a debate on these statements in the following lesson.

YEAR 10 GCSE CITIZENSHIP – RIGHTS AND RESPONSIBILITIES AT SCHOOL

(a) A Year 7 pupil is being bullied by a Year 9 pupil. She reports this to her form tutor. However, her tutor advises her to tell her parents as it is not a school issue.

Are teachers/schools legally responsible for dealing with bullying?

Who is normally responsible? Why?

(b) A pupil hears another pupil shouting in the toilets. As she walks past the toilet she sees a Year 8 pupil being beaten up by a group of girls. She carries on walking, as it's the teacher's responsibility to help the victim, not hers.

Are pupils legally responsible to intervene?

Morally who is in the wrong? Why?

(e) Selina is suspected of carrying weed in her school bag. Her form tutor asks her to empty her bag. Selina refuses, by saying that a teacher does not have the right to check anyone's bag.

Does the teacher legally have the right to check a pupils bag/belongings?

Morally who is in the wrong? Why?

Figure 4.3 Scenarios

LOOKING AT SOME OF THE SYDENHAM SCHOOL POLICIES

I. ANTI BULLYING POLICY

At Sydenham school we believe that everyone has the right to work and learn in a happy, secure and well-ordered environment.

We take a firm stand on undesirable behaviour and equal opportunities issues and those policies underpin our position that bullying behaviour of any kind can never be tolerated.

We see bullying as a systematic abuse of power; as behaviour which quite deliberately sets out to hurt, frighten and threaten. This definition, then, distinguishes bullying from occasional name calling or fighting which can erupt after a heated exchange.

2. ATTENDANCE POLICY

PRINCIPLES
- Every child has a fundamental right to be educated;
- Parents and teachers have a duty to ensure maximum attendance at school.

AIMS
- To enable maximum pupil attendance through valuing high attendance rates.
- To encourage students to take full advantage of their educational opportunity by attending regularly.
- To recognise the external factors which influence pupil attendance and work in partnership with parents, ESWS and other agencies to address difficulties.
- To create a culture in which attendance is valued and where students want to be punctual, are keen to attend and feel that they are missed when not here.

Figure 4.4 School policies

TASK BOX

1. In your own words explain what these policies mean and say why they are important.

2. What are agreed 'codes of conduct'? Why are they necessary?

3. What is the role of the student council? Do you think that it achieves its purpose? Explain your answer.

4. What do you think, 'We understand that having rights in the community also means that we must accept some responsibility' means?

5. Using the examples above (and any additional information from your planners) list the different ways in which Sydenham school policies can be improved?

Figure 4.5 Prompt questions

Evaluation

This unit represents our attempt to enable students to begin to make links between their personal world and the social and political world. We expected that many of our students, in common with young people elsewhere, would groan at the mention of politics, law or government and have great difficulty relating the legal and political system to their own lives. Our challenge with this unit was to make issues of rights, responsibilities, law and politics a challenging and relevant subject to our students as well as meeting the specifications of the examining board.

Our evaluation of this unit has taken the form of student feedback, both written and oral, as well as feedback from PSE staff teaching the unit. Students' written evaluations covered a range of aspects, from what students felt they expected to learn and what they had actually learnt, to what they had enjoyed and how it had affected their thoughts, beliefs and actions. We also asked students to suggest anything that needed adding and how the unit could be improved. The evaluation form can be seen in Figure 4.6.

Students identified that they had learnt about prejudice, racism, being a citizen, media, basic human rights and how our country is governed. One student commented that she had learnt 'that it is not only in one place or country we hear about racial discrimination, it is happening all over the world even though we might not notice it'. Many students

---

GCSE CITIZENSHIP STUDIES UNIT 1: RIGHTS AND RESPONSIBILITIES STUDENT EVALUATION

- What did you expect to learn about this unit? Be as specific as you can be.

- What did you learn about in this unit? Be as specific as you can be.

- What aspect(s) did you find most interesting and or/useful in this unit? Why?

- What aspect(s) did you find least interesting and or/useful in this unit? Why?

- What, if anything, needs adding or improving in this unit?

- What do you feel you improved on and/or achieved in this unit? Include skills as well as knowledge and understanding.

- What do you feel you still need to improve on in relation to this unit? Include skills as well as knowledge and understanding.

- How do you think this unit has or might affect your thoughts, beliefs and actions around your and others' rights and responsibilities?

Figure 4.6 Evaluation form

referred to learning about morals and rules and about government responsibilities as well as their own. Most students focused on how they had learnt about racial discrimination as well as the rights and responsibilities within their families and at school.

Students also wrote about which aspects of the unit they found most interesting. This was particularly useful as our concern had been that students may find this topic unapproachable and boring. Although many students focused on racism as the most interesting aspect, some students also identified the global aspect of their work on human rights as the most eye opening. One student commented on the lesson on the coffee industry. She said: 'The unfairness of employment and cheap labour in appalling conditions really shocked me because it makes me realise how awful life can be for children my age.' Several students also commented on the style of the lessons: 'It is all useful and the lessons are laid back and interesting.' I was pleased that some students had been interested in the political aspect of the unit. 'I found learning about the role of Parliament and the House of Lords the most interesting because it gave me insight into how our country is governed, I had not learnt this before.' Other students focused on the legal aspects of rights and referred specifically to criminal law: 'I like learning about the criminal law because I didn't know much about it at first and now I do.'

We also asked students to consider what they had achieved in the unit. These responses were very varied, including skills and attitudes as well as knowledge and understanding. In terms of attitudes, one student commented that: 'I understand that it doesn't matter where you come from, ethnicity, religion or skin colour, what matters is what is inside your character'. Another focused on progress she had made in her reading skills and confidence in exam questions, while others mentioned progress with group skills, for example, 'the skill to compromise within a group'. The knowledge and understanding focused on included a growing understanding of the importance of rights: 'Knowledge of the basic meaning of the term "rights" and how not to abuse them because I am fortunate enough to have them.' Another student said she had a better understanding of the reasons why we need rules and policies. Several students referred to the legal aspects of the work, in particular the criminal law as this was seen as relevant to their lives: 'I have improved on how much I understand the criminal law and now I will know what it means if I come across it in the future.'

The students' thoughts on the least interesting aspects of the unit were varied; some referred to particular learning styles, and one commented on a debate that she had not felt able to participate in. Others found that the need to apply their knowledge to exam questions was the least interesting part although they could identify good reason for doing this. A few students, though far fewer than we had anticipated, had found the legal and political aspects of the unit the least interesting. The responses to this question were the most varied and did include some students who could not identify a least interesting part. In some ways the variety of response to this question confirms the need to ensure a variety of teaching and learning styles as students clearly have a range of preferred ways of learning. Related to this question was one on how the unit could be improved. One student felt that we could look in more depth at the human rights abuses in different parts of the world; another wanted more discussion and more video resources. These issues will all form part of our teams review of the unit and we anticipate acting on a number of the suggestions.

Perhaps the most interesting part of the evaluation process for the PSE team were the comments on how it had affected students' thoughts, beliefs and actions, if at all. I had expected that a lot of students would be reluctant to talk or write about how the unit may have affected their views. However, many students expressed quite detailed and interesting thoughts. One student explained: 'I have realised how lucky I am compared to others in this world to have a free education, food, water and a safe home to live in.' Another remarked: 'I believe everyone should be treated equally and I don't see why some should endure discrimination. I have these advantages and I am happy to respect them by taking on my responsibilities.' I was interested to see that many students had made the link between the concepts of rights and responsibilities which we have found hard to establish in our lessons lower down the school. Some had also understood the global perspective of these ideas, linking their own experiences and choices to those of others. 'It makes you think twice about other people's feelings and beliefs.' One student commented on having greater confidence in tackling the issue of racism. She said: 'I am now more aware of it and why it is wrong . . . I now feel that if I see it happening that I can step in and try to help.' On a general level most students recognised that others have rights as well as themselves. 'Every person has got rights and other people have to respect that'. One student related the work to her life on a more practical level saying: 'I will make sure that I know all my rights and responsibilities and how to use them.' Although this unit did not focus heavily on government and parliament, it was nevertheless an aspect of the unit that some students found relevant and I was encouraged by the following point made: 'I didn't like the part about parliament but now I can see the importance of parliament.' There were few students who could not identify any effect on their beliefs, thoughts or actions. Perhaps this more than any other aspect of the evaluation was the most motivating for the teachers given that the aims of our unit included developing students' understanding of the concepts of mutual respect and understanding.

Conclusion

As the first unit in a new GCSE course the PSE team had a range of concerns and hopes in planning and teaching this unit. Firstly, we obviously wanted to cover some specific aspects of the Citizenship GCSE and to meet the aims initially set out for this unit. We were also concerned about making this work accessible and relevant to students' lives and learning needs. As PSE teachers, we needed to feel confident about teaching this unit and many of us were apprehensive about extending our own knowledge and skills in delivering this aspect of the PSHE and Citizenship curriculum.

A vital aspect of this work has been the use of active learning based resources such as case studies that often related to our students' own experiences. We have tried to continue to use the range of teaching and learning styles that have been so successful for our PSE curriculum in the past. The evaluations have shown that the unit has enabled many students to make the link between the political world on a national and international level and their own lives. Students' comments have given the PSE team ideas for developing this unit further by increasing the variety of resources and by including greater use of discussion and debates. The unit has resulted in greater teacher confidence in the teaching of citizenship at Key Stage 4 through a PSE programme. It has shown us that it is possible to introduce students to difficult concepts at the interface between the personal, political and social world. The PSE teachers have enjoyed the challenge of learning to teach a new aspect of the PSE curriculum and this will undoubtedly have an impact on our work at Key Stage 3. Despite our initial misgivings, teachers are clear that this unit represents an important and previously neglected element of our PSE curriculum. The challenge ahead for us will be to continue to develop schemes of work that meet the requirements for a dynamic and relevant PSE curriculum as well as meeting the requirements of the Citizenship curriculum. As a first attempt, students and teachers are optimistic.

Acknowledgements

I should like to acknowledge the contribution of Yvonne Brewster to this unit of work. Thanks also to the staff in the PSE Department and to the students from Sydenham School.

GCSE CITIZENSHIP STUDIES
UNIT 1: RIGHTS AND RESPONSIBILITIES

LESSON(S)/AIMS	ACTIVITIES	RESOURCES	ASSESSMENT FOCUS
1. To introduce the 'revised' GCSE. To introduce the concepts of citizenship, rights and responsibilities.	A. Read and explain new course overview. They need to replace the old one with this.	Course Overview sheet	K & U of:
	B. Explain the concept of citizenship, stressing the point that it is difficult to define. Show video clips 1 and 3 to illustrate the different views on citizenship. Get feedback.	Video clips 1 & 3 – The Citizenship Video Use Aims sheet.	• Course • Concepts of Citizenship, Rights & Responsibilities • Issues affecting our rights and responsibilities.
	C. Introduce the new unit and go over aims.	My Rights! My Responsibilities? Sheet.	
	D. Read Doug and Ug as a class. Ask them to draw a continuum as below.	Right & Responsibilities HW.	Skills
	They should then place a mark where their ideal world would be and finally add the following:		• Listening • Discussion • Explanation • Literacy
	Discuss and then explain this shows why we need a balance between rights and responsibilities as Doug or Ug are the alternative.		
	E. Complete the activities on My Right! Worksheet, either individual or pairs. Discuss examples for Q.4 as a class first.		
	HW: Complete CW and tasks on Rights and Responsibilities sheet.		

Year 10 GCSE CITIZENSHIP SOW – RIGHTS AND RESPONSIBILITIES (UNIT 1)

AIMS	ACTIVITIES	RESOURCES	LEARNING OBJECTIVES
2. To look at both the legal and moral rights and responsibilities of individuals within the family.	a) Sorting exercise, in pairs/small groups pupils should decide whether each statement is either true/false:	– Sorting cards	– To gain knowledge and understanding about the rights and responsibilities within the family.
	b) Call class together; ask each group for feedback, discussion.	– Information sheets ('Rights and resp., in the family, what is the law?')	
	c) Hand out information sheet, with some of the legal responsibilities of the family. Read with class. Each pupil to put into their folders for revision.	– 'Who should have the right?' Homework sheet.	– To understand some of the complexities involved in making distinctions between legal rights and responsibilities and moral ones.
	d)		
	– Divide class into 2 groups, either for/against.		
	– Copy statement 1 from 'Who should have the right?' Worksheet onto the board.		
	– Each group will have 2 minutes to produce an argument either for/against the statement.		
	– A pupil from each side will present argument to the class.		*Skills*
	– Whole class decides which was the strongest argument. (Keep scores on the board).		– Collaborative
	– Repeat above for all 4 statements.		– Decision making
			– Reasoning skills
	e) Set H/W – 'Who should have the right?' (Write up arguments for and against each statement).		– Communication
			– Team Building

AIMS	ACTIVITIES	RESOURCES	LEARNING OBJECTIVES
3. To know that members of the school community have both moral and legal rights and responsibilities.	a) Hand out scenario sheets, in small groups pupils should discuss each statement and answer the questions on the sheet. (Complete first scenario with the class to ensure pupils understand task). b) Call class together, ask for feedback. c) Handout school policy sheets and discuss why we have them, in pairs pupils complete questions. d) H/W – Complete Worksheet. – Find out about a different policy (This can be a policy in a shop, restaurant, retail, bank etc.) and write down its purpose/aims. Do you think it is effective? Why?	– Worksheets on rights and responsibilities at school. – School policy sheet.	To gain K and U about: – The purpose of school policies. – Understand the rights and responsibilities of members within the school. – Make distinctions between legal and moral responsibilities at school. *Skills* – Collaborative – Decision making – Reasoning skills – Communication

AIMS	ACTIVITIES	RESOURCES	LEARNING OBJECTIVES
4. To look at how rights and responsibilities vary between different cultures, religions and ethnic groups.	a) Look at the rights and responsibilities at home of a Muslim pupil Kaleeda. As a class, decide what factors affect Kaleeda's rights and responsibilities (i.e. religion, caste, traditional, parent values, ethnicity). b) Pupils list the different rights and responsibilities they have at home. c) Pupils should make comparisons between their rights and responsibilities at home and Kaleeda's. Divide class into small groups (possibly culturally/ethnically) or ask pupils to move around the room and compare their answers to 3 others. Pupils to look for pattern or similarities and differences between their list of rights and responsibilities within the family and other pupils. (Use Worksheet). d) Call class together, discuss any patterns and think about factors that influence people's rights and responsibilities. (i.e. religion/class etc). e) Set H/W – Interview an adult (either parent/guardian) find out the rights and responsibilities they have and what factors influence them.	– Work sheet 'Looking at different rights and responsibilities within the family'. 2 parts	– To gain knowledge and understanding about the different rights and responsibilities in the home of individuals from different cultures and religious backgrounds. – To be able to make comparisons between different rights and responsibilities. – Be able to identify different factors, which influence the rights and responsibilities of individuals. *Skills* – Collaborative – Decision making – Reasoning skills – Communication

YEAR 10 GCSE CITIZENSHIP SOW – RIGHTS AND RESPONSIBILITY

AIMS	ACTIVITIES	RESOURCES	LEARNING OBJECTIVES
5. To understand the interdependence of individuals, groups and global communities. The importance and need for mutual respect and understanding.	Explain aims of lesson and purpose of activity (Refer to learning objectives). a) Divide the class into 5 groups. Give each of the groups a role card, each group must think very carefully about their roles. Consider the points below: – How do they feel about it? – What sort of problems might they face? – What strengths do they need as a group? b) Call class together; hold up the coffee jar card, tell the groups that the jar is sold for £1.60 in the supermarket. Get the groups to discuss how much of the selling price they should get for the work they do, not what they think they get. c) Copy the table overleaf on the board, ask each group to tell the other groups how much they think they should get and the reasons why. Record the amount on the 'initial proportion' column. Repeat for all groups. d) Add up the amount, it will be more than £1.60! Ask each group to negotiate its position and reach a total of £1.60. Encourage groups to justify their claims – discussion. When agreement has been reached, record amounts into the 'Negotiated Proportion' column. e) Announce the actual amounts received by the people in each stage of production, by completing the last column. Discuss the 'Is?' there mutual respect on completed table. Ask pupils to discuss why this is the case? Although we are interdependent, is the situation fair? Is there mutual respect and equality? What can be done to improve the situation? Discuss – Explain H/W	– Role Cards – Coffee Jar Card – Table on the board. – H/W sheet. 'What can you do?'	– To understand how the trading system affects the coffee growers in Uganda, buyers and supermarket owners in the UK. Who benefits and who loses from trade? Is this fair? – To know that countries are interdependent on each other and have various different contributions to make to the global community. *Skills* – Communication – Discussion – Justification – Critical thinking – Reflection – Collaborative

GCSE CITIZENSHIP STUDIES
UNIT 1: RIGHTS AND RESPONSIBILITIES

LESSON(S)/AIMS	ACTIVITIES	RESOURCES	ASSESSMENT FOCUS
6. Rights & Responsibilities within the legal & justice system. Aims: To explore why we have laws, types of laws, specific laws in relation to human rights and where to get advice.	A. Recap over the unit so far, emphasising the point that we have moved from looking at R & R of individuals, within school, home, communities and internationally.	International agreements booklet.	K & U of: • Human rights legislation • Concepts civil and criminal law • Court and sentencing procedures
	B. Explain aims for today, with the initial focus on international agreements on R & R.	Civil vs. Criminal Law Booklet.	
		In the dock: a case study	Skills – Listening – Discussion – Evaluation – Explanation – Literacy
	C. Groups of 4: give them international agreements booklet. They need to skim over them and pick out the key themes that run through all of them, e.g. life, freedom, equality etc. Put these onto a brainstorm for their folders. Feedback.	Damien Thompson table	
		What is the law HW sheet.	
	D. Explain that we will now be looking at law more generally. Give out civil versus criminal booklet. Read over important aspects together. Ask class, which are civil, criminal or both; manslaughter (crim.) wills, (civ), property damage (both), libel (civ). Write as you go for them to copy.		
	E. Explain we will now use a case study to check their understanding. Give Damien case study and grids to groups. They need to use all the information in booklet to complete grid and come to a final punishment (sentence and damages to pay). Feedback. H/W: Read, fill gaps and tick sheet on Why Law.		

GCSE CITIZENSHIP STUDIES
UNIT 1: RIGHTS AND RESPONSIBILITIES

LESSON(S)/AIMS	ACTIVITIES	RESOURCES	ASSESSMENT FOCUS

7. Rights & Responsibilities of the media.
 	
Aims: To explore the importance of a free press, which investigates and reports on issues of public interest vs. their responsibility to be accurate and fair.
	A. Explain aims for today, emphasising the point that the media is another major institution in society that affects our R & R.
	
	B. Give definition of the media for them to copy down; means of communication that can reach a large number of people.
	
	C. Brainstorm forms of media (television, radio, newspapers, internet, satellite, music etc.).
	
	D. Explain that we will now look at the functions of the media and what the R & R of the media are in Britain. Handout 'Functions of Media' sheet and Media R & R 'articles'. Read over these as a class.
	
	E. With this information in mind, as a class briefly discuss the following statements; 'Celebrities shouldn't moan about the press. If you're in the public eye, you have to accept the bad press with the good'. You could bring in Princess Diana's death.
	
	F. Explain we will now look at how different newspapers use their functions and R & R. Groups of 4: give them a tabloid and broadsheet. They should compare them and discuss the content and space given to:
	
	  • Headlines/Main stories
	  • International news stories
	  • 'Showbiz' / Sports stories
	  • Finally, any evidence of bias
	
	H. Feedback on above points and what this says about how the press address:
	
	  • Their right to investigate and report
	  • Their responsibility to provide accurate information.
	  HW: Write up this feedback.
		Functions of R & R of Media sheet.
		
		Tabloid and broadsheet newspapers (6 of each, from same day).
			K & U of:
			
			• The concept of the media
			• The functions of the media
			• The rights & responsibilities of the media
			• The power of the free press
			
			Skills
			
			– Listening
			– Discussion
			– Content Analysis
			– Explanation
			– Literacy

LESSON(S)/AIMS	ACTIVITIES	RESOURCES	ASSESSMENT FOCUS
8. Resource-based questions on Racial Discrimination. Aims: To assess K & U and skills of R & R unit, using a current social issue.	A. Explain that this is the assessment for this unit. They will have this lesson to become familiar with the sources and to collect any missed CW and begin making notes. Their HW will be to write up their answers in neat and to complete an evaluation for this unit. They will have two weeks of HW time, but only today's lesson to prepare! B. Handout instructions sheet, source booklet and question sheet. Go through all three with class. C. Students must now begin the preparation for their assessment. They should: – read over sources and Q's carefully – check they have everything from the lessons/HW that they need. – Begin to make notes for each question with spider diagrams, bullet points in a list and / or annotating in the booklet. D. Five mins. Before end of lesson hand out evaluation sheet and go over it. State that it is very important that this is completed as well because this is a pilot course and we need to monitor it continuously. They will not get an attainment mark for it, but it will be marked for effort. The assessment is not complete without it! HW: As told at beginning of lesson – complete resource-based assessment questions and evaluation. Two weeks.	Instructions sheet Source booklet Questions sheet Evaluation sheet Lots of lined paper!	K & U of key themes that ran throughout rights and responsibilities unit (see instruction sheet) *Skills* – Literacy – Research – Analysis – Extended writing – Evaluation

Part II

Case studies of wider school practice

Chapter 5

Conflict resolution in schools: cases studies from an Inner London Borough

Sally Inman and Nola Turner

'I think hopefully, all the kids will soon realise that ultimately the idea of conflict resolution is not only about resolving conflicts, but preventing it from developing in the first place.'

(Co-ordinator, School A)

This chapter explores the potential of whole school initiatives around mediating and reducing conflict to contribute to, and be supported by PSHE and citizenship. The chapter is based on case studies of conflict resolution in practice and is drawn from an evaluation of a conflict reduction project in a number of secondary schools within an Inner London Borough – Tower Hamlets.[1] We are conscious that there is a welcome growth in conflict resolution work in primary and secondary schools and a growing literature in the area. We have chosen not to review this literature here, but rather to provide the reader with a glimpse of conflict resolution in action, using the words of the adults and young people involved in the work.

The evaluation

The evaluation was carried out between July 2000 and May 2001. The work in the schools formed part of a LEA wide, SRB funded project to develop conflict resolution in schools in the borough. The LEA conflict resolution project worked to a number of explicit success criteria as stated in the original SRB funding bid. These were:

- a change in ethos and culture in the schools;
- an increase in the understanding of staff in how to handle conflict;
- a reduction in the number of sanctions being given to young people.

The schools added success criteria of their own to those of the LEA.

Methodology

The evaluation took the form of a small-scale, qualitative study. We were concerned to explore the success or otherwise of the conflict resolution programmes through arriving at the understandings and experiences of those most involved. We were interested in the lived reality of the programmes for students and staff. A number of methods were used to collect evidence. These were:

- a review of the documentation at LEA and school level;
- semi-structured interviews in schools with senior managers, participating and non-participating staff, student trainers from Years 10 and 11, students identified as experiencing difficulty in resolving conflicts, Year 7 students who had received training from older peers, Year 8 students who had received training in the previous year;
- semi-structured interviews with the external facilitators for the projects and a school counsellor;
- observations of peer led training workshops, training sessions for student trainers led by external facilitators, a residential training session for staff led by a facilitator.

The limited time and funding available for the evaluation also played a part in determining the methodological approach adopted. While quantitative data relating to areas such as student achievement, exclusions, the incidence of bullying, etc. may be important indicators of the effectiveness of conflict reduction work, such data can only be built up over a measured period of time if it is to be meaningful. Our time-scale did not allow for this.

The conflict resolution programmes

Although there were variations in the history of the conflict resolution work across the schools with which we worked, the general pattern was one in which programmes had initially been set up to change the behaviour of a challenging group or class of students. At this early stage, students and staff in the schools had received training designed to impact on their ability to deal with conflicts in their lives and in the classroom. This typically included the experience of powerful residential sessions that took place over one or, in some cases, two weekends. A selected group of students then were given the responsibility of training Year 7 students and acting as their friends and mentors around the school, giving advice and dealing with less serious incidents of conflict as they arose. A variation of this involved students visiting local primary feeder schools where they ran a training session for Year 6 children in the term before they started secondary school.

The model was based on the desire to engage as many young people as possible in conflict resolution work, while at the same time ensuring that staff became more aware of conflict issues and acquired the skills for dealing with them. There were some common elements in all the schools. These were:

- Giving older students valued training and meaningful responsibilities.
- Enabling older students to become respected role models to younger students.
- Enhancing students' self-esteem.
- Giving staff in key roles the opportunities to learn advanced conflict resolution skills from professional trainers.
- Increasing all staff's awareness of conflict issues.
- Contributing to the potential of the school as a learning and achieving community.

Case study: School A

The conflict resolution work began in School A in 1996. The impetus for the project came from a number of concerns:

- Racial tensions among older students; there had been a particularly worrying racial incident outside the school.
- The LEA review of the school had indicated some negative features of the ethos as evidenced by high levels of vandalism, some reported student discontent, and staff perceptions of communication difficulties between staff and Senior Management.
- An external survey that recommended work on conflict resolution in school.

In School A older students are trained in conflict resolution and mediation.

> 'The aim of this programme is to provide skills to Year 10 students to enable them to work with Year 7 students on issues around conflict resolution.'
>
> (Co-ordinator's report 98/99)

The conflict resolution programme cycle in School A works in the following way. The conflict resolution work is discussed with Year 9 students and applications are invited for training. Normally around sixty students apply to be a volunteer and the names then go to a Year 9 staff team meeting. Teachers apply a number of selection criteria at this stage. These include:

- good attendance and punctuality;
- willingness to work after hours;
- willingness to catch up on other work missed.

The selection process normally reduces the numbers to around forty-six at this stage. The selected students are then required to attend selection workshops where they are engaged in role-play, group activities, discussion and reflection. External facilitators run the workshops. At this stage further criteria come into play. These include:

- ability to speak up;
- ability to discuss in small and large groups;
- ability to listen;
- ability to show empathy.

As a result of the workshops the numbers are further reduced to around twenty-four students. These students then attend a residential training weekend with an external trainer and a group of volunteer staff. The trained Year 10 students then work as groups of three, attached to Year 7 classes. At the start of the year they are introduced to the whole class, their photographs are displayed in the form room and they are attached to small groups. In addition, the students work with the external facilitator to plan and run workshops on conflict resolution for Year 7 students. Year 7 form tutors attend these workshops.

'From that residential everybody was given a pair or a three, and they were given each class, so like responsibility for a class. Like big brothers and sisters to them to guide them in year seven.'

'When we began to be trainers in charge of the year seven we were like teachers, we could do anything, anything a teacher could do. Like, if a person is in trouble, like we could phone home, if a person can't do that we could help them out.'

'We see them around school and everything and if they need help from us, then we just help them as well.'

'If they got a problem, they can come to us. We are like the parents to them.'

(Student trainers)

In the Spring Term there is a second residential weekend for the trainers focusing on the mentoring of Year 7 students. The intention of this residential is to further develop the skills whereby Year 10 students can create a long-term relationship with the younger students. The training aims to enable them to identify issues; for example, bullying or low self-esteem, and develop their skills so as to enable them to engage in early intervention strategies in situations of conflict. The student trainers we interviewed described some of the strategies they adopt:

'We don't tell them that they have to respect, we sort of teach it to them, explain to them, advising them, that kind of thing. We don't "tell" them what to do, that's not going to change it.'

(bullying) 'You talk to the person who is bullying them. Get them together, let them talk together and see if they stop bullying them and if he doesn't, we come in and we talk to both of them together, and get both points understood, and then see what's wrong. After that if he is still bullying, we have responsibility, after we talked about it. We have to go through the procedures with the teachers to sort it. That person will be excluded for whatever time.'

'The thing is, if we are in the playground and there is a fight there, we will have some responsibility. We have to get to help to get them inside, and like start the questions. If the matters get worse the teachers get involved. We are involved further, cause we got them inside. We talk to the person about why and everything. After that it's like sorted.'

Case study: School B

One of the original impetuses for the adoption of conflict resolution work within School B was a concern with an identified group of Year 9 and 10 students at risk of exclusion. The students were all boys, low achievers and were demonstrating difficulties in dealing with relationships with peers and adults in positive ways. Using SRB funding from the LEA the school engaged external facilitators to devise and run a training programme on anger management and conflict resolution with this group of young people. Three teachers and the school counsellor/home-school worker were also involved in the programme. The aims and objectives of this pilot programme were:

Aims:
- A reduction in 'bullying' behaviour by participants towards peers and staff.
- A reduction in loud aggressive behaviour between participants.
- An increase in conflict management skills among participants.
- An improvement in the emotional literacy of participants especially when dealing with anger and irritation.

Objectives:
- To facilitate several conflict resolution and anger management workshops with the six specifically selected participant students.
- To provide space and time to allow the participants to build up trust in each other, the facilitators and in the process.
- To engage these students in activities appropriate to their needs and to the aims of the pilot project.
- To help ensure sustainability and integration of the project by actively involving members of School B staff in the project at strategic stages.
- To involve the students in the evaluation of the project by encouraging them to monitor and self regulate their behaviour during the course of the project and in the future.

External facilitators

At the same time the school began to extend existing work on training young people to become peer counsellors. Year 9 and 10 students were selected for training. The project was advertised across the school and students were required to fill out application forms. The criteria for selection put emphasis on good attendance. Behaviour records were taken into account, though some young people who were 'risky' were selected on the grounds that involvement in the project may provide the stimulus for them to understand their own behaviour more and become better able to take responsibility.

The peer counselling training was delivered by a combination of external facilitators and the school counsellor/home-school worker. The training developed into the current structure whereby students from Years 9 and 10 are trained to work with Year 7 students. The peer counsellors are put into pairs and attached to Year 7 tutor groups. They work with the groups on a weekly basis providing support around friendships and conflicts and self-confidence and esteem. They are also available for one-to-one sessions with Year 7 students. A further development has been the involvement of the peer counsellors with Year 6 students as part of their induction programme before they start secondary school. Members of the school council are also involved in induction work with Year 6 students, as part of a larger school involvement with feeder primary schools.

Case study: School C

The origins of the conflict resolution work at School C can be traced to the early 1990s when the school went through a period of unrest, heightened by racial tension in the local community. This had a serious effect on levels of achievement throughout the school, and staff, parents and students wanted change. A feasibility study was conducted by external facilitators for developing a project that would train staff and students in 'practical skills and strategies for dealing with conflict'. The study found there was a general fear of conflict and a lack of skills for dealing with it in the school. However, it also stated that 'Staff and students shared the vision of a school which feels safe and where everyone takes responsibility for their own actions, and cares for and respects others' (Feasibility Study Report, July 1994).

In its initial phase, the work at School C ran for three years from 1994 to 1997. There was a positive evaluation on this work. A further programme was set up to run from September 1998 to December 1999. This too was deemed to be successful. Since then the project has continued year on year and it is thoroughly embedded in the school's strategic planning.

The pattern of the programme is as follows:

- All tutor groups in Year 9 receive training from external facilitators in the summer term.
- Year 9 students are invited to apply for further training to become peer trainers in Year 10.
- A group of about twenty students are selected.
- Early in the Autumn term this group receives training in preparation for a weekend residential course attended by volunteers drawn from the staff as well as the students.

- The group delivers training workshops to Year 7 students, supported by trained members of staff as well as external facilitators.
- Year 10 trainers have the opportunity to learn mediation skills at a second residential weekend in November in order to give further support to Year 7 around the school.
- The programme is reviewed annually.

The aims and objectives of the programme for 2000–2001 were:

Aims:
- To continue to provide a peer training scheme in confronting conflict work.
- To further develop a peer mediation scheme within the school.
- To further develop strategies to enable staff to support and run programmes in confronting conflict work.
- To explore the idea of Leadership with senior students in the school.

Objectives:
- To recruit and train a new group of peer trainers.
- To provide further training for the peer trainers in mediation skills.
- To provide peer trainers and mediators with opportunities to practise their skills in a structured and supported programme.
- To recruit and train a group of senior students in Leadership skills.

Outcomes of the conflict resolution work in the schools

The conflict resolution work in these schools has proved to be an important element of whole school provision for the PSD of the young people in their care. The student trainers we interviewed in the schools were all able to talk at length about the skills and understandings that they had learned through being trainers. They described feeling more confident, having higher self-esteem and having developed a range of negotiation skills that they felt would prove useful in their adult lives.

> 'This is the best stuff I have ever done in school. It has made me understand the school is on my side really if I can do something for the school. I used to hate coming here but I like it now and I don't want the little kids to be as bad as I was.'
>
> (Year 10 student, School B)

'I'm much better at putting things in a non-confrontational way. Like, I'm able to go up to people and ask what the trouble is and not get into fights myself. I'm like more cool!'

(Year 10 student, School C)

'I have learned a lot of new skills. Teamwork, how to deal with the younger children, resolving things. And another thing is like, participation with other people, like a person who doesn't wanna talk about a conflict or problem, sort of getting him into how it started, so they talk.'

'I am helping someone else how to grow up in a school.'

'We can be good parents, now cause we know how to be with young kids.'

(Years 9 and 10, School A)

'We are getting to know each other as friends; we can trust each other and we know how to work together.'

'I think we have more skills now for dealing with people and situations and they will always be there from now on.'

(Year 10 students, School C)

'I had a fight when we was at residential and we had to be an example to the rest . . . we had to learn to work together, we couldn't just, like, go to some other group and avoid each other. It was good for me. Like if I had a fight before, I'd just storm off in a huff and not speak to anybody, but I've learned it ain't no good. You just gotta get along with people.'

(Year 10 student, School C)

The younger students we interviewed were also positive about having older students trained in conflict resolution.

'They are encouraging to us, to want us to learn more.'

'If you have a problem, they help us solving it.'

'If someone is bullying you, they turn up to stop some.'

'If there is a problem with the playground you just find them and tell them and then they try to sort you out.'

'They wanted us to learn that people can have different opinions but still talk to each other, you don't have to fight to prove who is the best.'

(Year 7 students from Schools A, B and C)

One of the Year 7 students we interviewed had a very clear understanding of one of the reasons for training the older students

'[it] Makes them more experienced, in working with children. So if they come across a problem or something they can always help the person. It makes them better people when they grow up.'

Staff training in conflict resolution

One of the schools (School B) had put a lot of emphasis on the training of staff (teachers, learning mentors and classroom assistants) in conflict resolution. The training was described to us as being initially to do with 'damage limitation and crisis management' but has developed into a training programme that aims to support staff in developing a range of strategies and support mechanisms to help them sustain positive and inclusive relationships with young people. The residential staff training we observed was powerfully engaging the staff. The exercises required staff to give of themselves and to confront their own fears and anger. The work also provided opportunities for staff to support each other and get affirmation of their skills and achievements. The approaches used by the facilitators provided models of ways of working with students.

The aims of the residential programme for School B are set out below.

* To introduce a range of conflict resolution and anger management tools to staff members working with pupils in a variety of contexts.
* To explore appropriate methodology.
* To try out intervention strategies.
* To develop personal self-support mechanisms and model these to pupils.

External facilitators

The work required facilitators with expertise and experience, able to construct and sustain a safe learning environment. Several of the staff commented on the powerfulness of the workshop in relation to their own self-realisation and were clear that they would be able to use this self-awareness in their relationships with students.

'Well, it has given me an insight into how the students are developing. Not just thinking "Wow, so-and-so is more mature now", but understanding how they have got to that point . . . I see what they can achieve and how good our kids can become because it's so easy for them to write themselves off. And another thing is that having done work on conflict resolution I begin to think of conflict from the students' point of view. I understand why they get drawn in.'

'I think I have benefited a lot in managing behaviour. I think I handle conflicts better when they arise in the classroom as a teacher and as a form tutor. So a lot of children get the benefit of these skills. I am also more tolerant of the kids in general.'

Who benefits from conflict resolution programmes?

In the schools we worked with there were some tensions around which students should benefit from conflict resolution programmes. There was often a dilemma as to whether the training should be prioritised for those students who can demonstrate the potential for providing good role models for younger students, or whether the more challenging students should also receive the training, particularly when it could be argued that their needs are greatest. For the schools there is an unresolved issue around justifying the use of scarce resources on students with a poor reputation in school, especially when those resources are being used to purchase a weekend of residential training with highly skilled professional trainers. However, the most difficult students often have the most urgent need to confront the conflicts they create and to learn the skills of managing their own behaviour, yet it is clearly difficult to take a risk with those young people whose behaviour could undermine a conflict resolution programme.

The external facilitators we talked with were clear that working with more challenging students was important.

'I prefer to work with kids who have experienced conflict themselves because it gives me more to work with, and those kids have the voice of experience which is just what we want. Sometimes youngsters on the way to exclusion who have avoided being completely turned off school make the best material.'

(External Facilitator)

The schools too were aware of the need to include students whose behaviour is challenging. For example:

> 'The big worry about peer support is that it is seen as sad, boffin, rubbish. But you have to try to include kids who think like that. You can't just have the good kids. You have to have it centred on whom you are working with. You can't just have ordinary kids.'
>
> (Counsellor, School B)

> 'They didn't take on people who are really good at work. They took on people who were messing around and who changed. If they changed, they can change people in Year 7 as well!'
>
> (Year 10 student, School A)

The debate around which students should be prioritised for training in conflict resolution remains unresolved in the schools with which we worked. There is no doubt that all the adults were agreed that targeted work on confronting and resolving conflict should be part of the repertoire of what is offered to students on the margins. The issue is more to do with where to place such work in the face of competing demands and scarce resources.

The institutional context

One of the intentions of the project was to bring about lasting change to the culture and ethos of the schools. The vision was that of school communities where relationships were built on respect and sensitivity for the feelings of others. With this vision went the development of positive behaviour management practices which all staff have the skills to employ. This was clearly a tall order and teachers we spoke with were clear that conflict resolution could only form one aspect of building such communities, albeit an important one. They were clear that conflict resolution could not be a panacea for turning a school around. It had to be seen as one ingredient in a plan for school improvement:

> 'Conflict resolution and other similar programmes have to be seen an ingredient in the school's success rather than the main reason for it. *All* we do contributes to a growth in the students' confidence in themselves. The impact is implicit rather than explicit.'
>
> (Deputy Head, School C)

'It's very important that schools do not think that our work waves some kind of magic wand. A three year relationship is necessary to really *make* an impact (on school ethos).'

(Facilitator, School C)

'I think I want to say that the school does not want to inflate the importance of the conflict resolution work. It is part of a range of things we do. But, that said, I can say that the ethos of the school has changed. The children now enjoy being friendly rather than confrontational with each other, and that hasn't always been the case. What I might call an "anti-boffin" culture is diminishing, so it's much less common for kids to spend endless time and energy on cussing and seeking petty revenge.'

(Deputy Head, School C)

The wider school ethos and climate is a critical factor in the success or otherwise of conflict resolution work. However, this is not straightforward in that the schools in this study had developed conflict resolution projects partly to enhance the school ethos; yet their success was not unrelated to the fact that there was already well-developed elements of a positive and socially inclusive ethos in the schools. Conflict resolution programmes can clearly contribute towards a school climate and ethos that promotes the overall PSD of students. However, somewhat paradoxically they may be most effective where they form part of a coherent set of PSD structures and practices. Put crudely, conflict resolution programmes seem to be most effective in schools that are already partially 'successful' in relation to provision for their students' PSD.

Conflict resolution, PSHE and PSD

If conflict resolution is to have maximum effect in a school then it needs to be explicitly and coherently linked to other whole school initiatives for PSD and to the PSHE curriculum. In the schools we worked with it was clear that conflict resolution was one of a range of broad PSD curriculum initiatives aimed at raising self-esteem and confidence, enhancing student responsibility and participation. In these schools the initiatives included peer mentoring and counselling, using students to act as guides and interpreters within the school and local community and school councils. In all of the schools the conflict resolution work explicitly supported and linked into the PSHE taught curriculum. The

PSHE curriculum was used as a vehicle for developing the knowledge, skills and attitudes associated with mediation and conflict resolution and this work fed into the programme.

Key ingredients of successful conflict resolution in schools

In the evaluation study we noted some key ingredients of effective conflict resolution work in the schools in Tower Hamlets. These included:

- a desire for fundamental change (and to maintain that change) on behalf of the Senior Management Team, backed by full consultation with the school community including young people;
- the work is managed by staff with the power to see things through;
- an acknowledgement of the specialist skills of an external facilitator;
- effective communication between the school and the external facilitator;
- an explicit policy of keeping the whole school community well informed about the programme, by a variety of means including student presentations, and regular items at staff and governors meetings;
- a recognition by staff of the whole school demands of the programme and a will to find the time and resources to make it work on a permanent basis.

Just another initiative?

Conflict resolution has the potential to make an important contribution to students' PSD. The schools in the evaluation study demonstrate ways in which this potential can be realised. However, it is critical that work such as this becomes embedded in whole school structures and practices, rather than remain a somewhat 'bolt on' project or initiative. In some of the schools in the evaluation study there was a sense in which conflict resolution was still seen as a project sustained through the commitment of a few senior staff, rather than as a routine part of the school's activities. In all the schools relatively few members of staff were involved in the day-to-day running of the programmes. This limits the impact conflict resolution programmes can have on changing the ways in which all teachers deal with conflict in schools. Those teachers who volunteer for the role of trainers gain the most, and there is a danger that other staff will come to rely on these people to deal with conflicts as they arise. Similarly conflict resolution work needs to be explicitly built into the PSHE curriculum so as to ensure that all students get the opportunity to develop the very real knowledge, skills and values that come with this work.

Working in partnership

The schools in this study had all received external funding for conflict resolution. The funding had enabled them to bring in external expertise and pay for residential training for students and staff. Conflict resolution programmes are emotionally and intellectually demanding on students and staff. It is our view that the training teachers and young people require for this work is highly specialised and necessitates the use of external facilitators with appropriate expertise and experience.[2] Working with students without this level of training can be not just ineffective but harmful to young people.

> 'You *must* work with an outside agency. I cannot stress enough how important this is. Our staff do not have the time to plan and run the programmes to the same level. And it is good for the students to work with strangers. It adds a dimension to what we are trying to teach about respect and self-confidence. Our kids really respect the professionalism of the external team and they see them in a different light to the teachers. I suppose another aspect of this is that it is good for the school to have an external team working with us. It boosts our morale and is very good for the staff who are working in partnership with the team.'
>
> (Deputy Head, School C)

The teachers we interviewed were clear in that for conflict resolution to be effective and sustained there needs to be an ongoing, long-term partnership with external professionals.

Conclusion

Conflict resolution work is an important ingredient of a whole school approach to personal and social development. However, there is always a danger that work like this is short-lived, dependent on current 'fashions' and funding priorities. This study has convinced us that it should have a permanent place in all schools. For this to happen conflict resolution will need to become an integral part of the routine structures and practices of schools. PSHE should form one important context in which to embed this work.

Notes

1. Tower Hamlets Education commissioned the Centre for Cross Curricular Initiatives, South Bank University, to undertake the evaluation. The evaluation was carried out between the summer of 2000 and July 2001.
2. The three external trainers involved in the work described in this chapter are: LEAP Confronting Conflict, The Lab, 8 Lennox Road, London N43NW; Tig Land, Independent Consultant and Trainer, Email tigland@freeuk.com Phone 07958560685; Win Win Solutions (no longer operating).

Acknowledgements

We should like to thank the adults and young people in the schools involved in the project for their willingness to engage so positively and honestly in the evaluation. Thanks also to Tower Hamlets Education for supporting the projects and giving permission for us to use the evaluation study as the basis of this chapter.

Chapter 6

School councils and pupils' personal and social development

Sally Inman

Earlier chapters have taken the view that an effective PSHE and citizenship curriculum will both support and be supported by a range of whole school practices. We have argued that PSHE makes a very important contribution to the school's provision for pupils' personal and social development, but that it needs to have coherent links to other school structures and practices that also foster this development. We have also attempted to demonstrate how the learning outcomes for PSHE and citizenship describe broad areas of personal and social development, areas that should be promoted through an explicitly planned whole school approach in which the PSHE and citizenship curriculum play important roles.

This chapter looks at the capacity of school councils to play an important role in fostering the PSD of pupils. The chapter is a shortened and adapted version of a report of a three-year research project exploring the contribution of school councils to citizenship education. The research was commissioned and funded by the Association of Teachers and Lecturers (ATL).[1] In this chapter I attempt to demonstrate how school councils can both give support to, and be supported through, the PSHE and citizenship curriculum. In doing so I explore the need for a particular kind of institutional context – one that promotes democratic structures and practices.

School councils have a long, if chequered, history in primary and secondary schools in the UK. At a national level successive governments have recognised that school councils can play a useful role in fostering aspects of pupils' PSD in schools. National initiatives with respect to citizenship education since at least the Education Reform Act (ERA) 1988 have made reference to the capacity of school councils to promote knowledge, understanding and skills associated with democratic citizenship. There is not space here to list all these initiatives, but from the Speaker's Commission (1990), Curriculum Guidance 8, the Crick Report (1998), through to the National Curriculum (NC) 2000 we can find references to the important part that school councils can play in pupils' PSD. The non-statutory Framework for PSHE and citizenship at Key Stage 1 and 2, the non-statutory PSHE Framework at Key Stage 3 and 4, and the programme of study for citizenship in secondary schools all make explicit references to the contributions of school councils. The QCA schemes of work for citizenship include some useful guidance on pupil participation, including effective school councils. School Councils UK have provided some excellent materials for primary and secondary schools (School Councils UK 2002).

While school councils are still not given a statutory role in schools as they are elsewhere in Europe, schools are now being explicitly encouraged to develop school councils as an essential element of broad citizenship education, including PSHE.

What contributions can school councils make to PSHE and citizenship? How do they support the PSD of pupils? The literature on school councils would seem to indicate that in theory they could serve a number of inter-related purposes for pupils, teachers and schools:

- School councils can contribute to the promotion of *good relationships and discipline* by providing pupils with opportunities to participate and take on responsibilities within the school. In 1989 the Elton Enquiry Report (1989) recommended that students be given more responsibility and argued that where they participate in decisions about their own learning there were significant benefits for themselves and schools. The report argued that students behave better when they are given more responsibility. School councils can also encourage a sense of collective responsibility. The DfEE Circular 8/94 Pupil Behaviour and Discipline advocated school councils as a means of involving students in school life and taking responsibility. The evaluation of the pupil council initiatives undertaken by the Priority Area Development in Liverpool provides a similar picture of school councils contributing to a decrease in anti-social behaviour in pupils and enhancing the relationships between pupils and teachers (Khaleel 1993). Owen and Tarr's (1998) research in a school for students with disabilities suggests that school councils can be effective in combating anti-social behaviour. Trafford makes the same point in his work (Trafford 1993). A slightly different version of this position can be seen in the view that school councils provide opportunities for pupils to *learn to care for others and to engage in service to the community.*

- School councils can contribute to a more *inclusive school* and form part of a range of strategies to combat disaffection and alienation of some pupils. The Commission for Racial Equality Report on exclusions found that schools that had lowered their exclusion rates had established structures for involving students in the life of the school. Osler, in describing the findings of the report, says of such schools:

> They had effective structures for involving children in management and decision-making such as a school or class council.
> (Osler 1997, quoted in Davies 1998)

Research by Davies for School Councils UK provides further evidence that effective school councils can have an impact on *pupil exclusion and inclusion*. Her qualitative study of school councils in ten schools indicated that the impact of effective school councils on pupil inclusion/exclusion can be seen as a continuum, from what she describes as direct impact through measures such as peer control to a more indirect impact through the ability of the school council to convey important messages to pupils about, for example, being listened to and shown respect (Davies 1998).

- School councils provide a forum through *which pupils can have their voices heard and exercise their rights*. This view of school councils is based on a children's rights model (Franklin 1986; Davie 1989; Hart 1992). School councils are viewed within this model as one mechanism by which a school can ensure that their pupils have the opportunity to exercise their rights as described in the United Nations Convention on the Rights of the Child.

> The child who is capable of forming his or her own views (has) the right to express those views freely in all matters affecting the child.
> (UN Convention on the Rights of the Child, Article 12)

The Advisory Council on Education took this view of school councils when they said:

> School councils help schools become communities by giving everyone a stake in what is going on. What's more, it's a child's human right to be listened to, and to have his or her views taken seriously.
> (ACE 1994)

- School councils contribute to citizenship education through providing young people with *direct experience of the processes of democracy*. The decision-making mechanisms within school councils represent a site for the living out of participatory democracy, providing opportunities for pupils to explore matters of importance and to share in decisions about how to resolve such matters on an equal footing with adults (Holden and Clough 1998). School councils can form an important component of a set of social practices that encourage students to act, in Giroux's words, '*as if they lived in a real democracy*' (Giroux 1983 quoted in Ball). They promote a range of skills necessary for effective democratic living (ACE 1995).

> If a school council is to contribute to education for citizenship, pupils must be involved in the decision-making process, in exercising rights and responsibilities and in participating and contributing to the school community.
>
> (Holden and Clough 1998)

In this sense school councils can provide an 'apprenticeship in democracy'. This view of the purpose of school councils reflects the position of much of the current thinking about citizenship education within Europe.

> Democracy is best learned in a democratic setting where participation is encouraged, where views can be expressed openly and discussed, where there is freedom of expression for pupils and teachers, and where there is fairness and justice.
>
> (Council of Europe 1985)

Thus, school councils would appear to have the capacity to support PSHE and citizenship and contribute to PSD in a range of ways. They can:

- contribute to good relations and discipline and promote social inclusion;
- give expression to children's rights;
- provide a democratic experience and promote democratic skills.

However, as many teachers, children and young people know too well, school councils often fail to realise their potential. The literature would suggest that the reasons for their failure lie in a number of areas. On the surface it would seem that school councils often prove ineffective for what might appear on the surface to be structural or technical reasons. These include issues to do with size, administrative support, budgets, and involvement of teachers, reporting mechanisms, training of pupils, the scope and power of councils. The ACE survey (1995) revealed evidence that schools with school councils were more likely to involve students in management issues but these were often to do with a limited number of issues such as the physical environment, playground, uniform, behaviour, bullying. They found little evidence of consultation on areas such as the curriculum and school development plans. Pupils rarely exercised any control over budgets, though it was common for them to be involved in fund raising. The same survey also found that although many of the school councils had some kind of reporting procedures for council proposals and decisions these systems tended to be underdeveloped. They found that relatively few of the councils had effective and systematic methods for reporting outcomes, particularly to staff. The majority of councils had a staff presence, but none had representatives from support staff or site management. Few of the councils had access to the governing body on a regular basis.

What might at first sight appear to be technical weaknesses of school councils would seem to symbolise wider problems to do with the school ethos and climate. The literature would indicate that issues to do with reporting, scope and power of school councils often reflect and symbolise wider issues in the school to do with the level of participation and involvement of pupils. Ruddock, for example, has argued that councils are only effective if they are an explicit component of whole school democratic practice (Ruddock *et al.* 1996). Others have pointed to the tokenism of councils where the scope of issues debated is limited to areas such as toilets and uniform (Hart 1992). Research by Baginsky and Hannam for the NSPCC underlines the importance of school councils as part of the journey to democratise schools (Baginsky and Hannam 1999). Rowe's research for the Citizenship Foundation stressed the need for school councils to be accompanied by other methods of communication and consultation between staff and pupils including systematic use of pupil interviews and questionnaires. His work emphasised the importance of widening the scope of councils in relation to areas of real decision making and enhancing the quality of the dialogue between the members of the school community (Rowe 1996). Davies's research concludes with the remark that:

> What has become clear is that for a school council or other system of representation to work it must be embedded in a total ethos

of democracy, equity and concern for pupil and staff welfare and performance.

(Davies 1998)

A similar position is taken by ACE:

Whether the school regards student involvement in decision-making as a success will depend on its motivations. School councils which are tokens will become liabilities. School councils, student consultation and student involvement in planning and monitoring work all need to be part of a wider school ethos.

(ACE 1995)

School councils and broader democratic structures and practices

The effectiveness of school councils in relation to PSHE and citizenship and broader PSD is heavily influenced by the particular character of the wider school structures and practices within which they operate. School councils seem to be most effective where they are set within a particular school context; one in which the ethos structures and practices are democratic. Similarly, 'democratic schools' require either a school council or some other mechanism for student voices to be heard and listened to and for them to participate in decision making.

Any school that attempts to democratise must inevitably develop some kind of council or assembly in order that the students' – and possibly the teachers and other staff's – views can be voiced and discussed, unless the school is so small that every member can be involved in meetings.

(Trafford 1997)

Democratic schools require school structures in which pupils are consulted and given opportunities to experience responsibility. In theory then, school councils would seem to be an essential feature of a school that promotes PSD, including PSHE and citizenship. School councils have the capacity to send powerful messages to all pupils about the possibilities of their participation, taking responsibility and about their value and worth within the institution and beyond. Moreover, school councils at their best will raise fundamental questions for those who control and manage a school as to the nature of the institution they wish to promote.

What do democratic schools look like?

> Democratic schools are essentially defined in terms of the ways that they strive to engage the active participation of all members of the school community, including young people, in the decision-making processes.
>
> (Apple, M. and Beane, J. 1999)

The Scottish Consultative Council on the Curriculum describes school democracy in the following way:

> In school settings democracy is characterised by a willingness to allow and encourage young people to become involved in matters of decision making and choice within the community of the school. Through these experiences they come to see themselves as people who can effect the community in its widest sense in which they and others live and work. Like democracy itself democratic schools do not come about by chance. They result in explicit attempts by schools to put into place arrangements and opportunities that will bring democracy to life.
>
> (SCCC 1995)

So what might be the indicators of democratic practice within a school?

A commitment to the active participation of pupils will be evidenced across key areas of the school. Thus, in a democratic school we would expect to find particular defining characteristics within:

- values, ethos and climate;
- relationships;
- leadership and management;
- curriculum and pedagogy.

What might these defining characteristics look like?

Values, ethos and climate

Democratic schools are characterised by particular core values. These values include co-operation, mutual respect, autonomy, justice, and commitment to diversity (White 1991; Fielding 1997, 2001; Apple and Beane 1999). Such core values are not dissimilar to the central educational values identified in the rationale for the NC 2000. In a democratic school core values will be reflected in, and sustained through, the ethos and climate of the school (Eisner 1994). A democratic school will have an ethos and climate that sends positive messages to adults and young people about their worth and value and their right to be heard and consulted. The Scottish Consultative Council for the Curriculum describes the importance of a participatory climate when they say:

> Through the climate in which they operate, young people learn powerful lessons about justice, power, dignity and self-worth. It is important to ensure that these are positive messages. The school as a community needs to develop a climate and ethos consistent with ideals of co-operation and understanding, and based on democratic principles.
>
> (SCCC 1995)

Relationships

The nature of the relationships between adults and between adults and students is a critical indicator of a democratic school. The quality of the relationships between teachers and students is central and involves establishing and sustaining mutual trust and respect and the creation of conditions in which young people are enabled to feel good about themselves. Hay Mc Ber's research on effective teaching for the DfEE endorses this view of the centrality of trust and respect in effective relationships between pupils and teachers (Hay Mc Ber 2000).

Leadership and management

Democratic schools are characterised by particular forms of leadership and management. In democratic schools power is devolved or divested (Griffith 1998; Apple and Beane 1995) through participative and consultative structures and practices that enable others to have ownership over decisions. Collaborative practice is an essential feature of democratic management. Fullan has described this kind of leadership as a style that 'empowers others below you' (Fullan 1993). The Think Tank set up by the National College of School Leadership (NCSL) argues that effective school leadership involves what the report describes as 'distributed' leadership in which all members of the school community are empowered to take part in the decision making processes within the school (NCSL 2001).

Teaching and learning and the democratic curriculum

In a democratic school pupils are enabled to make and evaluate choices in relation to their own learning and are helped to take responsibility for the decisions they make. In an ideal world pupils are also enabled to become 'critical readers' of their society, recognising that all knowledge is socially constructed and challenging the taken for granted. However, a range of externally imposed constraints, including the National Curriculum, puts boundaries on such development. Despite these constraints, democratic schools will take all opportunities to promote teaching and learning styles in which pupils are given opportunities to actively participate, take responsibility and develop a range of 'democratic' skills (Holden and Clough 1998; Griffith 1998, Apple and Beane 1999; Inman and Stiasny 1987).

School councils in action: case studies

The argument so far would suggest that while school councils have the potential to make a significant contribution to PSD, including PSHE and citizenship, we need to be clear both about the most effective structure and form of school councils and the wider school context in which they operate. In other words, it is particular kinds of school councils within particular institutional settings that can contribute most effectively to PSD and citizenship. The research for the Association of Teachers and Lecturers (ATL) on which this chapter is based very much endorsed this view. The research included qualitative case studies of two schools, a primary school in central England and an inner city secondary school. The particular schools were chosen because they had many of the surface characteristics we thought might be necessary for providing the type of school council which could make the most effective contribution to citizenship. Two researchers spent three days in each school. The approach was ethnographic, documenting 'the lived reality' of school councils and democratic schools through first-hand observation and in-depth interviews with those directly involved. The fieldwork confirmed the position outlined earlier. In both the schools the school council played a significant role in promoting pupils PSD. The reasons for their effectiveness lie both in the structure and form of the council in these schools and in the particular nature of the wider school contexts in which they operate.

The structure and form of the school council

In both schools we looked at a number of aspects of the school council. These were school council meetings, representation and reporting mechanisms, the scope of the council and the effectiveness of the council within the school. To accomplish this we observed council meetings, interviewed pupils, teachers, senior managers, governors and support staff and reviewed all relevant documentation. Briefly, our conclusions were that in these two schools the school council was providing an important contribution to PSD and citizenship. Through the school council all pupils, not just counsellors, were learning the knowledge, skills and attitudes associated with wider democratic practice. In both schools the council acted as a vehicle of pupil empowerment – providing them with the right to be heard and consulted, the power to make decisions and giving them the responsibilities associated with these rights. In both schools the pupils were not involved in 'tokenistic' activity, but rather were engaged in a serious purpose. They were aware that the council makes decisions that can affect their lives, that it can change things in a real way and they have confidence in its power to do things.

> 'If you are actually in control of something, and then you know if you say this, you may be able to change it really big. It really makes you feel more easy . . . If you don't really have a chance to do that, you may actually think, "Oh, I might as well not try to do anything different and change anything, cause it's not going to work." '
>
> (Secondary pupil)

> 'You can change as well the way grown ups are, not only grown ups changing you . . . The grown ups are trying to change what you are doing, but you can change what they want you to do. They aren't just telling you.'
>
> (Primary pupil)

In the case study schools the structure and form of the school council played an important part in its effectiveness. The school councils shared some common characteristics and these are important ingredients of an effective school council. The characteristics are:

- meetings are time-tabled into lesson times;
- the council is whole school rather than being class or year based;
- there are explicit representation and reporting mechanisms.

'You have to bring other people's opinions to the council, rather than just your own. Say if somebody says something and you don't agree with it, you still have to mention it.'

[Interviewer] 'Is that true with everybody?'

'Yeah.'

[Interviewer] 'What about the younger ones?'

'We have to listen to what's given, because, if we don't hear, we don't know what to do.'

[Interviewer] 'And do you go and find out what other children think before you come to a meeting?'

'Yes.'

(Primary pupils)

'Soon after every school-council meeting, there is a governors' meeting. And two people from any year, every tutor group get to go to the governors' meeting. And they report back to the school council . . .'

(Secondary pupils)

- Meetings are run formally with agendas and minutes

'The students and adults are sitting in a circle. The meeting follows the familiar structure of adult meetings; minutes of the previous meeting, matters arising and main agenda items. The chair sits at a table covered in green baize, and uses a gavel to call order during the meeting. Students go through the minutes of the previous meeting, and at times challenge the accuracy of the minutes, when this happens the minutes are amended accordingly.'

(Observation notes of secondary council meeting)

- The council has a formal constitution.
- The council is formally consulted about major policy decisions.
- The scope of the agenda can be determined by pupils as well as staff.

'We can bring up really anything that we want. We need better facilities, better classrooms . . . The thing is we know how much money the school gets a year and have some control over how it is spent.'

(Secondary pupil)

'Our toilets are not very good. So we had to write to a man from the council and tell him what's wrong with our toilets. It [the toilet] overflows. Sometimes people put toilet tissues down the toilet and it over-floods, and some people can't get in our toilet because they are too small and so we had to write a letter. We try to call him every Friday, but he is never there. And when Miss gets through it's usually me who has to talk because Barry [other pupil] definitely doesn't want it.'

(Primary pupils)

(Describing the involvement of the school council in selecting a new deputy headteacher)

'I had to interview – I have been asking questions to the deputy head. There is like five or six questions we had to prepare. We made the questions up ourselves. So we had to be in the office and some of the teachers would come in, we have the questions that we were going to ask them. We were giving marks out of 10. Like how would you run the school. We had double meaning type of questions.'

(Secondary pupil)

• The council is under the direct oversight of the headteacher

Wider school structures and practices

The case studies provided confirmation that the nature of the institution is a critical factor in developing and sustaining effective school councils. In both schools the school council was set within a wider democratic climate and structures. This gave it a reality and power as the structures and ethos provide other ways in which pupils are listened to, consulted, asked to take responsibility, treated with respect and valued. In this way the seriousness of the council's role and power is affirmed and supported. The fieldwork supported the view that school councils can only be effective in institutions where there is a genuine and consistent commitment to pupil participation and where this commitment is practically realised through whole school structures and practices. In the case study schools we were convinced that the 'lived reality' for pupils was one in which they felt valued, listened to and empowered.

'What I also like is they give you your personal respect. Not like only if you're top of the class . . .'

(Secondary pupil)

'I am keen that young people come out empowered. If they are participating in a good school, which they're proud of, then it makes them feel that they are citizens of somewhere . . . important. [Then they] have standards, they can actually stand up for what they believe in and that there are fundamental underlying principles. Those things it seems to me, are what bring real citizenship: it's empowerment, it's a sense of worth, and it's a sense of actually being able to do things.'

(Headteacher secondary school)

'You can still be democratic. You can't be democratic in the curriculum, but you can be in the way you treat people, listen to the children and try to put some of their ideas into practice, the practical ones, you maybe channel them a bit. But I don't see any reason why you can't have children being responsible for things and being responsible for their own work, and their own action. Having self-esteem, all those sort of things. You can't have a school council if the rest of the time you ignore them and don't listen to them.'

(Primary teacher)

'We witnessed a circle time for Year 2 children at the beginning of the day. The children talked openly and with ease and confidence about their lives with a certainty that the teacher and other children would listen to them and take an interest in what they had been doing. This was clearly routinely done in that we saw children's stories being told in instalments with the teacher reminding other children about what had happened so far. The intimate connection between the teacher and pupils was striking; there was a strong sense of everyone sharing each other's lives. In this class all members share events and news from babies being born, one child's long struggle to persuade his mum to let him have a goldfish, two girls' ongoing story of their sleepovers, children talking about going on holiday, the winning of the football game the night before by West Ham, the giving out of party invitations. The teacher responds to all this news with genuine interest, laughter, reciprocity, sharing bits of herself and her family with them. She knows them intimately. Within this context democratic skills are being learned and sustained – children largely wait, listen, show respect, value others' news, and when they forget the teacher gently reminds them.'

(Observation notes of a circle time in the primary school)

Conclusion

School councils are likely to be an increasingly standard part of the structure of primary and secondary schools. This is obviously to be welcomed. However, if they are to realise their full potential in relation to PSD and citizenship and not become a short-lived initiative for many schools, then we need to think carefully at their form and structure so as to ensure that they are fully embedded in the wider school structure. As a result of the research for ATL we set out a number of recommendations about the structure and form of effective school councils. These are set out below.

If schools are to develop and sustain school councils that are effective in promoting citizenship then they need to ensure that the form and structure of the council fulfil a number of *criteria*. These include:

- whole school membership and representation;
- frequent and regular meetings planned for the year and held during lesson time;
- a written constitution;
- chaired meetings with formal agendas, minutes and agreed procedures for discussion and decision making;
- explicit and effective reporting mechanisms in relation to pupils, staff, governors and parents;
- a formal consultative role in major policies and decisions, including the selection of new staff;
- the scope and power to debate major issues within the school;
- a budget for the council and consultation over the uses of the school budget;
- direct involvement of senior management;
- formally structured involvement of other staff.

But most importantly we need to remain mindful that school councils can only operate effectively within an institution where all the adults share a commitment to the genuine participation of their young people in all the decisions that affect their lives.

Note

1. The full report for ATL is Inman, S. with Burke, H. *School Councils: an apprenticeship in democracy?* (2002), Association of Teachers and Lecturers.

References

Advisory Centre for Education (1994) *Discipline – how schools consult pupils*, ACE Bulletin, 61.

Apple, M. and Beane, J. (1995) *Democratic schools*, Association for Supervision and Curriculum Development, Alexandria, Virginia.

Apple, M. and Beane, J. (1999) *Democratic Schools*, Buckingham, Open University Press.

Baginsky, M. and Hannam, D. (1999) *School Councils*, London, NSPCC.

CRE (1997) *Exclusion from School and Racial Inequality*, London, Commission for Racial Equality/Central Books.

Crick Report (1998) *Education for Citizenship and the Teaching of Democracy in Schools*: Final Report of the Advisory Group on Citizenship, London, HMSO.

Davie, R. (1989) 'The National Children's Bureau: evidence to the Elton Committee', in N. Jones (ed.), *School management and Pupil Behaviour*, Lewes, Falmer Press.

Davies, L. (1998) *School Councils and Pupils Exclusions*, Birmingham, University of Birmingham.

Eisner, E. (1994) *Ethos and Education*, Scottish Consultative Council on the Curriculum, Dundee.

Elton Enquiry Report (1989) *Discipline in Schools*, London, HMSO.

Fielding, M. (1997) 'Beyond school effectiveness and school improvement: Lighting the slow fuse of possibility' *The Curriculum Journal* Vol. 8, No. 1.

Fielding, M. (2001) 'Beyond the rhetoric of student voice: New departures or new constraints in the transformation of 21st century schooling?' *Forum* Vol. 43, No. 2

Franklin, B. (1986) *The Rights of Children*, Oxford, Blackwells.

Fullan, M. (1993) *Change Forces*, London, Falmer Press.

Giroux, R. (1983) quoted in Ball, S. (1988) 'Costing democracy: Schooling, equality and democracy in Sweden', in Lauder, H. and Brown, P. *Education in Search of a Future*, Basingstoke, Falmer Press.

Griffith, R. (1998) *Educational Citizenship and Independent Learning*, London, Jessica Kingsley.

Hart, D. (1992) 'Children's Participation: from tokenism to citizenship', Innocenti Essays No. 4, Florence, UNICEF.

Hay McBer (2000) *Research into Teacher Effectiveness*, London, DfEE.

Holden, C. and Clough, N. (1998) (eds) *Children as Citizens: Education for Participation*, London, Jessica Kingsley.

Inman, S. and Stiasny, M. (1987) *Good Practice in Teacher Education*, London, Goldsmiths Publications.

Khaleel, M. (1993) *Pupil Councils First Independent Monitoring Programme*, Liverpool, Priority Area Development.

National College for School Leadership (2001) *Think Tank Report to Governing Council and Leadership Development Framework*, Nottingham, NCSL.

National Curriculum Council (1990) *Curriculum Guidance 8, Education for Citizenship*, London, National Curriculum Council.

Osler, A. (1997) *Exclusion from School and Race Equality*, London, Commission for Race Equality.

Owen, R. and Tarr, J. (1998) 'The voices of young people with disability', in Holden, C. and Clough, N. (1998) *Children as Citizens*, London, Jessica Kingsley.

Qualifications and Curriculum Council (2000) *Personal, social and health education and citizenship at Key Stages 1 and 2 and citizenship at Key Stage 3 and 4*, London, QCA.

Qualifications and Curriculum Council (2002) *Citizenship at Key Stage 3 and Key Stage 4*, London, QCA.

Rowe, D. (1996) *The Business of School Councils*, London, Citizenship Foundation.

Ruddock, J, Chaplain, R. and Wallace, G. (1996) *School Improvement: what can pupils tell us?* London, David Fulton.

School Councils UK (2002) *Secondary School Councils Toolkit, Primary Pupil Councils DIY Resource Pack*, London, School Councils, UK.

Scottish Consultative Council for the Curriculum (1995) *The Heart of the Matter*, SCCC.

Speakers Commission on Citizenship (1990) London, HMSO.

Trafford, B (1993) *Sharing Power in Schools: Raising Standards*, Education Now.

Trafford, B. (1997) *Participation, Power-sharing and School Improvement*, Nottingham, Heretics Press

UN *Convention on the Rights of the Child* (1989) London, HMSO.

White, J (1991) 'The justification of autonomy as an educational aim', in Spieker, B. and Straughan (eds), *Education: International Perspectives*, London, Cassell.

Chapter 7

Developing an approach towards emotional literacy: first steps in a whole school perspective

Martin Buck

This chapter describes the first year of development work in a three-year project between staff and students of Lister Community School and Antidote. Its focus is the enhancement of a more coherent and whole school approach towards emotional literacy within the institution, as part of the school's commitment to strengthening the place of personal and social development within learning and achievement.

The School

Lister Community School is situated in the centre of Plaistow, in the London Borough of Newham in East London. The school caters for students aged 11–16 and also offers a range of educational activities for parents/carers and other adults in the daytime and evening. The school has 1,350 students with 16 per cent more boys than girls. In 1998 it became the resourced provision for deaf and partial hearing students with a likely cohort of 30 students in September 2003.

Lister's student population reflects even more the cultural diversity of the area: 82 per cent of students speak English as an additional language; no one particular group predominates and fifty-four different languages are spoken at home; 11 per cent come from refugee or asylum seeker families; 51 per cent of students register for free school meals; 20 per cent are in the special needs register, and 3.5 per cent have a statement of educational need. Lister draws the large majority of its students from the local areas and in particular the Plaistow Ward, where the 33 per cent of children from overcrowded households represents the third highest figure in Newham. Only 6.5 per cent of adults have experienced higher education in a culturally diverse population made up of 62 per cent of children from ethnic minorities.

A rising crime rate, with a 40 per cent increase in offences carried out by young people on their peers in 2000–2001, offers further challenges to the school and the community. For some of our students, out-of-school influences, especially among their peer group, are powerful. Maintaining a focus on learning, achievement and attendance close to national expectations is an ongoing challenge for the school. The area is economically poor with small houses and flats (a mixture of private and council ownership), some corner shops and open spaces. There is little cultural provision and significant strategies are now being put in place through the New Deal for Communities (NDC) to regenerate a specific part of Plaistow. Lister has, over the last two years, played an active part in the NDC.

The school context and developments

The School Mission Statement states:

> As an inclusive school community we are committed to placing creativity at the heart of the learning experience. Our purpose is to ensure an educational experience, which promotes and achieves excellence and thereby raises achievement. By nurturing the values, confidence and skills of students, staff and the community, we will unleash the energy of individuals to prepare them for the opportunities of the 21st century.

Through the school mission statement and School Development (Improvement) Plan, Lister has set out a five-year intent, combined with a detailed strategic plan which itself contains four strands. The first strand focuses on the raising of achievement including attainment at Key Stage 3 and 4 developed through a high expectation and success culture. At present the schools A*–C grades have risen over a four-year period to a high of 32 per cent in September 2001. A–G grades have risen to a high of 92 per cent and the average points score show a proportionate rise. Similarly Key Stage 3 results have risen in English to 52 per cent, Maths to 48 per cent, Science to 45 per cent at levels 5 and above in 2001. Value added indicators are very positive in both Key Stages 3 and 4 especially when compared to similar schools in the Ofsted PANDA.

The second and interrelated strand involves developing a more relevant curriculum, which places creativity at the centre of the learning process and which gives priority to students' personal and social development. The third strand is concerned with strategies to revitalise Lister as a community school by strengthening links with partner primaries and post 16 providers as well as the community and business sectors. This objective has been central to the school gaining Performing Arts College Status in June 2001 and being able to play a role in supporting cultural regeneration in the immediate area, as part of a Borough and East London wide strategy.

The fourth strand addresses the strengthening of the professional role of our staff by building leadership throughout the organisation, through what has been described as 'distributed leadership' (NCSL 2001), in a move towards a more explicitly democratically oriented institution. This strand has also been linked in our work with our students in promoting with and for them a greater voice within the decision-making and consultation systems and processes of the school. The work on strengthening the School Council and Year Forum has been led by an Assistant Headteacher with lead responsibility for Personal and Social Development including the co-ordination of PSHE and Citizenship.

This initiative has seen over the last two years the School Council being given a budget of £5,000 per year, a twice yearly meeting with School Governors and attendance by senior students at the full Governing Body meeting once a term. Student representatives have also served on the Newham Youth Parliament, and the reporting of this body's work and that of the School Council has taken place in the school Newsletter. Nevertheless we are of the view, as are our students, that the role of the School Council needs to be further embedded in the day-to-day life of the school. For example, we are presently exploring ways, following the practice in other schools, in which our students can be more formally involved in the appointment of teaching staff within Lister.

A further component in our work is the enhancement of the role of peer mentors within the school. This programme has involved the selection, training and evaluation of the work of Year 10 students who work with two external agencies. The first is Life Line – a Newham based training charity which has delivered a comprehensive programme for peer mentors and peer advocates; the latter being trained to promote the programme in assemblies and other publicity and to co-ordinate times and schedules, while not actively engaging in one-to-one mentoring. The second training agency is Newham Education Business Partnership, who have provided training and guidance for a further group of our Year 10 students as well as support for our teacher school based mentor co-ordinators. In addition, these same Year 10 students have received a personal adult mentor from the business community who meets with them once per month during school time on the school premises.

Our programme of mentoring mirrors that which has taken place in many state schools across the country over the last ten years. It reflects many of the positive outcomes documented in Chapter 5. We are convinced that peer mentoring increases students' involvement in their school, increases their view of themselves as a genuine 'stakeholder', improves behaviour, and has an overall positive effect in raising students' self-esteem and desire to achieve. However, these programmes challenge schools such as our own to reflect in practice our commitment to deliver the mission statement and aims of the school. This is not always easy especially in a complex organisation which has resources to employ a growing number of adults to work with students alongside teachers, such as mentors, school councillors and teaching assistants. There is a need for all adults in the institution to value the work of peer mentors and to acknowledge and promote the range of skills and qualities being demonstrated by the young people. This includes the need to understand the necessity of students being withdrawn from lessons and to be trained to appreciate the importance of incorporating the systems for establishing peer mentoring in the way that they deal with behaviour issues. In short, 'keeping the system alive' and valuing the work in the way they speak about it as tutors and subject teachers, heads of year and senior staff, and the way in which this work is communicated throughout the institution, offers a real challenge to a school.

At Lister we have sought to ensure that our work with our students in increasing their voice and their more active role within decision making is embedded further into daily practices. This has not proved easy during a period when student behaviour within Lister has been of understandable concern to our staff. A period in which we have had one of the highest fixed term exclusions of students in Newham schools and during which we have faced more challenging behaviour in verbal abuse to teachers as well as not inconsiderable episodes of violent behaviour between students. Despite periods of calm, incidents that occur in the community in an evening or weekend between different factions of older students, mainly boys, feed back into school at times creating a destabilising effect on the institution.

We have sought to strengthen our Behaviour Management Policy during this period by clarifying the system of rewards and sanctions and by strengthening our work in the latter area. We have thus made accountability and expectations more explicit. We have worked closely with the Governing Body in understanding behaviour. We have codified sanctions including dealing with weapons in school and introduced a Governors' Warning System for behaviour. Most importantly we have as a school recognised the key link between learning styles, achievement and behaviour and the necessity of delivering a broader range of learning experiences. This has been made explicit in reviewed schemes of work and lesson planning, in which teachers recognise the importance of talking to students about their preferred learning styles and strategies to make progress in their work. We know from our own school evaluations, including in-depth interviews with our students, that students do have a dominant learning style; they are predominantly kynaesthetic and aural learners. This is by no means taking for granted the necessity of exploring which subsidiary learning styles they prefer to develop. We see this as our major work over the next two years; it links, we believe, with ongoing initiatives in academic tutoring, including a successful introduction of Academic Review days twice a year, introduced in 1999/2000 school year.

Our participation in the Healthy Schools Standard has supported much of the development work I have outlined above. The Healthy School initiative seeks to promote effective teaching on citizenship, drugs education, emotional health, healthy eating, physical activity, safety and sex education. It has also brought in additional resources for the Assistant Headteacher, Personal and Social Development, to lead a discussion through student questionnaires on healthy eating and diet and linking this work with our PSHE programme. It allowed us to reopen our Breakfast Club, which had previously withered on the vine, and negotiate with the School Meals Service on further improvements in the range of food offered at lunchtime. The Healthy Schools Programme also allowed us to run a highly effective Healthy Schools Week, focusing on both student and staff welfare issues including issues of stress in the work place and some strategies to deal with this significant personal and social issue. It has also provided additional resources for us to focus with our students on improving aspects of the school environment and introduce a quiet garden area which was designed and maintained by our students.

One further aspect of work which has proved difficult to manage in terms of competing priorities for staff release and training has been our participation in the Exeter University led 'A Pause' – Sex Education Project on Teenage Pregnancy delivered through our Year 10 PSHE programme. However, we have recommitted ourselves to the second year of the project and intend to strengthen aspects of the school-based management required for 'A Pause' in September 2002.

We do not claim that any of this work is unique or that we have established best practice. Nevertheless Lister has a growing reputation for tackling new initiatives and, by those who observe us, is a more dynamic institution in which to study and work than in the past. This makes the task of ensuring manageability, coherence and quality assurance as key elements of our work as a learning institution that wishes to promote genuine leadership for learning and learning for leadership both for our students and our staff.

The Antidote partnership – a critical friend

In the summer of 2001 we were approached by Antidote to participate in a school-based initiative as part of their campaign for emotional literacy in schools and in the wider institutions of our society; we were excited, but also apprehensive about their approach. We were aware that we were moving to a point of initiative overload in the school and that in the eighteen months of my leadership, a serious criticism could be made against me that I was overstretching the organisation rather than building the capacity for us to manage change effectively. We were very aware, however, of the need to bring together the range of developments into a more coherent whole to enable both staff and students to understand better their interrelationships and for the institution to better manage these important elements, all of which appeared to support our stated ethos.

We were aware also of the need to examine more deeply those aspects of our learning as adult and student learners, and as an organisation with an explicit commitment to learning. Our involvement in wanting to develop our collective and individual creativity in the range of initiatives that underpin our commitment to both our staffs' and students' personal and social development means that we deal explicitly with emotional intelligence and literacy. However, if we are serious about this crucial element of learning we need to provide further opportunities to examine our practice in the way we relate to each other.

We were not interested therefore in gaining a further label to our work in the pursuit of being a more creative school, a democratic school, or a healthy school, or a learning community; we did not need the label of an emotionally literate organisation. We, however, did need to recognise the significance of this important aspect of learning in addition to the cognitive and the rational and to attempt to deepen our capacity to build it in to our everyday interrelationships, communication and practices. I believe that Antidote are sufficiently wise to understand that their purpose is better served in not being precious over the title or label with an organisation. The test of their involvement is, surely, the extent to which they are able to support a school or a business in reflecting on its practices and to deepen an understanding of the emotional dimension.

Critical friend

Our relationship with Antidote is one where those working from the campaign organisation act as a critical friend. We have agreed a three-year commitment to pursuing our work on emotional literacy through our present initiatives and developments. This relatively long-term commitment in an open partnership was very important. We understand a critical friend to be:

> A trusted person who asks provocative questions, provides data to be examined through another lens and offers a critique of a person's work as a friend. A critical friend takes time to fully understand the context of the work presented and the outcomes that the person or group is working toward. The friend is an advocate for the success of the work.
>
> (Costa and Killick 1993)

We accept the assertion that a school needs a friend and that it is difficult, even unhealthy, for schools to be self-sufficient islands of excellence and that it is not easy to be a self-improving school in which change is accelerating and the growth of knowledge is exponential. There is indeed a value for a school in having an outside perspective (in addition to Ofsted!) a reference point and connection with a wider field of knowledge. External support and networking with an 'enlightened eye' can be challenging and motivating in any new relationship MacBeath *et al.* (2000). Work with Antidote has reflected these qualities.

Defining the concept of emotional literacy

> Learning is an emotional activity. We learn well when we are curious and engaged. We stop learning whenever we feel anxious; alienated or otherwise distressed. The more aware we are of our emotions the easier it is for us to appreciate the thoughts, feelings and experiences of others. This quality that we call emotional literacy is what enables us to engage in the sort of conversations,

with teachers or peers, through which we can take in facts, perceptions of which we were previously unaware.

(Antidote 2002)

In the Lister school context we want to understand better the emotional element of our students' learning and the ways in which we can better serve their learning needs by getting closer to the learning process. We also want to analyse what the conditions are which will allow our teachers to take cognisance of the emotional element of learning. Are they more open to such reflection, for example, when the behaviour of students in lessons is less threatening, or are they more likely to 'close down' if the behaviour is disruptive and challenging?

In short, we have a paradox. For while our staff's own emotional literacy is most challenged by negative behaviour linked to struggles in learning, it is also required to be at its most sophisticated in understanding and catering for students' feelings and emotional well-being. How can we better support the relationship element of learning between teacher and students, which the Hay McBer study (Hay McBer 2000) on teacher competencies prioritises?

As Antidote have identified:

Emotional Literacy develops when people feel sufficiently secure in themselves to hold on to their thinking capacities, even when they experience emotional pressure. They are able to communicate, collaborate and remain responsive to others in ways which will support them in their learning.

(Antidote 2002)

We believe that an important starting point for all teachers and professionals working with young people in a learning context is to understand the qualities and skills required to develop a capacity for sustained learning, underpinned by emotional literacy. Research at the Bristol University Graduate School of Education (University of Bristol 2002) suggest that effective lifelong learners display the following qualities: resilience, learnability, critical curiosity, playfulness, making connections, strategic reflections, and relationships. Antidote argues that an emotionally literate school supports the development of these qualities.

It does so by actively promoting *dynamic and supportive* relationships through which young people can learn from and with each other.

The awareness that they can call on the support of others helps students become more *resilient* in their learning.

Through their relationships young people learn to manage the different emotional states, so that they can enter states of *playfulness* and *strategic reflection* as these are appropriate to their current learning tasks.

Developing the capacity to take in both intuitive and cognitive information, students become more motivated to *make connections* between apparently disparate and contradictory pieces of data.

Increasing tolerance of what they know already is most likely to sustain states of critical curiosity. Made aware of the extent to which they can transform the ways they interact with others, they can more fully grasp the notion of learnability.

(Antidote 2002)

Initial steps: Perspectives and contradictions

In our initial meeting with Antidote we agreed that we had sufficiently similar approaches to form a positive partnership. We had no difficulty in subscribing to the Antidote 'charter' which asks that if we wish to develop more emotionally literate schools we need to:

- acknowledge the role that emotions play in shaping the processes and outcomes of teaching and learning;
- recognise that meaningful learning is a process that involves emotion as well as intellect;
- empower teachers to take control of the teaching and learning processes in their classrooms;
- ensure that the processes of change in our schools involve building respectful relationships, inclusive dialogue, and a valuing of pluralism and diversity;
- incorporate the emotional dimensions of learning into the training and assessment of teachers;
- ensure that the structures of schooling give teachers the time and the opportunity to establish the emotional bonds and understanding of their students, that are the foundations of effective learning;
- achieve a balance between challenge and security: stimulating teachers and pupils to realise their potential without risking damage to their confidence and pleasure in learning;
- acknowledge that all of us – parents, non-parents, policy-makers, pupils and teachers – have a role to play in shaping an energetic and creative education system.

We believe that the Antidote principles reflect closely our own thinking and commitment towards an enhanced approach to teaching and learning which has to reflect a whole school perspective.

Ours was an open agenda in which we had little preconception about precisely what should be our initial focus. We did however understand two principles. The first involved the need in our commitment to increasing emotional literacy to gain the perspective of staff and their perception of the institution as more or less enabling in terms of relationship building and democratic values involved in decision making, consultation and communication. The second principle involved not working with Antidote in a palliative mode sorting out short-term problems. We wanted to approach this work from a positive perspective and to establish a whole school framework on emotional literacy as soon as possible.

Antidote carried out a survey with both staff and students. The aims of the survey were to explore emotional and social factors that block and facilitate well-being and learning across the school. The first stage of the survey involved two versions of an open-ended questionnaire completed by 98 of the 150 staff and 236 out of 270 Year 8 pupils in order to gain a richer picture of staff and student experience. Antidote also interviewed 13 members of staff and 18 Year 8 students (1 boy and 1 girl from each tutor group). The questionnaire provides insights into the importance attached by our teachers of being able to teach well and to develop positive relationships with students and colleagues. It also shows the deep satisfaction that teachers get when observing students taking pride in their own work. Staff talked openly about the stress caused because of the conflict with students and the impact on their personal confidence. Staff responses also provide challenging interpretations with respect to comments over the tensions between monitoring performance and providing support.

Before the questionnaire we felt, as a senior management team, relatively optimistic that we were working on the right lines in strengthening systems and processes within the school. In the autumn of 2002 we had met the Investor in People (IIP) Standard, and therefore we were open to the outcomes of the questionnaire. The results of the data gathered by Antidote from our staff appeared at odds with the supportive commentary given by colleagues as part of the IIP process. Staff comments in the Antidote questionnaire appeared more negative in respect to some of the core principles we were seeking to develop around decision making, consultation and communication. It made us understand that this process was more fragile than we had judged and that we needed to attend closely to staff support through our line management, mentoring and buddy systems as well as through informal contacts and communication.

Our second principle of engaging in a positive manner with Antidote and not seeking short-term solutions was compromised by our decision to focus on Year 8 students for the survey. However, the pressure in school often means that we have to adapt and seek new learning in situations that appear problematic. We had, in short, to take a more pragmatic view than originally envisaged.

The survey reveals our students' desire to learn about each other and the wider world. Girls appear more openly eager to learn or at least comply with instructions, a quality recognised by some boys in their responses. For boys in particular it would seem that the challenge is to learn while not standing out from the crowd, an observation shared in much research in boys' schooling. Antidote posed an important hypothesis that the challenge of learning and of being in the same space together made boys and girls highly anxious. Calling each other 'boffin' for example might be an expression of this anxiety. There appears to be a yearning for someone to assuage the anxiety. Students are aware that teachers expect girls to act as agents of social control, but when girls actively take up this role their behaviour can accentuate this anxiety. These observations drawn from our students' comments have been helpful in assisting us to focus on learning activities that begin to provide safe opportunities for boys and girls to find out about each other and to share learning.

A major concern that we had begun to address was the behaviour in a number of our Year 8 classes during the summer term when they were in Year 7, and their first term in Year 8. This year group were in many ways 'troubled' in their relationships with each other and the breakdown in relationships in at least four of the nine classes was resulting in disruptive behaviour and a negative impact on learning. The year group had an excellent leadership team in the Director of Study, and Assistant Director of Study, with a strong set of tutors and co-tutors. They were well supported at Deputy Headteacher level through our line management system. Certain small groups of students were being identified by both staff and students as being involved in disruptive behaviour on a regular basis. Some of this was occurring because of the lack of an appropriate match in learning tasks with students' abilities, especially their skills in dealing with published texts which were often pitched above the reading age of those involved in disruption. Differentiation was a key issue. It was not, however, identified as the only factor. Those involved in sustained disruption were not all weak readers or those with poor literacy skills. The issue was more complex.

The Director of Study for Year 8 had decided to begin a student led Behaviour Review Group drawn from across the year group with at least two representatives from each form. They met on a weekly basis and discussed what they saw as the main features of the disruption to learning. A code of behaviour was agreed in line with the School's Charter For Learning and individual students were registered to meet the Student Behaviour Panel and describe their behaviour. A record was kept of the meeting, which was set up in the form of a circle time with a student who chairs the group. This work has empowered the students involved in the panel and made them more aware of their own behaviour. Those chosen for the panel were students who themselves had had problematic behaviour in lessons (and on occasions still do) but had committed themselves to reflect on their behaviour and wanted to succeed in their learning.

Those students who have been asked to attend have not enjoyed the process. They have been defensive about their behaviour and they have interpreted it as being held to account. Perhaps not surprisingly this student led management of behaviour has not been a miracle cure. It has, however, been valued by the student body in Year 8; those in the group have gained respect and self-esteem. The behaviour in the most difficult Year 8 classes has improved but not consistently. A more rounded approach to this issue has also required Lister staff to better understand that they need to support this process in their own lessons and contribute to the process through establishing more appropriately matched learning activities.

This important aspect of the jigsaw is now being put in place through work at a whole school level and a specific project being undertaken with two Year 8 classes. These two classes have undertaken the University of Bristol Effective Life Long Learning Inventory (ELLI) using the dimensions described above. These students have been discussing how they can be better learners. Each of them has been given their own learning profile that indicates whether they consider themselves to present strongly or weakly on each of the dimensions. They have found this process very difficult. The staff involved are still struggling with the Antidote team to find precisely how to turn this interesting research instrument into a meaningful, usable tool for increasing self-awareness in the process of learning by 12- and 13-year olds. These are early days. One potentially useful aid is that each student is requested to keep a learning journal. However, this in itself is a significant task in comprehending exactly what one needs to do to develop, for example, *greater resilience* and *strategic reflection*, particularly in a multicultural inner-city comprehensive where students are challenged as English as an Additional Language learners. Nevertheless we are committed to exploring ways in which we can make ELLI work. In addition, a tutor led intervention programme is being undertaken. This currently involves a weekly tutor time in which students use posters of a growing tree to symbolise aspects of their learning that are going well, and a brick wall that symbolises blockages to their learning that they have experienced. They have leaves or bricks with personal statements. These statements are used to focus the groups on their targets for the following week. One of the groups is also having a series of lessons based entirely on team building activities and co-operation skills. It is also envisaged that, with training, students from the groups and/or the Year 10 peer mentors attached to them will act as student researchers. This has yet to be put in place

This work is neither revolutionary nor unique. Rather, the colleagues working with these groups have used the Antidote project as a springboard for re-establishing a way of working with these young people which explicitly deals with the issue of the skills and qualities involved in becoming more effective learners.

Future perspective

We wish to progress to the second year of this project and to explore with Antidote ways in which they can support our work on learning styles within different curriculum teams. We want to develop strategies to promote effective techniques in tutoring to encourage further reflection on individual student progress, achievement and self-esteem. We also wish to work with Antidote to understand better the complexities of giving students a larger role, a bigger voice within the institution.

We are becoming more aware of the issues that Michael Fielding has posed about the extent to which we are willing to hear and encourage students' participation. We are finding his Student Voice checklist particularly helpful in ensuring that we do not become self-satisfied with our own progress but that it assists us in moving our commitment forward, doing our best to avoid tokenism in respect of students as stakeholders (Fielding 2001).

With our staff we wish to develop more robust and consistent strategies to support their own emotional well-being and welfare as part of our commitment to open decision making and consultation, thereby underpinning our aims of promoting leadership for learning and learning for leadership. This will require us to consider ways in which we can create more time and space for reflection and dialogue. How do we persuade ourselves that time devoted to reflection and dialogue is spent well? How do we find the time to reflect on who we are and what we are doing together and what is going on for us and between us? Can we create time for dialogue and reflection by saving time currently on less productive activities? How do we learn to trust that others with different levels of experience and power will join in dialogue with us and understand our point of view? How do we understand the complex interactions in any multicultural setting, the differences in other words, *within* as well as *between* different stakeholders?

We see our work with Antidote as part of our commitment to self-evaluation and the use of a critical friend to allow the benefit of gaining a heightened self-knowledge, affirming and celebrating the good things we are doing and enabling us to face issues and problems more adventurously.

Acknowledgements

I should like to acknowledge the contribution of Lesley Day to the writing of this chapter. I should also like to thank Antidote for their support and commitment to the work at Lister.

References

Antidote (2002) *The Quality of Learning – An Emotional Literacy Handbook*, Consultation Draft.

Costa, G. and Killick, T. (1993) quoted in MacBeath, J. *et al.* (2000) *Self-Evaluation in European Schools*, London: RoutledgeFalmer.

Deakin Crick, R., Broadfoot, P. and Claxton, G. (2002) *The Effective Lifelong Learning Inventory*, University of Bristol Graduate School of Education, Bristol.

Fielding, M. (2001) 'Beyond the rhetoric of student voice or new constraints in the transformation of 21st century schooling', *Forum* Vol. 43, No. 2.

Hay McBer (2000) *Research into Teacher Effectiveness*, London, DfEE.

MacBeath, J., Meuret, D., Soratz, M. (2000) *Self-Evaluation in European Schools*, London: RoutledgeFalmer.

National College for School Leadership (2001) *Think Tank Report to Governing Council and Leadership Development Framework*, Nottingham: NCSL.

Chapter 8

Dreaming for good: drama and personal and social development

Miles Tandy

In the course of my work, I often have conversations with primary school teachers about the role of the arts in education. Rarely does anyone express the view that the arts are unimportant. Many will argue a case on the basis of balance: the arts countering a perceived over-emphasis on the 'basics'. Often with this same notion of balance in mind, some will talk of enrichment: the 'something more' that the arts bring to the curriculum. There is also the widespread feeling that the arts offer means by which children can 'express themselves'. Perhaps reflecting its greater profile on the national agenda, the need to develop children's creativity also gets mentioned. And, most significantly in the context of this book, connections are frequently made between the arts and children's personal and social development. Whatever the range of reasons articulated, there seems to be a tacit understanding that the arts have an important role to play, but that discussing and explaining that role is a complex business.

If one is making a case for literacy and numeracy in the curriculum, the contrast could hardly be more marked. There is a clear connection between these 'basic' skills and the ability of the individual to function in society. To be illiterate or innumerate is to be unemployable and unable to manage even the most basic functions of everyday life. Unless an individual student plans a career in them, it is difficult to make a case for the arts in such a direct and common-sense way.

Yet although everyday discourse about education – even many recent government policies – might seem to make such simple connections between school, employability and the ability to function in everyday life, most people would also be prepared to acknowledge a much wider purpose for education, such as that expressed in the aims and values of the National Curriculum:

Foremost is a belief in education, at home and at school, as a route to the spiritual, moral, social, cultural, physical and mental develop-ment, and thus the well-being, of the individual.

(The National Curriculum 2000)

If this is what education seeks, a case for the arts might seem stronger: as important elements in the 'spiritual, moral, social, cultural, physical and mental development of the individual'. Yet even this role is not unproblematic. How, exactly, might the arts contribute to such development?

The idea of the arts as important means of self-expression has a long tradition in education. As far back as 1942, Wilhelm Viola (Viola 1942) drew on the work of Franz Cizek to develop the idea of 'Child Art', baldly stating that 'Child Art is expression' (Viola 1942: 54). Peter Slade (Slade 1954) proposed a similar notion of 'Child Drama': his approach might now be characterised as the most child-centred, progressive practice, inspired as it was by the writings of Rousseau and Froebel. The arts were regarded as media through which children might freely express them-selves, unhindered by inhibition, adult intervention or destructive judgement. Implicit in the case for these acts of self-expression is the idea that they are necessary for the psychological health of the individual: Viola, for example, cites the case of a boy who experienced terrifying dreams which only ceased once he had had the opportunity to draw the 'bogey man' who had disturbed him (Viola 1942: 59). In the past, I have been asked to lead drama workshops for children on 'fear' or 'anger', without any particular indication as to what they might be afraid of or angry about. I suggest that the underlying supposition was that if children were offered drama as a means of expression, it might serve to make them less angry or less afraid. Such a role for the arts is essentially therapeutic: media to make the individual better. While it is rare to encounter the view among teachers that self-expression is the *only* purpose for the arts in the curriculum, it is worth noting Kenneth Gergen's proposal that:

the vocabulary of moral feeling, loyalty and inner joy is largely derived from a *romanticist* conception of the self. Although it reached its zenith in the nineteenth century, this view remains very much alive in the present world.

(Gergen, 1991: 19)

If, as Gergen suggests, this view of the self remains alive, it should not be surprising that the idea of 'self-expression' survives with it. I would contend that it frequently lies behind some of the disquiet that teachers express about an over-emphasis on the 'basics' and consequent marginalisation of the arts.

In the present educational climate, making any case for the arts based on self-expression is a risky business. One is all too easily characterised as suggesting a return to the unstructured 'progressive' teaching of the 1960s, so readily demonised in the popular imagination. No wonder *All Our Futures*, the report of the National Advisory Committee on Creative and Cultural Education (DfEE / DCMS, 1999), is at such pains to stress that it makes no such case. While making it clear that the committee was not a lobby group for the arts, the report does have a great deal to say about the role of the arts in education.

The report is wide ranging, arguing for a 'new balance' in education. Education throughout the world, it argues, 'faces unprecedented challenges: economic, technological, social and personal'. Meeting these challenges will require a radical rethink of both the purposes and structures of education. The economic and technological challenges are already having, and will continue to have, a profound impact on young people's lives, demanding creativity, flexibility and adaptability on their part, and a much broader conception of ability on the part of those who seek to educate. The social and personal challenges are equally profound and require similar radical action. The report argues that the social challenge is:

> To provide forms of education that enable young people to engage positively and confidently with far-reaching processes of social and cultural change.

And the personal challenge:

> To develop the unique capacities of all young people, and to provide a basis on which they can each build lives that are purposeful and fulfilling.

The report argues strongly that current curriculum structures that make such clear distinctions between the arts and the sciences are flawed: relegating the arts to second-class subjects of lesser importance than the core curriculum will not help us to meet the challenges education faces. The arts are seen not so much as means of self-expression, but as part of the dazzling, ever growing array of forms which human creativity can take.

All Our Futures also makes strong connections between creativity and culture. 'Human culture', it argues, 'is as rich, complex and diverse as it is because of the richness, complexity and diversity of human creativity.' In his exploration of the diversity of human culture and his conception of 'art as a cultural system', social anthropologist Clifford Geertz suggests that:

> If there is commonality it lies in the fact that certain activities everywhere seem specifically designed to demonstrate that ideas are visible, audible, and – one needs to make up a word here – tactible, that they can be cast in forms where the senses, and through the senses the emotions, can reflectively address them. The variety of artistic expression stems from the variety of conceptions men have about the ways things are, and is indeed the same variety.
>
> (Geertz 1983: 119)

In Geertz's terms, *All Our Futures* suggests not only that children need to learn to 'cast ideas' in as many forms as possible, but that they need exposure to a wide variety of other 'castings'; other people's conceptions about the way things are. It is important though, that the role of the arts here is not so much to express something for the individual, rather to bring such expression – be it the work of an individual or a group – into a social domain.

So when in September 1999, I was approached by a school to work with a Year 6 class to devise and produce a piece of theatre on the theme of 'bullying', I imagined a range of possible intentions. One might be the hope that by 'doing some drama about it' there might be less bullying. Immediately my mind went back to an early experience of trying to use drama to this end. The lesson was before morning break and during their play time two children from the class I had been teaching were brought to the staffroom door: not only had they been fighting, but the fight had started over something that took place during the drama lesson. 'So much for that idea!' muttered the staffroom cynic in the corner. I felt more than a little sympathy.

But the school concerned with this work makes the value they place on the arts quite explicit. One of its stated aims is 'to put the expressive and creative arts at the centre of our curriculum'. My initial conversations with the headteacher indicated that there had been deep and serious thought about what the project might achieve. The school is in an area of relative socio-economic deprivation; some 49 per cent of the pupils receive free school meals. First and foremost was an expressed desire that the children should be involved in something that was successful and in which they might take pride: if all went well, their work would be performed to the acclaim of parents, families and fellow pupils. The head was quite explicit about the need to raise the self-esteem of this group of pupils and this project might make a significant contribution. It was also important that this was to be shared endeavour – the success of any outcome would depend on everyone contributing and fulfilling her or his particular role. But any of these aspirations might equally be met by all sorts of other projects – why a play about bullying? Although it had been identified as an issue in the school, we spared ourselves a quantitative target by which the project might be judged a success: there was no 'by the end of the project there will be no recorded incidence of bullying in Year 6'. My early experience of drama on the theme of bullying made me rather glad of that. To the great credit of both, the headteacher and the class teacher approached the venture in a spirit of openness to a range of possibilities. We had to start work and see where it led us.

In an era where those in education place such value on stating clear objectives and intended outcomes, working with a class in ways which genuinely value what they bring to the creative process can be difficult. But if the process were to be truly creative, and the resultant work genuinely collaborative, I had always to be mindful of the danger of over-planning. Classroom drama teaching has evolved pedagogy over a number of years (see, for example, Neelands, 1990 or Winston and Tandy, 2001) which allows the teacher to offer structures within which pupils can construct and develop their own work. Rather than present the class with a completed script, my intention was to use some of these structures to devise a performance with them.

My own thinking was stimulated by the discovery of a poem called *The Bully Asleep* by John Walsh (Wilson 1985: 75). Walsh evokes the scene of a child, known to his classmates as a bully, falling asleep one afternoon. Most of the children are tempted to seek revenge save one, Jane, who is more inclined to comfort him. The theme is common enough: that the bully is also a victim at least as much in need of our sympathy as our desire for revenge. But my interest was also taken by thoughts of him dreaming – of what does he dream, and why? Walsh offers no hint, but I thought it a good place to begin some speculation. Joe Winston (1998: 160) observes how a dream can serve 'the aesthetic function of placing symbol, and the interpretation of symbol, at the heart of the drama'. Exploring the idea of dreams might lead us all into deeper, more thoughtful reflection.

Of the dramatic conventions available in the primary school, the still image or tableau is one of the most widely used. It is a highly disciplined yet accessible form. Children arrange themselves in space to represent a moment frozen in time. Given that I wanted these children to prepare and present images of bullying, the quality of stillness had the additional benefit of making these images safe and controlled. Perhaps not surprisingly, the initial images the children produced were naturalistic scenes of physical violence being perpetrated on a 'victim' by one or more 'bullies'. As we reviewed and 'read' each others' images, they encouraged some immediate discussion about whether physical violence was the only form bullying could take: very quickly a consensus emerged that the *threat* of such violence was at least as intimidating. To explore this idea further, we used a device known as 'thought tracking' – as each image was 'frozen', we could speak and hear the thoughts of different people. Perhaps the most interesting and revealing were the thoughts of those apparently peripheral to the main action for whom the class spoke thoughts such as, 'At least it's not me', and 'I don't really want to be here'. Quite challenging for the class was the process of speaking the thoughts of the 'bully' – comments ranged from those that suggested out and out enjoyment of violence, through those that talked of a need to maintain a position 'at the top', to those that hinted at a deeper insecurity. The ensuing discussion dwelt on what might go on inside the bully's head – how important was it and how might we represent it?

We also used the children's original still images for a final activity using a strategy known as 'sound tracking'. As each image was held, the rest of the class could add sounds to accompany them. These sounds were a mixture of verbal and non-verbal, mostly made with voices, but with the possibility of adding tapping, stamping, clapping etc. as appropriate. Both the class and I were surprised by what emerged. Most of the chosen sounds were verbal, some naturalistically representing what was said, others suggesting voices in the heads of those involved. What we all agreed about was the power of layering these sounds together, then experimenting with bringing them to a crescendo.

By the end of the first half-day session with the class, we were able to record some important principles which they felt should guide our work towards a production. They were:

- It must be real: tell it like it is.
- It must show the point of view of the bully as well as the victim.
- It must show what goes on inside the heads of bully and victim.
- The victim must get revenge.

Given the work we had done that morning, I found their first principle interesting. It was never made explicit, but it draws a subtle distinction between the play being real, and it being realistic. The activities that had helped us get the deepest insight during the morning's work were those that were the least naturalistic. Could we devise drama that was 'hard hitting' in terms of its impact on an audience, without resorting to naturalistic depictions of violence? Quite apart from the desirability of putting such violence in front of an audience, we simply didn't have the specialist acting skills to make it possible. I also found the last principle worrying – could we avoid a simplified cautionary tale of 'bully gets his comeuppance and learns the hard way'? I certainly hoped so, but where does the effective teacher draw a line between allowing children to express their own ideas and leading them on to deeper thinking?

It's all well and good to talk of the danger of being too much driven by objectives and outcomes, but the fact was that we had a date in the diary by which a very clear outcome had to happen. We had promised a performance. With this in mind, I felt it necessary to take more control of the overall direction of the work towards the production, but still wanted to leave room for the children's creative contributions. One of the popular myths that *All Our Futures* is keen to dispel is the idea that creativity is simply a matter of 'letting go' and giving vent to free expression. Often it involves downright hard work, and creativity can thrive given tight constraints. The work I describe here demanded a delicate balance between the teacher's knowledge of what might be needed to make effective theatre, and a strong desire to allow the children's insights and 'voices' to come through. No doubt there were times when it was over-directed, but I would still suggest that the performance I describe owed its success to the extraordinary insights these children gave as we worked together.

We began the second morning's work by constructing an opening for our play. Individuals ran into the performance space and took up a still that suggested children at play. As they did so, they created a huge tableau which was brought to life when the last child joined the image. Through this teeming image of childhood play comes the child who is known only as 'the victim', followed closely by 'the bully'. Indicating a blend of apprehension and excitement about what might be about to happen, the other children form a semi-circle around 'bully' and 'victim'. The two of them improvised the following encounter which was then formalised into a script:

Bully: Hello.
(*Victim turns and falls backwards, cowering*)

Victim: What do you want?
Bully: I want to talk to you.
Victim: What about?
Bully: In the classroom.
Victim: What did I do?
Bully: You annoyed me.

The line 'annoyed me' is picked up by the semi-circle of children and spoken over and over until it reaches a crescendo at which point the 'victim' screams for it to stop. From the semi-circle the children then make individual comments including:

A bully is nasty.
A bully is violent.
A bully is intimidating.
A bully is manipulating.

The last few statements assert that a bully is 'tough', 'fierce' and 'fearless', but are met with looks of puzzlement from the rest of the semi-circle. When the last child states that 'a bully is weak', the statement is picked up and echoed by the whole group before they exit. In the last line of this first scene, the bully tells the victim: 'I'm gonna get you for this and you never know when.'

It is worth noting that none of these lines was written before it was spoken. The drama structures used offered children opportunities to make their own contribution within the constraints of the given form. Self-expression if you will, but also an opportunity to cast their ideas about bullying in forms which rendered them visible, audible and, to use Geertz's word, tactible.

In the next scene we represented the 'voices in the head' of both victim and bully. The children form a corridor down which each has to walk and as they do so the 'corridor' speaks. In the eventual performance, the children wore plain white masks for this, giving the effect of even greater distance from the words they spoke: they were 'faceless'. The voices in the victim's head include utterances that are quite chilling:

You'll never know when.
She might be round the corner.
Don't forget to look over your shoulder.
You'll never be alone.

And for the bully:

> You just can't stop.
> You're scared and they don't know.
> You can't do it yourself can you?
> You're addicted.

It was interesting to note that the children felt strongly that at this point we were fulfilling our aim to 'tell it like it was', even though this was one of the least naturalistic pieces in the play.

The next two scenes involved much more naturalism as we tried to present what might happen in the homes of both bully and victim. As we explored the scenes through improvisation, it was startling how distinct similarities between the two homes emerged. The scene used only a table and a few chairs to suggest the home. As 'the victim' comes home, she throws her coat down and leaves for her room. Called back, a short spat ensues which ends with the victim's mother declaring, 'I don't know what's got into her'. When told by the victim's sister that she is being picked on at school, the mother asks, 'Who's been picking on her?' The sister replies starkly, 'Just an ordinary bully'. Having devised a line such as this through improvisation, it would be unreasonable to probe into what might have led to it. It may have come from a child's direct experience, it may not; it may simply have 'felt right' at the time. Whatever its source, it says something uncomfortably true about the attitude taken to bullying by some: that it is simply part of life and we need to learn to live with it. Indeed, the sister's next line is, 'Learn to stick up for yourself.' Equally interesting is the line they gave to the victim's father. He leaves the scene saying, 'I've had enough of this,' and, grabbing his car keys, 'I'm off to work.'

On the other side of the performance space, the scene from the home life of 'the bully' is shown. It is an exact mirror image of the victim's house. Much the same scene ensues, except that the improvisation led to the bully being teased by her sister. 'What's the matter, Einstein?' she asks. 'Bad marks in a test? By the way, I T spells it!' Again, Dad leaves, this time he asks, 'Why can't you be more like your brother and sister? I haven't got time for *you*, I'm going to work!'

What I found most remarkable about the two short home scenes (they took but a few minutes each to perform) was how stark and concentrated they were. Free improvisation in drama will often lead to a great many words being spoken; but these were refined and crafted to a minimum, each of which carried particular weight.

The idea of mirroring from the home scenes was carried into the last scene of the play. Both bully and victim come into their respective room, this time using the tables to represent beds. They mirror each other's movements in the mundane routines of washing and preparing for sleep. Once asleep, the masked 'voices' in their heads return. The cacophony builds to a crescendo until both victim and bully sit up and scream for it to stop. Once silent, the victim stands and says, 'I have a dream and in that dream there's no such thing as a bully.' The bully states, 'I have a dream and in that dream I have a friend.' Alternately victim and bully speak the line 'I have a dream . . .' which in turn is taken up by one of the masked figures. Placing the mask on one of the beds, the figure takes up and completes the line, 'And in that dream . . .' On completing their line, they move into the space and take up a still which represents something of what they've said. There are a number of ways in which the statements are completed, ranging from 'I won't be lonely anymore' to 'and sometimes it frightens me' to 'we live without fear'.

As the statements are made and the still images completed, the bully and victim are left with a pile of masks on each bed. These they each collect in a bin bag. With the bags in hand they make their way round the still images and meet at the front. Both look bemused. 'I had a dream last night,' says the victim, 'and found these.' 'So did I,' replies the bully. 'Shall we chuck them away?' As they move through the stills the bully turns to the victim and says, 'Let's chuck them away for good.' The stills break, and each child points directly to a member of the audience and says 'For good!' Blackout.

Only after having worked the piece right through could we devise a title: we called the play *A Dream for Good*. Two performances were planned: one to the rest of the school, and one for the parents. The audience for the parents' performance, though small, was highly appreciative. At the end, after the children had left, a parent came to speak. Clearly moved by the children's work, he said, 'I used to be bullied at school,' and, pointing to the empty stage, 'that's just how it was'. Perhaps, in Geertz's terms, those children had succeeded in making some difficult ideas visible, audible, tactible.

More performances followed. The play was 'toured' to other local schools, it was taken to a county drama festival, and it was performed as part of the 2000 Conference of Local Education Authorities. Small wonder then, that the school was keen to do something similar in the next academic year.

By September 2000, the context had changed. Rather than a Year 6 class, there was a mixed Year 5 and Year 6. They were described, to use that splendid euphemism, as 'challenging'. The class were to be taught by the same teacher who had worked with me on *A Dream for Good*. We had discussed possibilities and decided to link the work to the National Literacy Strategy *Framework for Teaching*, specifically its suggestion that Year 6 pupils should study, 'where appropriate', a Shakespeare play (DfEE 1998: 50). We decided to work from *Romeo and Juliet*, possibly with a view to developing a contemporary parallel alongside our short version of the original play.

When I arrived to work with the class for the first time, their regular teacher was on sick leave. As things turned out, she was not to return. The class had already had a number of supply teachers; the teacher working with them on the first morning I visited had got them settled and well managed. I have described the approach I took to the first morning's work in some detail elsewhere (Winston and Tandy 2001: 82–4). Briefly, the children worked through a short scene from the beginning of the play which emphasises the hatred and tension between the two households. I then gave them titles to create eight tableaux which we then used to illustrate the story of the play as I narrated it in outline. It is, of course, a very powerful and moving story: one boy was, quite literally, moved to tears. We then moved on to create some images that began with the title 'if only . . .' in which the children explored the reasons behind the tragedy and the extent to which similar conditions exist in their own lives. There was agreement that there were many reasons for the kinds of divisions which form the background to the play: family enmities; race; even gender. We decided that two rival gangs would form the background to a contemporary story of friendship.

In the second session we explored these ideas further and began to devise an overall shape for the play. Though not as captivated as they had been by their introduction to the play, the class were nonetheless attentive and thoughtful throughout much of this second session. In the third they were less so, concentration began to wane and their behaviour deteriorated considerably. As the class became less and less focused, their belief – and mine – that we might ever reach a point where we were ready for performance diminished rapidly. And so their behaviour deteriorated further. I find it uncomfortable even to recall the fourth session. It will have to suffice to say that I was left wondering whether I had ever known anything about managing a class. The planned performance had to be postponed.

As I tried in vain to restore some sort of order at the end of that fourth session, one girl cried to her classmates, 'Shut up! You're only getting us into trouble.' 'So what?' came the matter-of-fact reply from another child, 'We're always in trouble.' I was left with the feeling that the self-esteem of these children had reached such a low that many of them felt that 'always being trouble' was all they were worth.

January saw the appointment of a new full-time teacher to the class. It is to her great credit that the stability she brought meant that we were soon talking about the possibility of another production in the summer term. She liked the idea of working with Shakespeare, but felt a fresh start was needed. On Midsummer's Day, we planned, they would perform a short version of A Midsummer Night's Dream. Their new teacher had considerable experience of devising and producing performances with children. Every bit of that experience was brought to bear on the eventual play, performed just as we had hoped, outside on a warm summer's evening. Aspects of the play were splendid, most notably, the two children who played Demetrius and Helena. As Helena pursued Demetrius through the wood, their lines tripped off with practised ease, and the energy in their performance was abundant. Others found the very act of performing in front of an audience much more difficult. For both the teacher and me, the most important thing was that they all got through it.

On the day of the performance, during the afternoon, we did a dress rehearsal for the rest of the school. There were still some problems and, by the end of the day, things were starting to get somewhat fraught. One child left for home at the end of the school day declaring that there was no way he was coming back for the evening performance. He did turn up, changed into his costume, and went out and played his part.

It was while reflecting on the play and its impact on the personal and social development of those children that I rediscovered some words of Iris Murdoch:

> Art and by 'art' . . . I mean good art, not fantasy art, affords us pure delight in the independent existence of what is excellent. Both in its genesis and in its enjoyment it is a thing totally opposed to selfish obsession.
>
> (Murdoch 1970: 85)

I certainly do not wish to claim that what those children had made amounted to 'good art', still less that it 'afforded pure delight in the independent existence of what is excellent'. A Midsummer Night's Dream is indeed a great play and fulfils Murdoch's criteria admirably. But a playscript, however great, needs to be brought to life by actors. To do this effectively, the performers must accept that the play is greater than any one player and *submit* to it accordingly. As I watched some of these children struggle to perform with commitment, even in front of their peers, let alone to a larger audience, it was tempting to put it all down to straightforward inexperience and embarrassment. But how much was due to an inability to *submit* themselves to the greater needs of the play? And if that inability was an important factor, how much did it in turn derive from low self-esteem? The submission holds out the eventual promise of involvement in something which might be successful and widely appreciated by others – as the acclaim for A *Dream for Good* had demonstrated so powerfully.

It is often taken as axiomatic that engagement in the arts generally, and drama specifically, increases confidence, raises self-esteem and so contributes to pupils' personal and social development. Just such claims are made in the 2001 Green Paper *Culture and Creativity: The Next Ten Years* (DCMS 2001: 21). The experience of A *Dream for Good* serves to bear the idea out: the class teacher commented that experience had 'made them as a class', filling them with a sense of their own individual worth and what they could achieve together. But the experience with the *Romeo and Juliet*, though it started with great promise, came close to having precisely the reverse effect. Was it too ambitious? Was it not sufficiently close to the children's everyday experience to engage them as effectively as a piece of work on bullying did? Either of these criticisms – and a great many more – might be justified. I'm certainly indebted to the teacher who refused to give up on them and worked with me to see their eventual performance of A *Midsummer Night's Dream* through. What does seem apparent is that the relationship between drama generally, and performance specifically, and personal and social development is complex and sometimes unpredictable.

When I run courses for primary teachers who are new to teaching drama, they often express an understandable anxiety about classroom management – how do you get children to commit to the work and behave accordingly. My stock answer is that the children need some experience of what good drama can do – experienced classes tend to want to get on because they know the eventual drama they make will be worth it. The problem is that they have to get there to know it was worth the effort of the journey.

The experience of A *Dream for Good* suggests how drama can offer means by which children can represent and explore ideas – ideas which can be profoundly relevant to their personal and social development. To engage in such work requires that those taking part focus outwards and give their individual attention to what is being created by the group as a whole. Whether drama is used in an exploratory way without the intention of developing the work as performance, or whether performance for an audience is the eventual aim, that outward focus is still fundamental. But it is also demanding – while drama may indeed *contribute* to increased confidence and self-esteem, it may also *demand* that same confidence and self-esteem for a class to work together effectively. It's a bit like the couch potato who isn't fit enough to start a fitness programme: walking to the gym might be too strenuous in the first place. You have, as they say, to start somewhere.

Acknowledgements

Thanks are due to Christine Gibbs, former teacher at All Saints Primary School, Nuneaton, Julia Vincent, teacher at the school for their involvement, commitment and support for the projects. Thanks also to Frances Evans and Tania Barras, teaching assistants, and to Robert Darling, student, all of whom made very significant contributions to the success of the work. Finally, to Sally Kaminsky Gaze, headteacher of the school, not just for her support throughout, but for having the vision to start the 'bullying' project in the first place.

References

DCMS (2001) *Culture and Creativity: The Next Ten Years*.

DfEE (1998) *The National Literacy Strategy Framework for Teaching*.

DfEE/DCMS (1999) *All Our Futures: Creativity, Culture and Education*. The Report of the National Advisory Committee on Creative and Cultural Education.

Geertz, Clifford (1983) *Local Knowledge: Further Essays in Interpretive Anthropology*, New York: Basic Books.

Gergen, Kenneth (1991) *The Saturated Self: Dilemmas of Identity in Contemporary Life*, New York: Basic Books.

Murdoch, Iris (1970) 'The sovereignty of good over other concepts', in *The Sovereignty of Good*, reprinted by Routledge, 1991.

Neelands, Jonothan (1990) *Structuring Drama Work: a handbook of available forms in theatre and drama*, Cambridge: Cambridge University Press.

Slade, Peter (1954) *Child Drama*, University of London Press.

Viola, Wilhelm (1942) *Child Art*, University of London Press.

Wilson, Raymond (ed.) (1985) *Nine O'clock Bell: Poems about School*, London: Viking.

Winston, Joe and Tandy, Miles (2001) *Beginning Drama 4–11* (2nd edition), London: David Fulton.

Winston, Joe (1998) *Drama, Narrative and Moral Education*, London: Falmer Press.

Part III

Case studies of whole school approaches

Chapter 9

Happy, calm and caring: ethos and PSHE at Park Lane Primary School

Mick Goodfellow and Jan Hamilton

We aim to provide a happy, calm and caring school where all children give of their best and acquire a sense of achievement through successful learning. We aim to provide for this within a broad, balanced, relevant and differentiated curriculum. We wish to create an atmosphere which promotes positive values of tolerance, kindness and understanding, where we encourage everyone to co-operate with and be considerate to others; a school in which we all feel valued. The staff and Governors of Park Lane Primary School, Nursery and Parents' Centre will strive to achieve this in partnership with parents and the local community.

All schools have aims statements, many display them prominently for all to see, and many echo the ambitions of this one. But, as all those involved with schools know only too well, developing the statement is one thing, making it a lived reality is quite another. Creating 'an atmosphere which promotes positive values of tolerance, kindness and understanding, where we encourage everyone to co-operate with and be considerate to others; a school in which we all feel valued' means taking steps so that such ambition can permeate all aspects of school life and apply equally to everyone involved. Ultimately, it is about consciously and deliberately developing those qualities of the institution that are often referred to as its ethos.

Developing an ethos at Park Lane Primary

What is an ethos? It is one of those words that everyone in education uses but rarely defines. It may therefore seem a nebulous idea which has no direct relationship with our daily lives.

The dictionary definition speaks of the characteristic spirit and beliefs of a community, system, or people. It is about the natural disposition of a place. One can immediately begin to feel how this may apply to a school since it is a community, a system and, most of all, people.

Park Lane is a mixed county primary school catering for about 280 infant and junior children. As a primary school, it has existed for six years and was the result of the amalgamation of two schools, Grove Farm Infants and Robinson's End Middle. Their closure and the opening as a new school came about because of Warwickshire County Council's reorganisation into infant, junior and primary schools. This meant changing the primary/secondary transition from 12 to 11 years of age. Both previous schools had served the local area for twenty-one years, a period which had seen demographic changes that had brought about intense levels of social and physical deprivation within the community. The local ward has a range of housing and population which, in statistical terms, can sometimes mask the problems faced by a large number of our children. We have, therefore, a range of wealth and poverty, a range of attitudes to school and learning among our parents and children. From our baseline assessments we know that many children enter the nursery unit with weak language, literacy, mathematical and communication skills. Their social and emotional development is often delayed. The school has a high special educational needs population with over half the pupils being identified on the SEN register mainly for general learning difficulties and emotional and behavioural difficulties.

Before the schools amalgamated Robinson's End was a school in crisis. The new headteacher was in post for a only term when she had the opportunity to appoint her own deputy. We learnt quickly to work as a team through keeping our vision alive in difficult circumstances. The challenge was to use and build on the good that was in the school as well as dissuade and deal with indiscipline and disruption from a significant number of children. To us, the ethos of the old Robinson's End Middle School was quite negative: it was about aggression and power, about disillusionment and anger. When Park Lane Primary came into being there had been a large-scale amelioration of these attitudes, but there was still much to do. Central to our thinking were two factors – the situation from which Park Lane came and the core importance of relationships.

What is it like to be in our school?

It is very like other schools. Any teacher would recognise the busy classrooms, the sudden surges of noise there, the children working. We could write many things about what we, as head and deputy, think about the school, but the ethos is built up from many perspectives.

For a pupil, there can be the range from the uncertain, the bullied (as with any school, some bullying does occur and is a fact of life for some children, which obviously affects their experience of the institution) to the enthusiast and the proud. For a period, the process of building up the sense of school esteem was through sport. This can, of course, have its drawbacks, particularly when the teams do not win! Nonetheless, being part of something that represented the school was an important way in which some children could show a commitment to it. In general, there are well-established routines and the children follow these set patterns well. They come to the teachers and the support staff expecting help. This expectation is a platform reached by the school.

For the parents, we aim at openness. With our Parents' Centre the depth of knowledge and companionship is quite astounding. Parents of older children find their children more involved and so become more involved in their children's day. There was hostility at first at a number of levels – those seeing teachers as just more representatives of authority, those who had lost faith in this particular school (both those basing it on evidence and ignorance) and those finding a sudden particular conflict about their children's behaviour.

So what did these parents find? We have an 'open door' policy, which meant and still means seeing parents who need, want, demand to see the staff, do see the head or deputy and if necessary the classroom teachers as soon as possible. Quite often this has been on demand, however inconvenient this can be for head and deputy. Talking, giving time to talking, is vital.

Then there are the classroom assistants: underpaid, hardworking, often dependent on the whims of others, often frustrated, sensitive to their role and status. We originally had some sense of segregation and apartness. Looking around the staffroom at a lunchtime last week, it would have been difficult to have picked out who was who between anyone. But the messages had to be repeated endlessly: everyone is part of the team; everybody is welcome in the staffroom. The policy has been to ensure that support staff are given training and most of our classroom assistants have undertaken and gained additional certification.

Not all members of staff have direct involvement with the children. A cleaner who worked at the school for many years before going on to a supervisory role in the county, spoke to us about our Ofsted report. She had noted the comments about the general good standard of cleanliness. She said that it was important for the cleaners to do their best and to go that extra bit to make sure they had done their part in making any inspection a success. The sense of commitment to the school was extraordinary. The deliberate and effective development of an ethos at Park Lane Primary really did mean taking account of and involving everyone.

So how does the ethos affect the curriculum?

In trying to raise the profile of science in the school, the science subject leader set a series of science challenges for the whole school, from Reception to Year 6. They took place each month and would consist of a simple project. Some would be quite open ended, such as making a musical instrument, while others would need detailed instructions – as in the making of a rocket challenge. These challenges were significant, not so much for the scientific understandings that resulted from them, but for the involvement of families in the learning of their children. It became clear that parents were enjoying doing the challenges as much as the children and that the talking and teaching going on at home was significant. Children could see that their parents were enthusiastic and knowledgeable and interested in learning. This was a more important outcome for the children than any increase in their scientific knowledge. It is also a pointer about the nature and aim of homework in the primary years.

A second illustration of the type of project undertaken which promoted and developed the ethos of the school through classroom work is what we nicknamed *The Railway Children*. During her work with the upper maths set of Years 4 and 5, the teacher decided that the children needed to put their thinking into a practical situation. She has a strong commitment to collective developmental work and set the children the task of organising their own day trip out. Together the group discussed possibilities and then had to check out costs and feasibility. Eventually they settled on a trip by train to Birmingham Airport, which, because of the bewitching nature of British transport, involved first organising a coach to Coventry. All the plans, costings, telephoning and organisation were kept firmly in the hands of the children: giving the responsibility to the children ensured not only a good day out but a powerful lasting message to the children about their own capabilities.

Many primary school teachers will readily recognise examples like these and see such approaches reflected in their own practice, but they do serve to illustrate how we try to ensure that our aims for the school, and the ethos we have worked to develop, permeate our approach to the taught curriculum.

Staff relationships

To find the sense of community, we needed to develop the common ground between us. When we began as Park Lane Primary School this was a process of learning which was probably harder for the staff than it was for the children. Infant and Junior staff had different histories and ways of doing things. It takes time to establish that the rule 'we always do it this way' may not actually apply to a new place. This process came about by talking and listening. It has to be a continuous conversation that goes on through the whole school, finding and building on that common sense of values and worth. There were lots of landmarks to be put in, such as peer mediation, the Respect[1] code of conduct, and even details like making sure everyone got the same standard of coffee available.

This is not a set of strategies that we have devised to produce a simple 'fits all' school ethos. It is not even a coherent set of strategies for our own school. We came into a situation and we tried out different projects and ideas to make the situation better. What holds it together is the way in which we have tried to establish a way of working and trying things out. This is about relationships. The need has been and continues to be to keep talking to everyone and make that conversation into one that develops over time so that ideas become the shared property of the school.

This process of talk is also important for the esteem of the school itself as we needed to develop the separate new sense of identity for Park Lane. We have continued the process so that we remain realistic about how we 'talk the school up'. Both children and staff have to have the means of talking and thinking about their school positively. This cannot properly be done by coercing or cutting off debate: there needs to be thought given not just to what we do, but to the way we do it.

Through always giving time to dialogue we have an effective feed-back process. It means knowing your school well and this means seeing more clearly how things will work and with whom. It also says that there is no quick fix. We always have great difficulty in keeping a straight face when we see the published league table results and find our place in the county. We can see and demonstrate the improvements in conditions, behaviour, commitment, and attainment that we have reached already, but we also know where we are and who we are. We have a commitment to changing our children's lives for the better and we know that there are things in school that can be done and that there are things that we have no control over. It means we take the long view. We take the home–school link very seriously, and one of our most successful ventures has been the appointment of a home–school worker. Originally this was with someone coming from a social services background and is now another professional with support services experience. This was part funded through a county project, but although that no longer exists the school has continued to wholly support it as it plays such an important part in the social growth of the children.

Becoming part of the school community

The children go back to their homes and their own milieu of lives and values, which differ considerably. The school is the area of common ground which is built up again every day and the more the values become shared the more the sense of community exists. The school has its set routines that are concerned with the overt learning tasks and there is the constant way things are done, but we have made conscious efforts to make parts of the day open to that sense of being part of the community.

Most of these examples will seem quite mundane, but are worth reflecting on as they deal with belonging and the structuring of relationships within the school. Like most schools, we begin the day with assemblies. We have separate infant and junior ones on Mondays and joint ones in the rest of the week, with frequent class assemblies on Wednesdays. Whole school assemblies have to be worth the logistical effort of tramping everyone into one place and out again. If things make us laugh we share it. If we make asides to colleagues, we enjoy it all the more. On Fridays we have achievement assemblies where infants receive certificates and juniors house point badges for good work, the children can have out-of-school awards presented and sometimes a music group will perform. At the end, children and staff with birthdays can come out to the front to get their badge, sweet and a rousing chorus. This may seem commonplace and even slightly 'naff'. There are times when the Friday assembly seems to be like a nightmare games show that never ends, but if there is a child beaming with the pleasure of their badge, their certificate, their achievement or that sense of belonging then it's worth its weight in gold. We do not pressure individuals to take part.

Then we have those spaces in the day: playtime and dinnertime. What are they for? For children to play in (and to forget to go to the toilet!) and to learn by themselves. This does not mean leaving a free-for-all where only the top-dog wins, but helping to structure the time and the expectations of what can and could happen and preventing what should not. Dinner supervisors are given training to help them introduce and use games with the children. We have meetings and encourage comment about procedures to follow or change to improve the level of socialisation on the playgrounds. The infant supervisors brought quite a degree of expertise in this from their previous school.

These children need space. They need to be allowed to find their own way of dealing with problems especially out on the playground. They cannot be dependent on the adult to solve all their problems. The home–school link set up the 'grey caps' system as a part of the peer mediation project with help from the County Support Services. This means selected children receive training to help other children resolve their disputes; a learning experience on all sides.

And through the whole day we try to weave into what we do the how of encouragement and insistence. The children need to find their own feet but they also need a supporting hand. They must have confidence that the staff will listen to them and will find the time to do so and respond. We never undervalue the small necessary moment of kindness to vulnerable children who have less of it in their lives than they should.

Designated time for PSHE and Citizenship

The approaches we have outlined so far support – and are supported by – the taught programme for PSHE and Citizenship. This is part of our curriculum provision across the school and includes:

- **Circle time** – the most widespread PSHE practice we have. It is a regular part of designated time for all pupils. Circle time can help pupils develop good listening skills, work successfully together and boost self-esteem. The underlying aim is to create a caring, supportive environment where both pupils and adults engage in respectful listening.

- **Social skills** – each year at least one group of children, which may be a whole class, works through a series of workshops on turn-taking, collaboration and tolerance using role-play, discussion and games. The heateacher and a number of other staff have been trained to do this.

- **Anger management** – a planned programme for specific children.

- **Relaxation classes** – these are voluntary and take place at lunch-times. Pupils learn to relax through a variety of techniques including breathing, movement and the use of imagery.

- **Music therapy** – we were able to purchase this through Warwick-shire's County Music Service. Children had the opportunity to be creative in a small group, making music in a way that would not be possible in a large group situation given their emotional and behavioural difficulties, their lack of confidence and poor self-image.

Special projects and interventions

These are a number of further interventions, some of which target particular groups of children, others which serve to enrich our overall provision for PSHE.

- **Nurture groups** – these help individual children to become more emotionally secure and better able to cope with social and learning situations. The sessions take place in the 'Rainbow Room' and are run by a trained and experienced Special Educational Needs Assistant.

- **Home/school support worker** – this worker has a number of roles, but is essentially a non-threatening point of contact for children and parents. She is known by her first name and engages with children by running the 'Grey Caps', teaching and playing games on the playground, and one-to-one contact. Vulnerable children are often referred to her by the headteacher.

- **Warwickshire Health Promoting School Scheme** – working together to achieve the Health Promoting School standard.[2]

- **Children's University** – these sessions began in September 1999. They take place on Saturday morning and children can choose from a variety of modules including dance and drama, ICT, art and drama, basketball, design technology and food technology.

- **Peer Mediation** – each year Year 5 pupils are given training in how to help each other resolve conflicts through paired talking and listening. A number of children are then chosen to be Peer Mediators (the Grey Caps – their identifying hats) who are available at lunch and breaks to help sort out squabbles. We plan to extend this idea further by training children as 'playground peacemakers'.

- **Parents' Centre** – now based in its own building and staffed by a teacher and a nursery nurse, it provides times for parents and toddlers to share experiences, work together with their children in a pre-nursery situation and learn from staff. Courses run by the outreach team from the local college range from computing to parenting to yoga.

- **Special days, weeks etc.** – Arts, Multi Cultural events, Performances, etc. Despite the pressures, the school still has days where a year group can commandeer the hall to paint Tudor portraits, learn to play African drums, etc. The events often involve bringing in artists and performers.

The ethos of Park Lane Primary which we have outlined and discussed in this chapter is about making our aims statement a reality for everyone involved: children, teaching and non-teaching staff, parents and community. Without the interventions we have referred to, it would be very difficult to make that aims statement a reality. But without the ethos which we have all worked to develop, it would not be possible for the other interventions to function as effectively as they do. We depend upon each other.

Notes

1. The Park Lane RESPECT Code of Conduct:
   - Remember the rules.
   - Enjoy our environment and keep it tidy.
   - Show that you can be safe and sensible in the playground as well as in the classroom.
   - Park Lane Pupils are polite, patient and kind.
   - Everyone looks after their own belongings.
   - Courtesy counts – remember to walk quietly and carefully through classroom areas.
   - Try to be helpful at all times.
2. See the Warwickshire Health Promoting Schools website at www.whpss.net

Chapter 10

A normal school soon?

Gill Winston

'The inspectors are here! And everyone has done a lot of work. Hopefully we will be a normal school soon.'

(Louise, aged 11)

This comment was one of many in our pupils' comments book, which traces the school's journey from its lowest point when it had just been placed in 'Special Measures' to its successful return to 'normality'. The school is a rural school, which serves the village of Stockton. As such it has a strong sense of community because all our pupils come from the village. The population of the village is mixed, with some families having lived in the village for generations – some of our pupils are among the fifth generation of their family to attend the school – while some are newcomers to the village, occupying the new housing recently built.

In September 1999, the school was placed in Special Measures. It was at this point that I joined the school as the new headteacher. There was only one permanent teacher in post with three temporary teachers working valiantly to carry the school through the turbulent term in which OFSTED had published their judgements of the school. They revealed that standards were very low, with all PANDA grades at E or E*, 25 per cent of teaching was judged as unsatisfactory, with no good teaching observed. In addition to this, the school was not teaching all aspects of the National Curriculum as required and resources were judged to be inadequate. Indeed, the resources of the school were completely outdated, tattered and dirty. The judgement of OFSTED was stark:

In order to improve standards and the quality of education in the school, the governors, headteacher and staff should:

- improve pupils' standards of attainment and progress in all subjects;
- review the quality of leadership and management of the school;
- improve the quality of teaching;
- improve the quality and range of resources in school.

These key issues related to every aspect of the school's work and meant that everything we did would be under scrutiny. The publication of these facts lowered the morale and confidence of the whole school community. The pupils had a strong sense of being 'behind', parents were angry about the failings their children had suffered and, although they all wanted to see the school recover and succeed, many doubted whether this would happen soon enough to benefit their children, particularly because the three new staff needed had not yet been appointed. There was a strong sense of disappointment throughout the village that the school, which had served so many generations of their families, was once again under threat: only two years earlier the village had fought hard against the school's closure as part of Warwickshire's re-organisation of primary education. Their campaign was successful and the school was kept open, changing from a 4–8 'First School' to an all-through primary. When I started at the school in September the very first cohort of KS2 pupils had taken their SATs the previous May. Many features of the building, resourcing and pedagogy of the school reflected the fact that the school had catered for KS1 pupils for many years up until this point.

Having fought so hard to keep their school, many villagers did not believe that the LEA would now be in support of keeping the school open in its current circumstances. The possibility that large numbers of children would now begin to leave was very high, with several parents coming to see me daily to discuss the possibility of moving their children. Three new teachers had to be found for January and only one of the posts would offer promotion, the other two would be a sideways move for anyone already in post – how could the school attract good staff in these circumstances?

However, there were positive elements to the situation:

- Everyone understood that there was an urgent need for change.
- The village did not want to lose their school and knew that their only chance of avoiding this lay in solidarity – if people started taking their children away closure would be more likely. This led to an understanding that the community would have to support the school if they wanted it to succeed.

- Additional money and support was now available to us.
- New staff appointed to the school may bring skills which will help accelerate school improvement.

Most importantly, the three new teaching posts could be in fact *the* most positive element to the situation. If we could attract good teachers, the process of improvement would be accelerated. They would have had no part in the factors which caused the school to go into Special Measures and would have *chosen* to come to our school, with full knowledge of the professional commitment they were taking on in the work they would have to do in order to raise standards rapidly and ensure that Special Measures were no longer required. The parents' decision to put their trust in the school and support it in the medium term, along with the good behaviour of the pupils, gave us strengths in the way we were able to present ourselves.

Through this process, which included encouraging prospective candidates to visit the school to discuss the challenges that lay ahead, we were able to appoint three experienced, confident and able teachers to the school. By the following term a fourth new teacher was appointed of an equally high calibre. Although steps had already been taken to begin to address the many and varied needs of the school, key challenges needed to be addressed quickly so that we could begin to make headway and measure impact. The new teachers found that pupils' learning behaviours were poor. The ethos pervading the classrooms could be summed up as:

- Noisy.
- Lots of movement (children were not used to sitting and staying on task for long).
- Lacking in purpose.
- Lack of care shown towards work (particularly recorded work).
- The children's work lacked pace.
- Untidy (most resources were too old to be of any use and were stored in a haphazard fashion).

Our initial work together as a staff brought about a clarity as to how we would approach the key 'hidden' issues as we perceived them – to raise the pupils' morale, teach them how to become good learners, motivate them to take an active part in their own learning and, through this, make accelerated progress. We agreed together what we considered to be the qualities of good teaching and prepared evaluation formats so that responses to scrutiny of planning and observations of teaching would be firmly grounded within these criteria. This exercise also gave teachers the tools for self-evaluation relating to our whole-school agreement on what we had agreed were the characteristics of quality teaching. What came through loud and clear from these early discussions was a strongly held belief that we would not raise morale or motivate and enthuse our pupils into good learning habits if we confined our energies to teaching the core curriculum. We set ourselves against trying to raise standards in the subjects which would come under HMI's greatest scrutiny by giving them additional curriculum time, as this would inevitably mean paying lip service to 'less important' subjects such as the arts. We were all in agreement that the curriculum should be broad and rich. We believed that it would not only be possible to raise standards in literacy and numeracy within and throughout such a curriculum, but that a thin and narrow curriculum would be unlikely to grow the attitudes we needed the children to adopt.

In our discussions about what a good lesson should look like, the following criteria were listed:

What does a good lesson look like – what are the essential elements?

- Well planned.
- Objectives – teacher + adults + *children clear about what they should be learning.*
- Good use of resources.
- Secure understanding of subject.
- *Matching teaching style to children's needs* and subject.
- Manage pupils well – *promote good behaviour.*
- *To have high expectations of what the children can achieve.*
- *To develop children's self-esteem through positive reinforcement.*
- Use of effective and supportive questioning.
- Assess pupils' work thoroughly and use assessment to help pupils overcome difficulties and inform next steps in learning.
- Lesson introduction: *remind them of what they already know*, indicate what we are going to learn next, stimulating, challenging and inspiring, brisk and definitive start.
- Use time, support staff and resources (including ICT) effectively.
- *Use homework effectively to reinforce and/or extend what is learned in school.*
- *Pupils acquire new knowledge or skills, develop ideas and increase their understanding.*

- *Pupils apply intellectual, physical or creative effort in their work.*
- *Pupils are productive and work at a good pace.*
- *Pupils show interest in their work, are able to sustain concentration and think and learn for themselves.*
- *Pupils understand what they are doing, how well they have done and what they can do to improve.*
- Both staff and *pupils show enthusiasm.*
- Familiar, high quality resources.
- Modelling.
- Practical experiences.
- *Promote good working relationships in the classroom.*
- *Pupils are given opportunities to learn in a variety of ways* – practical, open ended questioning – range of resources – investigative.

These statements are rather untidy grammatically and have not been placed in any order of importance. There was so much to do in such a short time that we spent little time 'tidying up' written policies and documents – the crucial thing was to articulate and agree goals and direction and then get on with the practicalities of getting there. The criteria in italics show that the teachers' thinking was already very much grounded in the understanding that the pupils had to be *active participants* in the process of improvement rather than recipients of it. Interestingly, since this ethos of good teaching and learning has become embedded, the children's contribution to our teaching and learning policy in response to the question, 'What do good learners do?' very much reflects those early criteria brainstormed by the new staff:

- Listen.
- Think.
- Concentrate.
- Look.
- Know where to find things.
- Know what to do when they get stuck.
- Can get on by themselves.
- Always try their best.
- Work hard.
- Work carefully.
- Are not nasty.
- Take their turn.
- Help each other.
- Take care of things in school.

- Are kind and helpful.
- Sit nicely.
- Focus on what they are doing.
- Do what they are told.

It is interesting to note that the children are quite clear that learning involves a lot more than just the acquisition of knowledge. They identify criteria, which are very definitely rooted in PHSE and Citizenship, criteria much more about being part of a supportive community that is *enabling*, as can be seen through the children's statements that good learners are helpful, kind, co-operative, behave well and know how to help themselves and others.

I believe that the early discussions between the school staff helped us to articulate a strong vision, which included not only a sense of where we wanted to take the school, but also an idea of how we thought we would get there, who would be responsible for what and when and where to all pull together as a team effort. This, in turn, brought a clarity of intention to the pupils, giving them clear objectives to work towards and measure themselves against. The staff watched for signs of improving learning behaviours across the school, and were quick to recognise and reward pupils' efforts, through a simple whole school reward system which was consistently and rigorously implemented. This brought about an infectious drive among the pupils to improve their approach to learning.

It was important that the commitment and enthusiasm of staff and pupils was backed up by the necessary improvements in the resources and environment they had to support their learning. This not only involved the more conspicuous actions, like the provision of new furniture, but also matters as mundane as seeing that all the children had new books, pens and pencils. The message that their work mattered was important. We also put a great deal of effort into more general improvements to the learning environment: putting up displays; organising and tidying resources; throwing away anything that had become old and tatty. And creating a decent learning environment also meant increasing the hours for cleaning. It all mattered and had a direct impact on how the children understood the importance of what we were all doing.

In addition, we developed specific interventions to improve children's learning behaviours. We increased teaching assistant's hours so that they could be more actively involved in this process. As a whole staff, we undertook training in the use of circle time and introduced this across the school. The introduction of the Literacy and Numeracy Strategies helped by providing a structure that was regularly reinforced. The teaching assistants sat with children on the carpet and helped them to understand how to 'sit in a learning sort of way' during whole class time.

The curriculum was another key area to which we turned our attention. The introduction of Curriculum 2000 coincided with the school's need to design a curriculum from scratch. As a new staff we had already agreed a basic set of principles upon which to base quality teaching and learning; now it was time to apply those principles to a brand new curriculum tailored to the needs of the school and the requirements of Curriculum 2000, a curriculum which would play to the strengths of the staff and, most importantly, raise standards of attainment in all areas by 'hooking' children in to learning through interesting and exciting work.

First and foremost were the principles on which we were not prepared to compromise – the practicalities would have to be worked around these. These principles were agreed in discussions during staff meetings, the notes of which were used to form policy. Our 'Teaching and Learning Policy' begins:

> At Stockton School, we aim for all children to receive a broad, well-balanced curriculum. The staff team share strong values and principles, which underpin curriculum planning. We believe that the curriculum should . . . We express our principles clearly in the curriculum planning rationale:

- *A broad and rich curriculum which ensures that the core curriculum is well taught and that links with, and between, the foundation subjects are fully exploited.*
- *Learning opportunities should be varied with maximum potential for motivation and enjoyment (both for pupils and teachers).*
- *The arts and humanities should be strong in themselves and should serve to strengthen the core curriculum.*
- *Learning should be meaningful, placed within strong contexts that are, wherever possible, familiar to the children.*

As a small village school, contacts with the wider world were to be an important aspect of our planning, so, as well as ensuring a good curriculum balance in the long-term plan, we also wanted to incorporate a balance of visits out of school and visitors into the school. This involved juggling topics about to ensure that costly visits were spread out, as were topics with a specific subject focus such as arts or history based work.

Another key area in which we worked to raise pupil morale was through our use of assessment. Initially this was used to give a clear picture of what the pupils knew and understood and where the gaps in their learning were. This analysis enabled us to establish a baseline from which we could both plan for progress and begin to measure it. The involvement of the pupils in this process brought about target setting, which proved to be a powerful tool in moving the children's learning and self-esteem forwards rapidly. Target setting remains one of the most important aspects of the interaction between the pupils, teachers and parents relating to the children's learning, and as such it is still evolving as we continually refine the process.

We all felt that it was important for the children to have a voice and to tell us about how they wanted the school to improve. If we wanted the children to be active participants in the process of school improvement they would need to be given tools with which to participate and this meant giving them a voice so that they could tell us what they wanted to improve and inform us of the effect our attempts at improvement were having. We introduced a comments book in which they were invited to record their feelings and opinions about their school. Many expressed positive comments about their new teachers and there were many positive comments about their new curriculum, with pupils in particular referring to their enjoyment of art, drama and PE. The following are examples from the book:

- *I like better work.*
- *The school is getting better than it was. The children get better at work. We get better learning.*
- *The school has changed a lot.*
- *I liked the people who performed today.*
- *Toy monitors aren't out on time.*
- *We want to play more.*

In addition to the comments book, we introduced a suggestion box, where children were invited to give their own ideas of how improvements could be made to the school. The suggestion box revealed a strong desire throughout the school for the simple comfort of soft toilet paper. Large quantities of the crisp, hard type filled several shelves in the caretaker's cupboard. These joined much of the school's other outdated equipment in one of a succession of skips, and soft toilet paper became the next item on our full order books. Several parents used the box to inform us that older pupils did not like to use the toilets because taller children could see over the doors: the toilets had not been changed since the school had been an infant school. Builders were drafted in and alterations were made to the heights of the doors. Seeing a quick and positive response to their suggestions, the pupils became more interested in the box, several of the older boys orchestrated a number of requests for proper football posts and were thrilled to see them installed soon afterwards in the school playing field. Requests for toys at playtime were responded to by the 'Friends of Stockton School' and a recent request for more toys will also be funded by them – the pupils are currently carrying out a survey to see which toys are most popularly requested and will be in charge of ordering within the budget they have been allocated. Of course there are limits, and requests for a swimming pool and play-park with swing and a slide have not been successful so far!

These features of citizenship exercised within their own school are now having a wider effect on the children, who actively seek to improve the quality of life of other children. They recently raised money to help pay for clean water, a safe place to sleep and education for street children in Kenya, who they heard of through a grandfather of one of the pupils who works as part of a joint church project there – the 'Kabare' project. One girl brought in a bag full of sugar lollypops, which she bought with her own pocket money after hearing that the street children in Kenya only receive such sweets on Christmas day. These are children who have learned that they can make a difference and actively seek to do so.

In summary, the key ways in which we built a strong positive ethos and fostered an enthusiasm for learning in our pupils were:

- Everyone connected with the school shared common goals and worked towards them as a team. This began with the teaching staff initially but quickly spread to support staff, pupils, governors and parents.
- Quality teaching and learning was at the heart of everything we did, with all the stakeholders understanding what this meant and how they could both contribute to it and benefit from it. Again, as I stated earlier, this involved the active participation of the pupils, and in order to bring this about, the shape this participation would take had to be articulated clearly.
- There was consistency in everything we did. Consistency was gained through discussion leading to agreement and then strong communication of that agreement, with teachers embodying the vision for the rest of the school community.
- The strong principles and values we shared were built into every aspect of the school.

- A good long-term curriculum was developed and schemes of work written.
- The pupils were actively involved in the process of improvement.

In the final report that removed us from special measures, HMI says:

> The school is a happy and welcoming community. A positive ethos extends to all aspects of its life. Relationships between the pupils, and between the pupils and adults are good. Classroom assistants and teachers are consistent in their dealings with the pupils, and form a close knit and affirmative team. The pupils' behaviour is good in lessons and around the school. In all classes, the pupils have positive attitudes to learning and work hard.

What has been the impact of this on personal and social development?

As I try to unpick the strategies and their effects, the extent to which everything is tightly woven together and interdependent becomes clear. The rewards system could not have worked as well if pupil progress had not been so dramatic, but the recognition through the rewards themselves accelerated the progress. This progress would not have been made without high quality teaching, which in turn needed the firm baseline that our assessment and analysis provided. The assessment and analysis gave us good quality information, providing a clear picture of what the next steps in the pupils' learning had to be. Sharing this information with the pupils and parents through target setting gave the pupils purpose, direction and pace in their learning and enabled parents to share and contribute to their child's progress. The quality of the curriculum and its impact on teaching and learning cannot be underestimated, nor can its contribution to the enthusiasm and motivation of both pupils and teachers. None of the strategies would have been as powerful if the teachers and teaching assistants were not all giving the same messages consistently across the school, and if they did not share the values and principles in which everything was rooted, principally that the quality of experience for our pupils had to be central to everything we did. Even the introduction of soft toilet paper reinforced the message to pupils that they mattered and showed them that their voices were listened to and taken into account.

There has been a sea change in the way in which the school perceives itself, how it is perceived by the community it serves, and how the pupils operate within it. This has taken place over a relatively short period of time and is now secure and sustainable.

We recently carried out surveys of how the school is perceived by our pupils. Gathering this sort of information is as important to us as the assessment data we collect. As with all our data it gives us information about what we are doing well, but also tells us where we need to make improvements: 96 per cent of our pupils tell us that they know how well they are doing and what they must do to improve, and most of our other questions elicited an equally positive response. However, the pupils filled in the survey anonymously and were invited to make further personal comments on the back of the sheet. Many of them chose to do this, 25 per cent wrote positive comments, largely about enjoying school: 'I like coming to school and I enjoy learning and I have no problems'. But, 21 per cent raised issues regarding playtime provision and the behaviour of other pupils during this time. This is clearly our next issue to address thoroughly – and to do so in partnership with the pupils. If we are sincere about the quality of the pupils' experience being central to everything we do, this must extend to every aspect of the school's life and not just those related to academic standards.

Because we had not carried out such a survey when we began the process of school improvement, there was nothing to measure against when considering the impact our work had had on the children. In an attempt to do this we asked the children to tape child-led group discussions relating to the changes in school. In these discussions the pupils refer continually to the improvements in teaching and learning, their ability to learn and make good progress, the new decorations and structural improvements to the school, the much-improved resources they now work with, and their positive feelings about school generally. In response to the question: 'What would you tell a new child in the village about your school?' almost all responded: 'I would say it's a good school.' About the teachers, the most common comments are: 'They make learning interesting', and: 'They can take a laugh'.

We also carried out a survey of parental attitudes along the lines of the OFSTED questionnaire. In comparison to the figures of 1999, there is a significant shift in the parents' views of the school with a very strong positive view of the school in key areas of its work. Interestingly, the pupils' comments regarding playtime provision were echoed by the parents, who had also been invited to make further comment about the life of the school. These surveys have given us a good measure about how far we have come and about how much further we must continue to go. The surveys, and in particular our response to them, will reinforce the message to the children that they have worth and that by expressing their views and offering suggestions they can have a real effect on the quality of their experiences at school. In the report, which brought us out of special measures, the inspector also wrote:

> The teachers have high expectations about the pupils' behaviour and attitudes to work and have established suitable routines to enable teaching to proceed smoothly. The teachers are knowledgeable, confident and conscientious. They respect the children and show this in the way they question them, respond to their ideas, and promote a positive view about their potential.

And what about standards? In 1999 our PANDA grades were all E and E*. For 2001, it contains A*, A, B, C and D.

In the end of Key Stage 1 SATS for 2001, 63 per cent of our pupils achieved Level 3 in maths. Before 2000 there had been no Level 3s in maths at Stockton. For Key Stage 2 there is a similar pattern of improvement. While there is no comparison to make with 1999 as there were no Key Stage 2 results in the PANDA at that time, our prior attainment grades are all As and Bs.

On one level, ours is a straightforward story of 'school improvement': addressing low expectations, improving the quality of teaching and learning, raising standards. I would argue though, that such dramatic improvement over such a short period of time would not have been possible if we had not placed the personal and social development of the children at the heart of the process. One approach might have been to 'sort out behaviour' and go straight for standards, leaving PSHE and Citizenship issues to their place in Curriculum 2000 – at the end. We all knew them to be much more central than that.

Returning to Louise's opening comment: 'The inspectors are here! . . . hopefully we will be a normal school soon.' I would add my wish that we become an exceptional school, which brings richness, success and joy to the community it serves. As one child in the taped discussions said:

'I feel as though there is a brighter future in front of me now.'

Establishing a community of practice for citizenship education at Deptford Green School

Anna Douglas and Anne Hudson

This chapter provides an account of how a school in south-east London has begun to develop a community of practice in the area of citizenship education. The joint authorship of the chapter has its origins in a paper written for a conference in March 2001.[1] At that point the school was in its early stages of developing its citizenship focus. Anne Hudson, Assistant Headteacher Coordinating Citizenship Education, and Anna Douglas, PGCE Social Science Tutor at Goldsmiths College, had begun to share ideas about citizenship education and planned to work collaboratively in the training of student teachers. The school has moved on considerably since then. This chapter aims to reflect emerging practice, and our thoughts about the pedagogy that might support citizenship education. We do not claim that these ideas are ours alone. They have been informed by our involvement and interaction with students, teachers, trainers and community practitioners.[2] We use the term 'community of practice' to indicate the important link between social relations and knowledge which develops through activity (Lave and Wenger 1991). A community of practice represents, as Mercer suggests, 'the way in which groups of people use their ability to share past experience to create joint understanding and co-ordinate ways of dealing with new experience' (2000: 116). We note, as the school progresses with becoming a school for citizenship, that there is a great deal of thinking and discussion about what is being done and why. This chapter intends to give a sense of this social learning through involvement in practices, indicating where theory has helped us reflect more deeply about evolving practice.

Deciding to become a school for citizenship

Deptford Green School is, in many ways, a typical inner city compre-hensive,11–18 school with 1,216 pupils on roll; 56 per cent boys; 50 per cent free school meals; 55 pupils with Stage 5 SEN statements; a large ethnic mix (55 per cent with English as an additional language) and a catchment area with high index of social and economic deprivation. The staff are committed to promoting equality of opportunity and its members have found themselves uncomfortable with the implications of some aspects of current government policy. Among these is the specialist schools agenda, which many perceive to be divisive. The proliferation of schools specialising in areas like technology, sport and art can undermine the notion of comprehensive education within a geographical area, attracting some pupils away from what should be their local schools. In 1999, the senior team decided to endorse a risky idea put forward by one of its members. The proposal was that, recognising the gathering momentum of the specialist schools agenda, Deptford Green begin a campaign for a category of specialism appropriate for inner city schools like this: one which could cement the links with the local community and create the context for developing an appropriate ethos.

The arguments in favour of becoming a school for citizenship remain powerful. First, it invites an important focus on affective as well as cognitive development. Awareness of evidence for the link between academic attainment and emotional intelligence, promoted by Daniel Goleman (1996) and the advocates of accelerated learning, has piled up during the past decade. The development of emotional intelligence is an important dimension of citizenship education. Second, there is evidence that breaking down the walls between schools and their local communities by bringing parents and carers into schools and making them centres of lifelong learning across the generations has had an impact on attainment in several community schools. Initially the school's citizenship agenda was very much inspired by the success of community schools and informed by Hargreaves and Fullan (1998) who state:

> In turning schools into stronger communities, school reforms should not be separated from wider urban reform. They depend on each other. . . . Schools should build not any kind of community, but democratic communities which value participation, equality, inclusiveness and social justice, in addition to loyalty and service among all their members. These communities should start in the

classrooms in which pupils share responsibility for their own and for regulating each other's behaviour. Involving students and parents in decision making, teaching and learning decisions, parent conferences and assessment of achievement extend these democratic principles further.

(Hargreaves and Fullan 1998: 98)

The aims behind the school's citizenship agenda are seen as a means to:

- raise achievement in ways which are tangible, measurable and lasting;
- change the culture of the school and its interaction with the community;
- pioneer, demonstrate and disseminate good practice;
- develop new ways of thinking and learning;
- draw together key initiatives across the school;
- challenge social exclusion and celebrate cultural diversity.

Audit, consultation and construction

The introduction of the citizenship agenda at Deptford Green consciously followed the School Improvement model of audit, consultation, construction, implementation, and review. Later on in the chapter we consider how other models might also inform the process. The process began by taking stock of what was already in existence, positively identifying the following: an openness to collaboration with the community; a commitment to supporting the development of students' voice in the school; some efforts to redevelop the pastoral curriculum; work with local community forums and SRB (Single Regeneration Budget) regeneration. In various staff and middle management meetings there was wider discussion around the proposal to seek specialist status. Next, following the procedures required for conventional specialist schools, the school secured £50,000 worth of private sector funding from a large investment bank, UBS Warburg, already working in partnership on a mentoring scheme. The bid followed the Specialist Schools format, including a mission statement, school and community aims, and a four-year development plan. This was presented to the DfES. A commitment to a new category of specialism was not secured, but innovation funding was awarded.

At this point further staff involvement was needed and to this end two voluntary weekend residentials were organised in January and July

2000. Both were attended by over 20 staff, teaching and non-teaching, and generated a wealth of ideas about how different curriculum areas could 'own' citizenship and provide relevant opportunities for young people. Later in the year, when the senior team firmed up proposals for action, a questionnaire to colleagues to ascertain their views was completed, and the proposals were overwhelmingly endorsed. The next stage involved two kinds of audit of existing provision. The first was a curriculum audit, which got indications from all departments of how they perceived their current delivery. Although the findings from this were useful in giving all teachers confidence that they were already dealing with aspects of citizenship education, the school has now moved beyond that model, as suggested in a later section entitled 'Citizenship and the curriculum'. A sample of students across all year groups also completed a questionnaire, to ascertain their understanding of aspects of citizenship education. Findings from these were insufficient to build up a clear picture of pupils' experiences and insights at that stage.

The community context

Prior to approaching the DfES with its request that citizenship become a specialist category, the school had been working to consolidate links with the local community. The process of regeneration in the local area had led members of the school management to participate in local organisations like the Deptford Community Forum and two local SRBs. Significantly, the Evelyn SRB had developed a reputation for genuine community consultation and involvement. This partnership between such organisations and the school has provided funding for facilities, services and activities in the school and simultaneously raised the school's profile in the area. Members of the various forums had begun to call upon the school for advice and support. The membership of these forums tends to overlap, and several of the same personnel became involved in a new 'Get Set for Citizenship' SRB which developed in consultation with members of the school's senior management team. The Assistant Headteacher and a member of the Get Set Partners group, came up with a bid for a citizenship outreach worker to be based at Deptford Green. Funding for the post was secured, and by February 2001 the worker had been appointed. His role is to work on the interface between the school and the community. It is anticipated that this will help the school to sustain its involvement in community regeneration and enable pupils from the school to be actively involved in the process.

This work adds to other links with various outside agencies supporting pupils through mentoring, advocacy, and attendance projects which were drawn together in 1999, when the school set up a Community Department. That department is overseen by an employee of the Children's Society, has an office on school premises, and forms an important part of the community context. The issue of sustainability of projects and contact seems a crucial one to raise at this point. If a school is really to maintain its links with the local community it is important to consider ways in which mutual interests can interact to support each others' wider goals. A proposed outcome of 'Get Set for Citizenship' is to regenerate through maximising community participation. In tandem with this the school wants to encourage more concern and interest among its students for the local community. To date students' GCSE coursework research into local community issues has been presented to a panel of local representatives including, councillors, borough safety personnel, a Community Policing Officer and members of the school's senior team. It is hoped that students' future research will feed into a wider forum and be of use to communities outside the school. This is a dimension that could be important in consolidating the school's interaction with local community issues.

Launching citizenship awareness through Citizenship Day

In order to raise the profile of citizenship among students, it was decided that a Citizenship Day would be organised in December 2000. The normal timetable was suspended and the whole school was involved in activities linked to the citizenship theme. The morning began with upper and lower school assemblies addressed by key speakers including MP Joan Ruddock, representatives of local community organisations and representatives of the School Council. During the rest of the day students could opt for activities as diverse as considering how the Tate Modern reflects twenty-first century culture, visiting the Houses of Parliament, being part of a newspaper production team, hands-on experience of environmentally sound gardening and recycling, sharing citizenship learning with local primary school pupils, running an EC café and exploring human rights issues. In all there were 41 different activities on offer. These were undertaken in mixed age groups. A survey of students before and after the event found that their insights into and enthusiasm for citizenship benefited from the day. Surveys of students and teachers indicated that they enjoyed it enough to want to make it a regular feature of school life. They also showed that students believed they understood more about citizenship education. The following quotes reflect some of the students' sentiments:

'The day was good and I wish we could do the same day again.'

'Citizenship was good because I worked with different people.'

'We should have a day like that once a month so we learn to work with different classes.'

'Citizenship Day is a good day to find out what citizenship is all about.'

'It should be every month.'

'This was the best day in school.'

'It was very enjoyable and I got to know some other people that I didn't know working together with different age groups.'

'The day was fun, yet it helped me to learn about the meaning of citizenship.'

'I found the day very enjoyable and an exciting learning experience.'

'It was one of the best ideas the school has come up with.'

'I learned about how the youth parliament works and we had to make a video on fox hunting and had an argument about it, like it was real.'

'I loved the day so much I wish we could do it two times each month.'

'It was very interesting and even though it was hard work, especially for teachers I think most people enjoyed themselves.'

Attempts like this day or other single events to promote citizenship are open to criticism. First, it might be asked whether all the activities (which included learning circus skills) really fulfilled the criteria for the knowledge and skills in the Citizenship National Curriculum. Second, such events are not seen to have a sustainable impact where the citizenship agenda is not being addressed as part of more regular school life. It is acknowledged that some of the activities might fall short of promoting the political literacy dimension and other aspects of knowledge and enquiry which are part of the National Curriculum. However, the intention is to develop these aspects of citizenship education throughout the curriculum, including through specialist citizenship lessons at KS4. A major aim of the day was to convince all participants that citizenship can be fun. Feedback from the questionnaires provided evidence of enjoyment, and pupils and staff are looking forward to the next Citizenship Day. Interestingly, it also showed that one of the aspects the pupils enjoyed most was working in mixed age groups and the sense it engendered of the school as a community.

Citizenship and the culture of the school

In this section, we explain how the school has moved forward with increasing the extent to which young people feel they participate within the school community. This starts with listening to young people and taking their views seriously. Article 12 of the UN Convention on the Rights of the Child states that, 'All young people have the right to express their views in all decisions that affect them'. We believe that the level of participation could be seen as a key indicator of successful citizenship education. In attempting to promote wider student involvement in the life of the school and developing a culture of shared ownership, the school looked at ways in which the School Council could become a vehicle for this. Before 1999 there was a small-scale council, but its effects had been limited. Various steps to further empower the School Council have been taken:

- Getting School Councils UK to run training days for both staff and students.
- Devoting a PSHE lesson across the school to planning the elections.
- Proper elections with hustings and secret ballots.
- Holding meetings in school time.
- Developing a firm three weekly cycle of meetings – each year council meeting in the first week; whole school council in the second week; meeting with senior management in the third week.
- An awayday for students' evaluation.
- School Council representatives produced a Power Point presentation for the senior team detailing their achievements and recommendations for further empowering the student during the following academic year.
- Using assembly time for interactive assemblies during which the

representatives summarise achievements to their year group and members of the audience have a say via a roving microphone.

The achievements of the council include:

- Persuading governors to spend over £10,000 improving toilets.
- Arranging for an ice-cream and burger van to sell refreshments at the annexe playground every break.
- Some concessions on rules to do with uniform.
- Statements from school council representatives indicate that their experience has boosted their self-esteem and helped cultivate the young people's sense of themselves as agents of change.

Contrary to the findings in some other schools, Alderson (2000), the year councils and whole School Council often devote more that 25 per cent of their meeting time to issues to do with curriculum and learning. However, there is more work to be done on developing structures and processes that enable students to contribute to decisions about curriculum and learning issues. Students' comments about their involvement in the School Council show that they value the citizenship skills and attitudes they are acquiring, as suggested in the quotes below:

'I am able to recognise the process and procedure which we have to go through to change a certain thing.'

'I have learned that I can make a big difference and that if I listen to what people's opinions are then we can make them be heard.'

'There is much more than just going to school because us pupils can change the school.'

'I have learned to listen to other people, to say what I think and to work as a team.'

'I have become more interested in the school, its environment and the local community.'

'Having learnt that I have great importance in school makes me feel acknowledged.'

Some issues in widening participation

Participation is clearly a key underpinning concept in relation to citizenship education and links with daring young people to think critically about the world around them. As Fielding argues, there needs to be the development of 'students as agents of their own and each others' educational transformation' (Fielding 2001a: 150). Holden and Clough (1998) in their edited book *Children as Citizens: Education for Participation*, explore how participation can be encouraged. They use the term 'action competence' to describe the opportunities that may be provided, and skills that need to be developed, by both teachers and pupils (1998: 19). Hart's (1992) 'ladder of participation' is often referred to in literature on this subject. We would also see this as a useful model to think around when looking at how student participation can move forward. Ultimately, we would want to shift participation to the higher rungs of Hart's ladder where there are more student 'initiated and directed activities' or to the highest level of student 'initiated with decisions shared with adults'. Much of the student involvement described earlier is 'adult initiated'. Within this model we would assume that at some stages teachers would structure and assist the learning process.

A social theory of learning should underpin citizenship education. This suggests that knowledge, skills and activity are socioculturally organised, and must not be viewed as attributes of individuals. Assuming that the introduction of citizenship education in many schools is likely to be led by non-specialist teachers, we might want to talk about teachers and learners working within a 'construction zone' of learning. Thus as Newman *et al.* (1989: 2) suggest, 'When people with different goals, roles and resources interact, the differences in interpretation provide occasion for the construction of new knowledge'. The potential here is that *shared* thinking about knowledge arising from participation in activities will occur. Wenger (1998: 267) refers to 'interaction between the planned and the emergent – that is the ability, of teaching and learning to interact as structuring resources for each other'. One interesting example of this process is to be found in the effects on the school community of the anti-bullying projects that some students undertook as part of their GCSE coursework. Out of this student research a critique of the school's existing anti-bullying policy emerged. One of the main criticisms was that the policy was not sufficiently publicised. The students urged the senior team to address this. Later, three groups presented their investigations at a National Conference on bullying. Here they began to reconsider their notion of punishment as the only way of dealing with bullies. In discussion with a well-known psychotherapist they concluded that some form of support must be provided for bullies, who are often damaged individuals. They took this idea back to the school where the senior team has begun to investigate the possibilities of setting up a professional counselling service for bullies. A further, perhaps ambitious, idea is to consider how participation extends to enabling students to find the confidence to interact within their local communities, so that learning does not remain situated within the 'cosiness' of the school context.

Arguably, the process is also about enabling teachers to have ongoing experience of participation themselves. Given the lack of democracy within the education system generally, teachers may not have had much opportunity to really exercise their rights as citizens either within a school or beyond. The value system embedded in the tightly controlled curriculum does not easily lend itself to learner or teacher autonomy. In his recent critique of education policy Fielding (2001a) makes a useful distinction between the Person-centred School and the Effective School. Based on different assumptions and contrasting practices, Fielding describes the two constructs:

> The Person-centred School is expressive of education in its wider, more expansive sense, is centrally concerned with the relationship between ends and means and is infused by the reciprocally conditioning values of freedom and equality which are constitutive of schools as learning communities whilst the Effective School is preoccupied with certain kinds of outcomes of schooling, is concerned mainly with the reality of their achievement rather than the rhetoric of their intended processes, and is driven by the necessity of performance and productivity, which are central to schools as learning organisations.
>
> (Fielding 2001a: 150)

The Person-centred School is likely to provide a more sympathetic context for the development of participation.

Citizenship and the community

The work of the citizenship outreach worker has been partly that of a 'school-community broker'. This includes building contacts with the local community and facilitating interaction between the community and our school. Links with local feeder primary schools have been strengthened through students leading citizenship lessons and an assembly. They have interviewed primary school students to inform their design and technology coursework and hosted Year 6 students for the afternoon to introduce them to life at secondary school. Year 8 students put on a special performance of their end of term pantomime for a local primary school.

Avenues for student involvement in the local community have begun to open. In Spring 2000 a mixed age group of students produced the centre spread of *New Cross News*, airing their ideas for improvement in the local area. Their suggestions included ideas on transport: 'trams would be a good idea' in order to reduce pollution; 'lower bus and train ticket fares'; and a clear recognition of the need to improve public transport to reduce the number of cars being used. Other concerns were: improving the quality of green spaces, 'we ought to plant more trees and flowers and have dog free and dog only parks'; providing facilities for young people, 'if children do want to take up graffiti as an art there should be a place for them to do it'; and a desire that 'people should respect each other for their colour or their race and have fun together'. They have set up a project to recycle aluminium cans (and donated the proceeds to a local special needs school). They have supported local children in developing their skills in music and drama through the Young Arts Leaders Award. With a grant from Sport England and Learning Through Landscapes, students are also leading a project to improve the school's grounds. They are regularly involved in consultations and events at local and national forums. These include consultation on the DfES citizenship website, speaking at the Carnegie Young People's Initiative, sitting on interview panels with the National Children's Bureau and The Children's Society, leading workshops at conferences and advising on issues such as crime and the environment in London. (See Figure 11.1 and Figure 11.2.)

Consolidating links with the local community involves allowing the school to become a resource for life-long learning in the local area. Thus, some of the DfES funding has contributed to developing a new computer suite, 'the Community IT room'. The room is a useful base for meetings of various citizenship-linked projects. It is used for cross-curricular IT based learning during much of the day, enabling students to develop computer literacy and transferable skills. Two evenings a week it is used by parents and carers following IT courses, now with the support of students in Year 10 who have been trained as IT mentors. The parents have been positive about the work of the IT mentors as reflected in the quotes below:

Figure 11.1 Student interview on aspects of the environment in the local area

Figure 11.2 Students collecting views on school grounds

> 'They are helpful, polite and earn great respect most of the time. They have the patience to explain things to you, they never get tired when their assistance is required.'
>
> 'Far too clever for their age! They are very pleasant, proficient and smiley!'
>
> 'They are very helpful and courteous. Their knowledge of IT was very high and they explained items clearly.'

In addition to the IT mentors, a group of Year 10 students have been trained as mentors on the issues of bullying and have run sessions for Year 7 students. The Community Department has trained twenty sixth form students as mentors to work with small groups of students in Deptford Green and local primary schools.

One development that is hoped for here is that these activities will become part of sustained community involvement which acts in a dialogic way, so that the community and students initiate projects and use each other as a resource. If active citizenship is to be transformative, partnerships must be based on mutual need and relationships of trust. Importantly, the process may enable young citizens to seize opportunities outside of the school community and use their understanding and skills in a wider community context.

The school's citizenship work has attracted wider interest and has enabled it to intervene in a wider local and national dialogue about citizenship education. Locally, this has included a session for Lewisham curriculum deputies on implementing citizenship education. During 2001 the school initiated a Lewisham wide *Citizenship for All* Conference planned with colleagues from local schools and the Professional Development Centre. Links have also developed with the Institute for Citizenship since through the piloting teaching materials and exploring resources for GCSE Citizenship Studies. There have been discussions about subject specifications and assessment with the QCA and collaboration with an exam board on the new GCSE Citizenship Studies short course. The school has also worked in different ways with three teacher training institutions (Goldsmiths, Institute of Education and University of North London). Collaboration with teacher trainers has led school staff to contribute substantially to the citizenship component of the Goldsmiths Social Science PGCE course. In this way, two educational communities have been able to interact in mapping out a training course and in that process reflect jointly upon implementing citizenship education in schools. In addition, trainee teachers, through their experience in a range of schools, have provided insights into different models of delivery. We feel we are in the very early stages of devising an effective training process and it will be important to evaluate this first year with all those involved.

Citizenship and the curriculum

The emphasis on 'active citizenship' in the most recent QCA documentation and other official pronouncements indicate a proposed shift, in this instance, away from a transmission model of education towards learning that is more situated. A situated learning approach implies that knowledge and understanding emerges out of the learner's participation in practices and activities, not as a result of being taught via a formal, decontextualised, curriculum. From the point of view of the school this means creating frameworks for participation, some of which have been described earlier. The challenge for schools introducing 'active citizenship' is to enable learners and teachers to connect knowledge that emerges out of participation in activities, with knowledge taught in a more formal classroom context. If young people are to transfer their understanding of how they can change something in a school environment to the wider local, national, and global community, they need to have both practical and abstract understanding of 'real life' political processes. In addition, if knowledge and understanding emerges out of participation in activities, then learning, rather than being individualised, becomes part of a social process. Herein lies another pedagogical challenge, given the dominance of individualistic assumptions about the nature of learning.

In reflecting upon the curriculum audit, it became clear that really transforming citizenship education cannot be achieved without experiential learning. The best citizenship education must be rooted in the potential to initiate and effect change. This must be informed by a holistic approach that embodies learning *about*, *through*, and *for* citizenship. There is recognition of the need to provide opportunities for students, as part of their citizenship learning, to actively research local community needs. The 'active learning in the community' GCSE coursework has proved both challenging and rewarding. Many students have embraced the opportunities to investigate an issue that concerns them directly. They have chosen to engage in a variety of projects. They have researched their issue using surveys, photographs and video and have presented recommendations to panels of local decision-makers. They have evaluated their own work, and reflected on how they collaborated with other students. Some have researched crime in the local area, making proposals for improved safety. Others explored the problem of teenagers smoking, attributing its continuation to unprincipled shop-keepers. They presented video evidence of this, which they showed to the local police. Yet another group produced an engaging video about the students' desire for a skateboard park. They argued that this would help reduce crime locally. Their presentation was enthusiastically received by a Lewisham councillor, who promised to take the recommendation back to the council. These are three examples among many.

Twilight INSET sessions have been run to support the work of all departments in developing their own Schemes of Work which can be shown to deliver education *about*, *for* and *through* citizenship. This has resulted in some unique developments in the school's curriculum, some of them gaining momentum from the Citizenship Day when departments pioneered citizenship activities linked to their own subject areas. For example, there are Maths Schemes of Work entitled *Citizenship through Maths* which explore data on human rights and poverty. A Year 8 PSHE Scheme of Work looks at fair trade and has led to the pupils' marketing of Fair Trade chocolate at break times. Year 7 Geography groups have explored safer routes to schools and made proposals to influential local personnel. ICT at KS4 and KS5 includes a critical look at the Data Protection Act.

The notion of curriculum content explicitly organised around pressing worldwide issues is appealing. We are exploring the implications of this vision, outlined in Cogan and Derricott's (2000) book *Citizenship for the 21st Century*. They draw together the findings from an international research project by 182 policy experts and scholars over an eighteen-month period. Parker *et al.*, in Cogan and Derricott (2000), propose that the essential subject matter of the curriculum should be derived from a set of six ethical questions. These provide a possible framework for thinking about citizenship issues from a local to global level. The questions they suggest are:

1   What should be done in order to promote equity and fairness within and among societies?
2   What should be the balance between the right to privacy and free and open access to information in information-based societies?
3   What should be the balance between protecting the environment and meeting human needs?

4 What should be done to cope with population growth, genetic engineering, and children in poverty?
5 What should be done to develop shared (universal; global) values while respecting local values?
6 What should be done to secure an ethically based distribution of power for deciding policy and action on the above issues?

(Parker et al. in Cogan and Derricott 2000: 153)

The school is using these questions for its citizenship schemes of work.

Citizenship and pedagogy: the challenges ahead

The pedagogical implications of citizenship education go way beyond simply transforming curriculum content. It brings a multiplicity of challenges for teaching and learning, namely:

- Planning to engage a multiplicity of intelligences.
- Developing higher order thinking skills – analysis, synthesis, evaluation, metacognition.
- Collective thinking and a deliberation-based approach.
- Building teachers' and students' political literacy.
- Introducing opportunities for situated learning.
- Promoting students' sense of themselves as agents of change.

Several writers have touched on the interface between citizenship education and the current interest in 'accelerated learning' and the 'learning revolution'. Citizenship education specifically and simultaneously invites both cognitive and affective engagement: the exercise of emotional intelligence or, in Gardner's (1983) terms, interpersonal and intrapersonal intelligence, as well as a range of others such as linguistic and logical.

Citizenship education is increasingly recognised as a fertile area for developing thinking skills such as synthesis and evaluation. Teachers need to develop skills in teaching thinking and in questioning to promote thinking. There are many bullet point lists in the literature on thinking skills, but one that encapsulates a characterisation of high quality thinking, was advanced by Resnick (1987):

High Quality Thinking
- is not routine – the solution is not fully known in advance;

- tends to be complex – a solution is not obvious from a single viewpoint;
- can offer several solutions to a problem not just one;
- involves considered judgement and interpretation;
- can involve the application of different criteria to the same problem that may conflict with each other;
- involves uncertainty;
- involves improving meaning;
- requires mental effort;
- involves self-regulation/reflection on the thinking process.

(Quoted in McGuiness 1999: 6)

Importantly, citizenship education demands a reassessment of the nature of classroom dialogue and interaction. It challenges us to move away from the notion of the teacher as the source and mediator of knowledge. As Paulo Freire (Freire and Macedo 1998) would argue, we need to develop in our lessons empowering dialogue based on respect. It should not involve one person acting *on* another, but rather people working *with* each other. In his book *Words and Minds*, Neil Mercer (2000) provides useful insights into how teachers can create communities that enable collective thinking. He discusses classroom based activities for developing language as a 'tool for thinking collectively' (2000: 149). Importantly, the focus is on ways of developing students 'co-reasoning' and the kind of talk that would be very appropriate in a citizenship classroom:

> *Exploratory talk* is that in which partners engage critically but constructively with each other's ideas. Relevant information is offered for joint consideration. Proposals may be challenged, and counter-challenged, but if so reasons are given and alternatives are offered. Agreement is sought on the basis for joint progress. Knowledge is made publicly accountable and reasoning is visible in the talk.
>
> (Mercer 2000: 153)

Success depends on creating 'communities of enquiry'. Drawing on Vygotsky's ideas Mercer refers to an 'intermental development zone' where teacher and learner 'must use talk and joint activity to create a shared communicative space' and 'negotiate their way through the activity in which they are involved' (Mercer 2000: 141). Cogan and Derricott (2000) argue that the citizenship curriculum should be 'deliberation-based'. This means that the core practice in the curriculum is discussion of the ethical questions themselves with the intention of recommending suitable public action.

In addition, the citizenship curriculum does have to include a notion of developing politically literate citizens. This strand of citizenship is one which must not be turned into 'old rote learning civics'. It should, as Crick (2000: 62) suggests, be about enabling an individual, 'to think in terms of change . . . We are confident that political action is worthy of encouragement if it is based on knowledge and understanding'. This presents several pedagogic challenges. The first is to develop teacher confidence and real understanding of the concepts and knowledge that underpin citizenship education. This is not a new knowledge base, as there are already numerous existing traditions to be drawn upon from those who have been involved in political, social, global and rights education. Second, school learning has to enable students to use their citizenship knowledge in contexts outside the school. As Wells (1999) states:

> The manner in which classroom activities are selected and organized should not only lead students to construct a personal understanding of the topics involved that equips them to participate effectively and responsibly in similar and related activities beyond the classroom, but it should encourage the development of a disposition and the necessary strategies to adopt the same stance independently in new and unfamiliar situations.
>
> (Wells 1999: 91)

Schooled learning is criticised because it often decontextualises knowledge from the communities of practice which produce and use the knowledge. Wenger characterises schooled knowledge as stripped of its social complexity and leading to 'a brittle kind of understanding with very narrow applicability' (1998: 265). Thus, as educators we have to look at how we can build knowledge, understanding and skills through participation in the classroom, school and wider community. The latter is essential if we are not to disconnect our learning from the world in which all citizens have to operate.

The school is developing schemes of work which are informed by principles perhaps best encapsulated in the TASC (Thinking Actively in a Social Context) method, developed by Wallace and Adams (Wallace, 2000). At every stage in this approach, learners should be given time to engage in reflection upon their thinking processes. The emphasis is also on transferring skills to other contexts. Many lessons centre on deliberation over current affairs. The 11 September 2001 attacks on New York provided a tragic but important opportunity to engage students in dialogue on global issues, which up till then may have seemed irrelevant. Through discussion and role play, this dialogue led in some instances to 'public action' with some students writing to the Prime Minister to express their concerns about the attacks and the response to them. Yet another example is the globalisation scheme of work, which explores environmental issues and world trade, and invites students to design the 'global citizens' fair trade supermarket. They are invited to take action to promote ethical consumption which may include writing to the local supermarket about the sources of its stock.

How the citizenship agenda has contributed to PSD

In many schools, as is reflected in the whole range of textbooks for Citizenship and PSHE, citizenship education is being delivered largely through PSHE. In this school, the focus on citizenship has presented ideal opportunities to enhance the PSD offer through the three dimensions of curriculum, culture and community.

The PSHE schemes of work which pre-dated the citizenship agenda had a strand entitled 'Rights and Responsibilities', which included units on equal opportunities, disability, bullying, human rights and environmental issues. The citizenship curriculum audit led to a day of developmental work between teachers who had volunteered to lead on citizenship education and the Head of PSHE. Together, they outlined what could be delivered separately from PSHE in Year 10 and Year 11 GCSE Citizenship Studies. They then revisited and rewrote citizenship learning outcomes for PSHE across KS3 and KS4. This led to the introduction of some new lesson plans and schemes of work informed by the same principles of active citizenship and, where appropriate, global awareness.

The process of election of the School Council representatives has become part of PSHE lessons, where students are learning about secret ballots, how to make speeches, and taking part in hustings. Year 7 PSHE now includes a unit on safer routes to school, which involves pupils surveying routes locally, producing presentations on their findings using a variety of media (including rap) and getting responses from the borough council on their suggestion. In Year 8 the unit on chocolate and world trade culminated in a decision to regularly sell Fairtrade chocolate at the annexe building. A new Year 9 PSHE unit draws upon some ideas from the Citizenship Foundation and uses the issue of football to explore layers of identity, working together as a team, and wider issues of child labour raised through football stitching (see Appendix 11.1 and Appendix 11.2).

As explained earlier in this chapter, the School Council, due to the frequency of meetings, links with senior staff and its own raft of achievements, has begun to have an impact on school culture, making it more participative. The main transmission belt for these democratic ideas and values is the relationship between students and their form teachers, particularly the learning about the School Council's processes and structures that happens in PSHE lessons. The discussion that takes place in PSHE lessons about the matters that are taken to the School Council impacts in turn upon the culture of tutor groups. Devoting time and energy to developing this process has created among the students a sense that they are listened to. After a January 2002 meeting with students from other schools, School Council representatives fed back to the School Council, saying, 'Our school is much better than other schools because they don't listen to their pupils'. For young people who are often struggling to find a voice, these experiences are vital parts of PSD. As the school moves on to produce shared statements of aims and values and a code of conduct involving all members of the school community, these developments should also help to nurture a culture conducive to effective PSD.

Links with the community through the whole citizenship agenda have been outlined elsewhere, but it should also be noted that the pastoral curriculum does draw upon the local community, increasingly, because of the citizenship education agenda. Hence workers from various locally based environmental organisations like Groundwork are increasing inputting into PSHE learning. The local sexual health clinic supports and leads some of the lessons on safer sex, and community policing officers contribute to lessons on crime and safety. More direct input from such personnel is envisaged in the years ahead.

In this school's experience, therefore, the quality and status of PSHE has been enhanced through the focus on citizenship. The parts of PSHE which are not being addressed by citizenship here are, however, vital. These include drug and sex education. It is the school's belief that while citizenship teachers may have a propensity to focus on political literacy, they are not necessarily well equipped to address these areas and certain other aspects of emotional literacy. For this reason, PSHE is very much still on the agenda, and teachers here share the concerns expressed by John Bennett (2002: 3) that the government White Paper *Schools: Achieving Success* marginalises PSHE. To this they would add that there are areas specific to both PSHE and Citizenship that are better addressed as such. However, they would also endorse an approach to PSHE learning which respects young people as citizens and decision makers here and now and addresses the diversity of their experiences. The school, which now has a specialist citizenship teaching team, is currently exploring arguments for and against specialist PSHE teachers.

Areas for development and unresolved issues

We would not want to present this account of how the school has moved forward with citizenship as unproblematic. The process has encountered many of the barriers and tensions that surround any new initiative. For example, additional time has had to be found to deliver citizenship sessions, and active citizenship is likely to demand more curriculum time. Thus, a dialogue about which subject area should release time may enhance the perceived status of citizenship education, but it might also create resistance towards opting for discrete provision. Along the way, negotiation mediates the parameters of change. Activity that has led to change within the school has emerged out of existing practices that in turn have helped to frame new ideas and approaches.

One major challenge for the school is to develop a viable framework for assessing citizenship education and planning for development, coherence and continuity in pupils' learning experiences across the key stages. Beyond doubt, more flesh will need to be added to the bones of the 'can do' statements comprising the KS3 attainment target. Students' own involvement in mapping their progress is clearly vital.

Another, perhaps more difficult task, is to explore more thoroughly a set of indicators for citizenship education. These would be linked to criteria by which we might judge the success and quality of citizenship education in the formal curriculum, in the school's culture and ethos, and in its interaction with the community. The school is anxious to see the global perspective, 'the ability to look at and approach problems as a member of a global society', be given its proper status as the overarching frame of reference for all citizenship education. Students should be involved in these efforts to identify, develop and use indicators.

There is still a long way to go in terms of developing a democratic culture in the school. In order for the young people in the school community to have a voice, teachers themselves need to feel influential too. There must be a sense of a shared agenda and a jointly constructed set of values to which all subscribe. There is a great deal that the school can learn about democratic practice from other schools and from the developing research and literature on improving student voice. There are also limitations to active democracy and empowerment outside the school. Pearce and Hallgarten (2000) ask:

> How far can schools forge a common citizenship if the social and economic forces outside the school gates are pulling in the opposite direction? To warp a famous phrase, *can schools, and the citizenship education they teach, compensate for society?*
>
> (Pearce and Hallgarten 2000: 9)

In terms of sustaining the energy of the present initiative, the school has to embed within its own structures the opportunity and ability to reflect, critique and change practices. Teachers have been engaged in ongoing review of their implementation of the development plan for citizenship. Next, the school needs to extend and deepen the review process, involving students more thoroughly. Ideally, it will mean the whole school community interrogates its curriculum together. Creative and research orientated teachers will be able to help develop and sustain the school as a centre of enquiry. This is part of the model that Porter (1999) calls the *reflexive school*, defined as one that offers:

> a secure and confident environment, that values flexibility and creativity, that encourages cooperation in problem solving and acknowledge the uniqueness of individuals. It would also be an institution that recognises the importance of the local community as a source of security and personal identity.
>
> (Porter 1999: 95)

The school has established itself as one that is committed to citizenship education. We have used the term 'community of practice' to indicate that it is in the process of creating a joint understanding of what that means. Beyond what has actually happened we have highlighted areas of theoretical knowledge that can be drawn upon to support thinking about the process. Implementing many of the ideas discussed here require a high level of collaboration among participants, particularly in creating Mercer's 'intermental development zone' of thinking about how to bring about changes in institutional practices which enable teachers and learners to work in a more dialogic way. We conclude with two visions that may inform future development of practice. Fielding

(2001b) writes of 'new communities of practice shaped by an essentially dialogic form of engagement' and suggests that:

> Teachers cannot create new roles and realities without the support and encouragement of their students: students cannot construct more imaginative and fulfilling realities of learning without reciprocal engagement with their teachers. We need each other to be and become ourselves, to be and become both learners and teachers of each other together.
>
> (Fielding 2001b: 108)

Porter highlights the importance of the wider community of practice:

> The wider research and evaluative network in the centers of teacher preparation and support, and within the local community, will need to interact with schools in the unending task of making learning more relevant and the schools more responsive to changes at the local and national level.
>
> (Porter 1999:102)

Notes

1. Conference *Diverse Citizenships?* held at the University of North London, in March 2001.
2. We would like to credit here Pete Pattisson, the school's Citizenship Outreach worker, and Keith Ajegbo, Headteacher of Deptford Green, both of whom are very much a part of this process of an emerging community of practice.

References

Alderson, P. (2000) 'Practising democracy in two inner city schools', in A. Osler (ed.) *Citizenship and Democracy in Schools: diversity, identity, equality*, London: Trentham.

Bennett, J. (2002) *PSHE & Citizenship Update*, Dec 2001/Jan 2002, Issue 13. London: Optimus.

Cogan, J.J. and Derricott, R. (2000) *Citizenship for the 21st Century: an international perspective on education*, London: Kogan Page.

Crick, B. (2000) *Essays on Citizenship*, London: Continuum.

Fielding, M. (ed.) (2001a) *Taking Education Really Seriously*, London: RoutledgeFalmer.

Fielding, M. (2001b) 'Beyond the rhetoric of student voice: new departures or constraints in the transformation of 21st century schooling?' *Forum*, 43 (2).

Friere, A. and Macedo, D. (eds) (1998) *The Paulo Freire Reader*, New York: Contiuum.

Gardner, H. (1983) *Frames of Mind: the theory of multiple intelligences*, New York: Basic Books.

Goleman, D. (1996) *Emotional Intelligence*, London: Bloomsbury.

Hargreaves A. and Fullan M. (1998) *What's Worth Fighting For in Education?* Buckingham: Open University Press.

Hargreaves, D. and Hopkins D. (eds) (1994) *Development Planning for School Improvement*, London: Cassell.

Hart, R. (1992) *Children's Participation – from tokenism to citizenship*, Innocenti Essays No. 4, Florence: UNICEF International Development Centre.

Holden, C. and Clough, N. (eds) (1998) *Children as Citizens: Education for Participation*, London: Jessica Kingsley.

Lave, J. and Wenger, E. (1991) *Situated Learning*, Cambridge: Cambridge University Press.

Mercer, N. (2000) *Words and Minds*, London: Routledge.

McGuiness, C. (1999) *From Thinking Skills to Thinking Classrooms*, Nottingham: DfEE Publications.

Newman, D., Griffin, P. and Cole, M. (1989) *The Construction Zone: working for change in school*, Cambridge: Cambridge University Press.

Parker, W., Grossman, D., Kubow, P., Kuth-Schai, R. and Nakayama, S. 'Making it work: implementing multidimensional citizenship', in J.J. Cogan and R. Derricott (2000) *Citizenship for the 21st Century*, London: Kogan Page.

Pearce, N. and Hallgarten, J. (2000) *Tomorrow's Citizens: Critical debates in citizenship and education*, London: IPPR.

Porter, J. (1999) *Reschooling in the Global Future: politics, economics and the English experience*, Oxford: Symposium Books.

Resnick, L.B. (1987) *Education and Learning to Think*, Washington: National Academy Press.

Wallace B. (2000) 'Able and talented learners from socio-economically disadvantaged communities', in M.J. Stopper (ed.) (2000) *Meeting the Social and Emotional Needs of Gifted and Talented Children*, London: David Fulton.

Wells, G. (1999) *Dialogic Enquiry:Towards a Sociocultural Practice and Theory of Education*, Cambridge: Cambridge University Press.

Wenger, E. (1998) *Communities of Practice: Learning, Meaning and Identity*, Cambridge/New York/Melbourne: Cambridge University Press.

Appendix 11.1

Year 9 PSHE Unit: Identity, football and global issues

About the unit

This unit is designed to explore layers of identity, the importance of team-work and global issues related to football. It explores students' perceptions of themselves and invites them to be aware of the dangers of stereotyping. It links the notion of identity to teams and teamwork. It explores notions of fairness and disadvantage. It introduces students to the Convention on the Rights of the Child. This sets the context for considering the issue of child labour focusing on football stitchers. It challenges young people's conventional wisdom about child labour in southern Asia and underlines the importance of poverty as a factor in child labour.

Where the unit fits in

The unit addresses the following aspects of the Key Stage 3 citizenship programme of study:

Knowledge and understanding about becoming informed citizens

Pupils should be taught about:

1b) the diversity of national, regional, religious and ethnic identities within the UK and the need for mutual respect and understanding

1f) the work of community based, national and international voluntary groups

1l) the world as a global community and the political, economic, environmental and social implications of this.

Skills of enquiry and communication

Pupils should be taught to:

2a) think about topical political, moral, social and cultural issues, problems and events by analysing information and its sources;

2b) justify orally and in writing a personal opinion about such issues, problems or events;

2c) contribute to group and exploratory class discussion and take part in debates.

Skills of participation and responsible action

3a) to use their imagination to consider other people's experiences and be able to think about, express and explain views that are not their own;

3b) to negotiate, decide and take part responsibly in both school and community-based activities;

3c) reflect on the process of participating.

The unit links with other 'Rights and responsibilities' strands of PSHE and with the exploration of child labour in the Year 9 History curriculum.

Expectations.

At the end of this unit most pupils know about the concept of multiple layers of identity and the importance of fairness and team work. They have considered the notion of young people's rights and how this relates to child labour. They understand that global economic factors affect the quality of young people's lives.

Some pupils will not have made so much progress and understand that identity has various dimensions. They know that teams are important. They understand that young people in different parts of the world have a different quality of life.

Some pupils will have progressed further and know and understand that there is often conflict between our different layers of identity. They are aware of the need to protect young people's rights and some of the key provisions of the Convention. They understand that for young football stitchers child labour can be a desirable necessity due to their economic circumstances. They consider other positive responses to these issues.

Note: Resources for this unit include videos and packs produced by Save the Children and CAFOD. The unit also uses resources produced by the Institute for Citizenship.

Appendix 11.2

DGS PSHE SOW: Topic: Football, identity and global issues, Year 9

Learning objectives	Activities	Resources	Differentiation
Who am I? For pupils to understand the complex nature of personal identity: To understand that identity is not single and fixed Think about the different aspects to our own individual identities Reflect on how well the class knows each other Place football in this complex of identities	☐ Pupils work through sheets on individual identities ☐ Try to guess who the others are ☐ Debrief ☐ Explore layers of identity	• 'I am . . .' sheet • Layers of identity sheet and OHP of the example (or an enlarged version) • Response sheet	*Collaborative learning activity – differentiation through pupil interaction*
In the frame To examine our attitudes to Africa and how they are formed To consider football and teams in a different light	☐ Brainstorm looking at photos in groups ☐ Follow worksheet tasks ☐ Discussion on our images ☐ Video ☐ Discussion	• Worksheet: Images of Africa • Laminated photos and answer cards – one for each group of 3–5 pupils. • Lined paper – can simply be one per group if scribes are appointed. • Millennium Stars Video	

Learning objectives	Activities	Resources	Differentiation
The real me; talking points *To allow young people to explore and communicate their identity creatively* *To explore ways in which people are prevented from realising their full potential and expressing their identity*	☐ Pupils making collages of themselves ☐ Discussing these and the issue of stereotyping	• Sugar paper • Magazines, newspapers • Glue • Scissors • Sheets: *Introducing the real me.*	
Team work and team talk *To explore teamwork and co-operation* *To examine what happens when there is tension between the needs of the individual and those of the team* *To examine the influence that sport has on individuals and society*	☐ Musical chairs type activity ☐ Discussion about collaboration ☐ Discussion based on 'quote' cards.	• Going for gold instruction sheet • 6 sheets of A1 paper (a broadsheet newspaper will do fine) • Tape/CD player and music • Desks pushed to the sides of the classroom. • Set of 'quote' cards.	*Collaborative learning activity – differentiation through pupil interaction*

continued

Appendix 11.2 continued

Learning objectives	Activities	Resources	Differentiation
Bonus ball **To show how difficult it is to succeed against the odds** **To reflect on human needs and consider the link between basic needs and basic rights**	☐ Experience of physical disability and unfairness through 3 legged football ☐ Discussion of issues of equality and rights ☐ Looking at Convention on Rights of the Child	• Sugar paper • Magazines, newspapers • Glue • Scissors • Sheets: Introducing the real me.	
Investigating child labour **To explore our notions of child labour** **To discover the issues affecting child workers in South East Asia** **To reconsider the factors leading to child labour.**	☐ Discussion of preconceptions about child labour ☐ Watching video about chidlren talking about child labour ☐ Exploring global issues underlying child labour	• Video: Children talking about child labour. • Worksheet: Who wants to ban child labour? • Whiteboard pen.	

Part IV

Bringing things together

Chapter 12

Leadership and management of PSHE to support a whole school approach

Martin Buck

This chapter analyses the leadership and management skills required for those in primary and secondary schools responsible for PSHE and citizenship. It sets out the organisational delivery of PSHE/citizenship within primary schools and then examines organisational arrangements best suited to secondary schools, before applying Michael Fullan's leadership themes to a PSHE-citizenship context (Fullan 2001).

Leadership and management in the context of curriculum change

As the previous chapters have indicated, PSHE is a discrete area of taught curriculum provision that has undergone and continues to undergo considerable change within state schooling in England and Wales. These changes are a result of a central government expectation that PSHE should be an entitlement for all pupils in both primary and secondary schools. Its depth and range has been left to schools to determine, with national guidance and advice.

In addition, in the primary sector PSHE is expected to support the teaching of a more explicit approach to citizenship (as a non-statutory requirement) while in the secondary phase citizenship is a statutory area of the curriculum with its own assessment programme as of September 2002. The Crick report (1998) views the relationship between PSHE and citizenship as being more distant, which has led to a subsequent separate and scaled down legislation for citizenship. Nevertheless, the revised Curriculum 2000 legislation makes clear that both areas are required to contribute to an enhanced emphasis given to pupils' personal and social development.

In this context, the management and leadership of PSHE requires a greater focus and role to support the delivery of a more coherent, enhanced and sustained approach towards PSHE and citizenship. This has clear implications for a number of aspects of school organisation including:

- The location of the leadership and management post or posts within both primary and secondary schools.
- The delivery of the PSHE and citizenship curriculum.
- The organisation of the PSHE and citizenship curriculum, including the amount of time devoted to it.

These elements will be explored in greater depth below. Before doing so it is important to summarise and acknowledge the present range of curriculum and organisational issues that are presently being addressed within the primary and secondary sectors, which give a context to PSHE/citizenship developments.

The range of initiatives include statutory responsibilities to deliver improved SATs at Key Stage 3, including the setting of targets and more recently a Key Stage 3 Strategy which involves literacy, numeracy, ICT and a cross-curricular dimension. At Key Stage 4 we have a revised curriculum with further changes in the 14–19 age range. There is a revised SEN code of practice, a strengthening of the Race Relations Act and the introduction of a Disability Rights Act, all of which schools must address. Performance management and an enhanced school self-review process are being developed alongside continued external accountability provided by Ofsted. In terms of teaching and learning there is research and guidance on gifted and talented students, thinking skills, emotional literacy, learning styles, mentoring and guidance and behaviour management.

Many of these initiatives are progressive and helpful to schools and can provide the possibility of increased positive outcomes for pupils, including enhanced attainment and broader achievement and a greater number of sustained learners. However, these developments cannot be taken for granted, since they operate within a time of considerable pressure for schools in regard to staff recruitment and retention and pressure on resources to deliver the desired outcomes. Many staff experience the pressure of 'initiative overload', not because they don't welcome them theoretically, but because increased accountability and workload make it difficult to embrace them positively.

Separately, these initiatives fail to take into account the daily pressures within schools – many of them are working within communities in which poverty, poor housing, rising youth crime and the intrusion of an anti-learning street culture into school life, drains the energy of those working within them. Excessive expectations from the centre, whether it be central government or an LEA, that change needs to happen at a pace dictated by them, can be counterproductive. Crucially, within a systematic and coherent framework, a way must be found to incorporate recent PSHE/citizenship requirements within these other major change elements cited above, so that the implementation of the overall package is not an add-on, but rather a welcome pulling together of different areas of the curriculum, that makes good sense to both teachers and learners alike.

The typical structure of management is often inadequate to meet the challenge of a more demanding curriculum framework which requires explicit links between various aspects of taught curriculum and the broader curriculum within the school. A coherent, whole school approach towards styles of learning and a broader range of learning opportunities must be the future model if schools are to continue to narrow the gap between their stated mission or intent statement and the daily experience of students. Both primary and secondary schools are making progress in delivering better examination results, but with the introduction of a revised Curriculum 2000 with greater demands and expectations, schools have to be more than examination factories.

Leadership and management of PSHE/citizenship in the primary school

Traditional management structure

In the primary sector a traditional management structure has varied according to the size of the school and whether the school is infant, junior or an all-through primary. In a typical small infant school, PSHE will be understood to be integrated into the induction programme and form a part of the regular strategies of teaching and learning within the school. Typically there is not a specific post holder, with perhaps the exception of the headteacher to overview the work.

In a larger junior school setting the post holder might be a deputy headteacher, depending on their skills and interest, or alternatively it could be a specific post holder who might be responsible for RE, paid on a plus one allowance. In a larger primary a PSHE co-ordinator might similarly be identified within Key Stage 2. The specialist programme of sex and relationships education, along with health development initiatives would typically involve the post holder in establishing links with an LEA Advisory Team member, and a Community Care Health Service professional, ensuring that each year team follows a flexible programme supported with resources. This programme might well have been squeezed over the last three years with the pressures placed on delivering a core curriculum programme alongside humanities, technology and PE especially where a modern foreign language has been introduced into the Year 5 or 6 curriculum.

Strengthening the leadership

The issue for the management and leadership within a primary school is to ensure that PSHE is located more firmly within a whole school approach to PSD. Leadership has to come from the headteacher or a designated member of the leadership team with strong support from the headteacher and school governors. If a PSHE co-ordinator is identified outside the leadership team then this person needs to have leadership and management skills. These will include:

- An ability to display a vision owned and shared by colleagues in support of school aims.
- Being recognised as a good teacher of the PSHE elements of the curriculum.
- Keeping abreast of local and national initiatives.
- Being recognised as a person who champions the work of PSHE within the curriculum.
- Displaying good personal and social skills with adults and children.
- Keeping aware of their own professional needs and encouraging others to specify their needs and seeking to support them.

Management skills

These will need to be discernible in the day-to-day management of the PSHE elements of the curriculum; through the use of resources and the liaison and use made of outside agencies. They are likely to include:

- The writing of PSHE policy that informs the curriculum and makes links with other aspects of school life.
- Ensuring a well understood programme of study which is recorded through a scheme of work ensuring that the PSHE elements are given sufficient time along with the management of available resources.

The organisation of the PSHE/Citizenship curriculum

The organisation of the primary PSHE curriculum is distinct from that in the secondary sector. A crucial factor is that in the primary phase, pupils are taught mainly by a class teacher for all subjects throughout the year. More specialist work can take place outside the classroom in maths, science and even humanities and PE in Years 5 and 6, but this is still a minority of the curriculum time in the school week. The integration of the primary curriculum, especially through topics and themes, still exists especially in the early years despite the impact of the subject-based National Curriculum. Primary practice at its best will incorporate PSHE work, providing the opportunity for teachers to demonstrate the continued pupil centredness which has been, and remains, a hallmark of the primary curriculum.

The organisation of the primary curriculum can take place through the following elements:

- Teaching PSHE within the national curriculum subjects.
- PSHE as a topic.
- PSHE as a strand within a topic.
- A timetabled PSHE slot.
- PSHE as an 'experiential' challenge.
- Circle time.

Teaching PSHE within the National Curriculum subjects

This delivery method has certain advantages in that little additional time has to be created for a separate PSHE and citizenship slot. However, there are specific topics on sexual and personal relationships and drugs awareness with older primary pupils that do require a discrete and sustained teaching programme.

PSHE as a topic

The advantages of the PSHE topic such as 'ourselves' is that it does have a clear link to key aspects of the PSHE curriculum and it lends itself to straightforward planning. Conversely, it is not possible to incorporate all the learning outcomes of PSHE into a topic. Schools will need to ensure that they do not ignore other opportunities provided by the 'experiential' challenge or the use of expert visitors.

PSHE as a strand within a topic

This is a variation on the above in which a topic such as the 'School Environment', which will cover aspects of geography, science, English and mathematics, can also address relationships, bullying, mental health, physical health and exercise. This approach can increase the relevance to other parts of the curriculum, but without adequate time and planning it has dangers of being marginalised.

A planned timetable slot

The advantage of this approach is that the PSHE learning outcomes can be planned for in a coherent manner; it will especially support a potentially better delivery of sexual and personal relationships and drugs education. However, in the context of the primary curriculum PSHE can be perceived as just another whole school programme unless careful planning, monitoring and evaluation takes place.

PSHE as an 'experiential' challenge

This has considerable advantages especially for older primary pupils in that they are given an opportunity to engage in 'real' learning through, for example, attending a residential field trip which gives them opportunities to take on responsibility for planning and delivering some aspects of the programme with their peers. The development of personal and social skills and qualities can be significant. The disadvantage is that not all pupils will have the opportunity to engage in this type of activity, so that other types of perhaps more modest experiential learning need to be developed, such as fund raising for a charity.

Circle time

Circle time is regarded by most, if not all, primary practitioners as an important tool for learning in PSHE. It also contributes towards improved behaviour and supports opportunities for pupils to participate in aspects of school consultation and decision making.

In primary schools the delivery of the PSHE curriculum will understandably still remain class teacher led. However, increasingly this work will be supplemented by the role of the co-ordinator as expert practitioner in sensitive areas such as sexual relations and sexuality. Co-ordinators themselves may be supported by an LEA Advisory

Teacher or Health professional, especially if the school is involved in the Healthy School's Standard. The focus on a Health Awareness Week, for example, in the summer term will allow a range of experts to work together to support a class teacher and whole school approach.

Leadership and management in the secondary school

A traditional management structure

Management posts for PSHE within the secondary sector have typically been set at MPS +2 or 3. The post holder writes the scheme of work and operates as the main provider of lesson materials for tutors who deliver the programme with their own tutor group one period per week. Less frequently a specialist Key Stage 4 team is established in which the working relationship and the team is more dynamic, with responsibilities for planning and delivery of lessons shared. In a minority of schools a specialist team such as that developed at Sydenham School in Lewisham deliver the whole school programme at both key stages, as described in Chapter 4.

The traditional model has important weaknesses. These centre around the lack of clout held by the PSHE co-ordinator to effect change either within the PSHE curriculum and/or between the wider curriculum and PSHE. The isolated role of the PSHE co-ordinator has periodically been documented by HMI and Ofsted. It has also been evidenced in the work undertaken by the Centre for Cross-curricular Initiatives at its national conferences and through its school-based support work over the last eleven years. The PSHE post holder is often without adequate line management and support and therefore experiences powerlessness to effect curriculum and organisational change. She/he is often expected to deliver processes such as learning through group work, talk, presentations and pupil responsibilities for welcoming and receiving visitors, that are not typically embedded in practices of other curriculum teams. In addition to this, PSHE is often seen as the area that can be endlessly manoeuvred to meet other people's needs. On the one hand it is perceived as a subject where students can be removed from lessons to undertake other activities that are deemed more important; and on the other hand it is expected to be able to undertake the delivery of new initiatives in an otherwise inflexible curriculum. In short, PSHE is both valued and tolerated, expectations are both high and minimal.

Legitimate concerns to introduce assessment processes and procedures are thwarted in the name of time shortage and complexity of issues.

Often the curriculum delivery is highly dependent on worksheets or teacher led discussion, with some evidence of pair and small group work encouraged by more experienced practitioners. Tutors have varying degrees of confidence in delivering the programme that challenges those staff with less knowledge and skills to deal with sensitive issues around sexual relationships, drugs education, health matters, sexuality and abortion.

Even when training time is given through year meetings and staff training days, pressure of competing initiatives at the whole school level, can result in this support being sparse or appearing 'on the run'. The co-ordinator, even when highly skilled and committed, is considerably challenged to meet the requirements of the post. This is more than a case of human frailty; it raises serious structural issues in respect to:

- the position of the PSHE post holder within the school's leadership and management structure;
- the organisation of the PSHE and its links with citizenship education curriculum including the time allocated to it;
- the delivery of the PSHE curriculum.

Alternative models for the leadership and organisation of PSHE – possibilities in the secondary school

Setting the context

The requirement for all schools in England to commit themselves to ensuring that each student's personal and social development is enhanced within the school is a major challenge to all school leaders. This legislative requirement, if undertaken seriously, will require a review of the taught curriculum, alongside pedagogical practices and the relationship with extra curricular activities (out of hours learning) and student participation, including links with the neighbourhood community, as well as national and international ties.

This broadening agenda, welcomed by many within schools, requires leadership from the top, including strong support from the headteacher and active involvement of the Governing Body. It requires a school to focus on the issues of coherence, rigour and commitment in relation to both PSD and PSHE/citizenship. Such an agenda is intimately tied in with a school's values, its cultural experiences for both pupils and staff, and its aims translated into everyday practices. It is, however, fundamentally in delivery terms a systemic question that requires 'collective' school leadership and management valuing PSHE and supporting the link between the taught programme and a set of wider school priorities and initiatives that need to complement one another. For this to be best achieved PSHE/citizenship needs to have an explicit link with PSD commitments of the school through a member of the school leadership team having the lead responsibility for PSD and PSHE. This should be the case in both primary and secondary schools, as I have already indicated.

If this management structure is rejected on the grounds of cost, logistics, division of labour or historical problems, I believe there is a strong argument to support a PSHE co-ordinator on a significant management allowance being directly managed by a member of the school's leadership group, who themselves have a strategic lead responsibility for PSD initiatives across the school, which might include equal opportunities practice and monitoring systems for student achievement and reward. The PSHE co-ordinators require systems so that their work can be communicated and adequate liaison and support for those delivering the PSHE programme can be developed. The exact nature of these systems will depend on the organisation of the PSHE/citizenship curriculum.

Organisation of PSHE/citizenship – tutor led or specialist team?

In deciding which is the best mode of organisation for PSHE/citizenship, schools will inevitably take account of the following factors:

- The skills, confidence and capabilities of its teaching staff in respect of tutoring, guidance, subject knowledge and teaching and learning styles.
- Cultural traditions that give value to tutoring, and guidance through a Year Team or House System approach.

There is an increasingly strong argument that the challenge for PSHE is to develop a coherent framework that builds in progression in the form of a spiral curriculum in which students are taught to see the interrelationship between the personal (and the private) and the social and political. For example, a person's sexuality should be understood both as the most intimate and personal aspect of an individual's being, and as socially constructed in the way that the self is viewed by that individual and by the wider social grouping in which they exist. A full under-standing of what it means to be 'gay' has to deal therefore with both dimensions; exploring concepts of identity, self, society, power, status, as well as notions of normality, equality and discrimination. This work requires a whole school perspective and commitment. This should involve agreed policy development that is led by Governors and involve all the stakeholders of the school. It could be argued that all staff should be willing to engage with pupils on personal, social and political issues. If the school ethos is to be delivered through everyday social interaction and practice, institutional ownership has to be demonstrated. This appears to be a powerful argument for retaining the role of the tutor to deliver the PSHE programme. In this context teacher-tutors are supported with a training programme, and aided with advice and guidance from experienced practitioners.

When discussions take place over the pedagogy to be employed within PSHE/citizenship lessons, the argument goes that the teachers of PSHE cannot be expected to act as vanguard for teaching and learning styles such as group work, presentation debate, research and study skills, and using drama techniques. If these approaches are evidenced across the curriculum already then fine, otherwise PSHE doesn't have to be 'special'. What sets it apart is not its pedagogy, but the focus and context of its subject matter, which all teachers as adult learners can experience and share with their pupils. The argument continues that, if a secondary school has a strong tradition of tutor led PSHE work with good co-ordinators, opportunities for sustained training, and a willingness to incorporate elements of the citizenship curriculum, then it may well be advised to build on this, and not go for a radical change. However, such effective practice is rare in my experience and in the experience of those who have contributed to this publication.

I believe there are compelling arguments to move to establishing a specialist team for PSHE/citizenship either in Key Stage 3 and 4 or a transition piloted model for one Key Stage with a review and then the introduction of a second Key Stage. The argument in favour of developing a specialist team is based on two assertions. The first involves the specialist knowledge and understanding now required to deliver the PSHE/citizenship curriculum; the second involves the central place given to academic tutoring within the broader tutoring role. It is unrealistic and counter-productive to expect teachers who are under pressure in their own preferred discipline to deliver high quality PSHE lessons.

The development of academic tutoring in secondary schools has increased considerably over the last five years with the further extension of statistical analysis of pupil performance at GCSE/GNVQ and Key Stage 3 SATs, in part supported by the DFES Autumn Package. This has been linked to the introduction of Academic Review Days and the use of target setting by individual students, either to set process or attainment targets in conjunction with their tutor or a school mentor, often in a meeting attended by the parent/carer. Ofsted (2001) has commented upon this development in the Chief Inspectors' Annual Report and in the Improving Inner City Schools Report 2000 which identifies 'the setting and review of academic targets communicated to all staff and parents' as a key feature of the curriculum in successful inner city schools.

The training and support of teachers to develop interviewing and questioning skills, as well as the time allocated through tutor time, can assist these significant developments in tracking student performance, including liaison with subject targets and attainment on a regular basis, using ICT systems. These important developments have in my experience only recently become firmly established in secondary schools, and still for many schools practices are embryonic or tentative. Tutoring then, in extending academic support and guidance still needs to ensure that opportunities are provided for students to reflect upon their general well-being and the issues which face them in adolescence. Effective tutoring will therefore make a significant contribution towards students' personal and social development but it cannot be left to the tutor to deliver the taught PSHE programme, as well as providing all the above.

A school which prides itself in supporting students' personal and social development, as a reflection of its stated ethos, will already be requiring its tutors to be skilled negotiators, listeners and problem solvers, working with young people who have the confidence in the tutor to share possibly intimate concerns and to help guide them to other professionals when the need arises. There need be no contradiction in the complementary work carried out by a class tutor and the work led by a PSHE teacher on supporting the needs of young people within a school. The communication systems between the class tutor and the teacher of PSHE, however, need to be clear and explicit. In part they are no different from those required between the tutor and the teacher of mathematics. However, the nature of the work within PSHE/citizenship with its direct requirement to gain pupils' understanding and emotional responses on a range of personal and sensitive issues does add an additional dimension for the need to ensure regular feedback sessions between tutor and PSHE teacher. This is best achieved as a timetabled slot, alternatively as part of a Year Team meeting, or as a scheduled after-school meeting. An informal arrangement in non-contact time is unlikely to succeed over the longer term.

Schools in general need to develop skilled tutors in most secondary schools. Trying to develop skilled tutors and expert teachers of PSHE-citizenship as well as asking the same people to extend themselves in their own discipline areas is perhaps a step too far.

A specialist team approach for the delivery of PSHE-citizenship

The arguments in favour of a specialist team include:

- Qualified and trained staff to deliver a coherent approach across all classes, through a regular planning and review, commensurate with the work of other curriculum teams within the school.
- Improved communication processes supported by the school's meeting cycle.
- Clearer line management responsibility.
- Improved levels of commitment towards agreed learning styles and classroom management approaches.

The establishment of a PSHE/citizenship team will not necessarily be straightforward. School budget constraints may prevent the appointment of new staff including Newly Qualified Teachers who are now being trained in specialist PGCE courses. It may require the identification of colleagues who might be interested in transferring their teaching or at least a sizeable part of their week to the PSHE activities programme. Senior colleagues may need to make a strategic decision to introduce a specialist team over a two or three year phased programme with either Key Stage 3 or Key Stage 4 being introduced as a pilot, with a built-in review process before any second stage commences. The advantage of spreading the timescale for specific years to be taught by specialists is that it allows time to review the existing PSHE programme, and to strengthen the teaching and learning procedures as you develop the team.

Conversely, the danger of a single move from a tutor based delivery approach towards a specialist team is the level of expectations it can generate. There is a further danger that the PSHE/citizenship curriculum is too identified with the specialist team and that other staff may feel that they have very little investment in understanding what happens in PSHE/citizenship. The solution to this very real danger lies in the links between PSHE/citizenship and the subjects of the National Curriculum being made explicit, albeit in a manageable and visible form. The links between the tutor and the teacher of PSHE/citizenship must be formalised. The whole school approach to personal and social development must be a living reality with visible and real co-ordination and links that need to be publicly communicated, and celebrated.

Curriculum organisation and time

The organisation of the PSHE/citizenship curriculum can take place in a number of ways:

- A weekly or fortnightly slot.
- A programme that is tied to another area of the curriculum and operated on a termly or half-yearly programme, with an enhanced time allocation in the taught period. For example, a two period time slot in which PSHE/citizenship is backed against RE or ICT with half a year group with transfer in December or February.
- A weekly or fortnightly slot which is supplemented by a collapsed timetable day for each group on a rotational basis.

Teaching PSHE/citizenship through the subjects of the National Curriculum

Elements of the PSHE/citizenship curriculum can and should be promoted through other subjects. A degree of co-ordination is, however, required which allows both subject teachers to be able to say, 'I know you have covered this in your PSHE/citizenship lessons', and, conversely, PSHE teachers must be able to acknowledge linked work undertaken in subjects. There are huge possibilities, and experience suggests that manageable links with quality input best serve pupils.

These approaches at Key Stage 3 are challenging but possible. In Key Stage 4 PSHE/citizenship is an entitlement in the curriculum, and because not all students will undertake the subjects outlined above, schools will need to adopt clear systems and procedures to ensure that this entitlement is delivered in as a coherent a way as possible.

Effective leadership in the promotion of PSD, PSHE/citizenship

I have argued that effective leadership for PSHE/citizenship needs to involve good leadership and management and I have set out a series of qualities that the PSHE Co-ordinator will need to demonstrate in examining her/his role within a primary school. These same qualities will be required in the secondary school. However, I believe that senior leaders will at best need to understand a further set of leadership aspects. Effective school leadership can be analysed following Fullan into five key change themes (Fullan 2001). These are:

- Moral purpose.
- Understanding change.
- Developing relationships.
- Knowledge building.
- Coherence making.

These are independent but mutually reinforcing for positive change in schools and other institutions.

I. Leaders with a moral purpose

Moral purpose is concerned with acting with the intention of making a positive difference. In the case of schools this means a difference to the lives of pupils, staff, parents and other stakeholders where possible. It assumes the need for the school leaders to reflect a style of leadership that promotes certain values and beliefs within the organisation. A school leadership which seeks to promote its students' personal and social development will need to demonstrate characteristics involving democratic processes in consultation, decision making and active participation of its stakeholders in the life of the school.

If a school is seriously committed to PSD and PSHE/citizenship then this will be reflected in those at the heart of school leadership. The key postholder in the leadership team responsible for PSD will be supported by a collective responsibility explicitly guided by a shared moral purpose.

2. Leadership that understands change

The second element involves school leadership understanding the complexity of the change process. Implementing change within the taught and wider personal and social development curriculum requires, as I have argued, a whole school approach in which all staff can recognise and contribute to a series of learning experiences for their pupils and themselves that promote personal and social knowledge, skills understanding, dispositions and qualities outlined in the various chapters of this book. It will require an understanding from leadership that there will be resistance from both staff and pupils and that 'opposition' will need to be given a voice to enable concerns and anxieties to be explored and overcome.

In the case of the PSHE/citizenship curriculum, there will be legitimate concerns over:

- How do we fit it all in, even with increased time?
- How do we overcome pupil apathy or resistance to specific aspects of the programme?
- In the case of the specialist delivery PSHE/citizenship team, how are we going to set up systems to ensure that there is a manageable and meaningful relationship between the class tutor and the specialist teacher?
- What systems do we need in place to monitor pupils' involvement in the wider life of the school (extra curricular, out of hours learning). Who is going to do this?
- How are we going to manage the implementation dip for our new courses if it occurs?

3. Leadership that builds relationships

Fullan gives considerable emphasis to the importance of his third key change theme, that of building relationships. Leaders of PSD in the school, including the PSHE/citizenship Co-ordinator, have to be able to build relationships with a wide range of others and be given the time to do so. Our effective PSD/PSHE leader has constantly to build purposeful interaction and problem solve and to be aware that easy consensus is false and undesirable.

4. Leadership that develops new knowledge

Our PSD/PSHE leader, with others in the school leadership organisation, will need to understand the importance of building new knowledge, both inside and outside the institution. This will involve various types of data collection – including quantitative and qualitative, through a process of self-review with others. They will need to understand the difficulty of collecting and interpreting this new knowledge, especially in an area as complex and sensitive as personal and social development. This requires information to be turned into socially useful knowledge. For example:

- How are we going to assess the impact of the peer mentoring scheme?
- How has our work on emotional literacy in Key Stage 3 progressed?
- How can we evaluate the work of the school council?
- What impact has PSHE had on the school anti-bullying work?

Our school leader for PSD/PSHE will need to demonstrate a mature and varied set of interpersonal skills, and have the ability to foster these in other key players if relationship building is to progress, with the purpose of underpinning the school's approach to PSD.

5.   Leadership that develops coherence

Our school leader also has to demonstrate the ability to frame coherence in our approach towards PSD and PSHE/citizenship, especially in the complexities of the relationship between the taught and the wider curriculum experiences of pupils. She or he will also need to manage the tension between the creative juices that change and innovation brings, and a lack of equilibrium which can occur if others cannot see the big picture.

- How will we keep people informed about the various elements that generate the pursuit of an enhanced PSD?
- How will these elements be expressed in our School Development Plan?
- What other forms of communication will need to be utilised to keep staff and pupils abreast of change?
- How will we use staff meetings and training days?
- How will we use our website and/or school newsletter?
- What about the role of assemblies?
- How are we going to keep parents and governors and community agencies informed and able to participate in the various elements of our PSD work?

In addition to our PSD Leader having the required knowledge, skills and personal qualities to manage this process of change, she or he will also have personal characteristics centring on 'energy, enthusiasm and hopefulness' (Fullan 2001).

These characteristics are clearly not the exclusive preserve of leaders of PSD, PSHE/citizenship, but they are essential qualities for a leader to demonstrate to young people and colleagues alike, the school's commitment to personal and social development, and to an effective integrated PSHE/citizenship curriculum.

References

DfEE/QCA (1998) *Education for Citizenship and the Teaching of Democracy in Schools*, London: DfEE.

Fullan, M. (2001) *Leading in a Culture of Change*, USA: Jossey-Bass.

Ofsted (2001) *Improving Inner City Schools*, London: Ofsted.

Chapter 13

Looking to the future

Miles Tandy, Martin Buck and Sally Inman

Those who work in education do well to think about the future: investing in the future is in large part what the whole business is about. The institutions in which we educate young people – the buildings and general environment, the deployment of teaching and non-teaching staff, the curriculum, activities outside the taught curriculum – all speak volumes about the aspirations we have for the young people who attend schools day by day.

In her recent speech to the BETT conference,[1] Secretary of State for Education and Skills Estelle Morris began with a computer-generated video showing 'the school and classroom of the future'. The video opens with gently soothing computer-generated music and a reassuring voice that tells we are about to see:

> ICT transforming the way we learn . . .
>
> . . . a fusion of teaching, learning and technology.

Education, we are told, is 'a constantly evolving process'. The viewer is led up to the door of a building much like those we see on any high-tech business park; steel, glass and yellow brick. Admission is by swipe card, presumably able to record who has come in and when – no need for old-fashioned registration here. Inside the building we are greeted by an adult figure, perhaps a teacher, looking like Lara Croft[2] might if she worked in a library.

The overall impression is one of light and space. There are open steel stairways, high-level galleries and plenty of healthy-looking pot plants. There certainly seems a very different 'pupil to space' ratio from those applied in some recent school building. The voice-over tells us this is 'an open layout for open minds'. It is a place 'where light and space combine to produce an atmosphere where teachers can reflect and plan and students can learn and enjoy leisure time'. There is an open courtyard with a semi-circular arrangement of benches under shady trees. At least they will be shady when they are in leaf – this is a school for all seasons. Some computer-generated students sit quietly on the seats, others walk steadily across the space. No one runs, shouts or fights.

Then we get to the classroom of the future, entering through grand double doors to another airy space in which students sit singly and in small groups in front of computer screens. There are few straight lines – windows, furniture, low-level shelving all follow gentle, elegant curves. 'The intelligent design', we are told, 'uses space to accommodate different class sizes and learning methods.' Technology is everywhere; 'from plasma screens to lap-tops and palm-tops, headsets and electronic links to facilitate self-directed learning'. The technology offers 'children of all abilities to learn at their own pace alongside one another, studying individually or in groups'. Teachers 'can offer leadership to pupils with the support of a classroom assistant'. It is a 'fully inclusive space, accessible to all with ramps and low-level desk tops for wheelchair users'.

There is something ghostly about the figures that populate this space. They are all more or less the same; fair-haired and in navy-blue uniform. One group of five students sits with their teacher around what looks like an interactive whiteboard. The teacher's ghostly appearance is emphasised by the way in which you can see through her to the screen when she stands in front of it. This 'unique environment' is one which 'brings the world into the classroom where students and teachers can engage with other cultures, share common experience, and exchange ideas and where we can prepare our children to fully participate [sic] in the world of tomorrow by enabling them to utilise information and communication technology'.

The final shot is of a printer which silently delivers the message that 'The future is here, ICT is already transforming our classrooms'. And the last slide proclaims that:

> . . . this opportunity is heralding a new era for education.

It is a grand vision of progress. Things, go the words of the song, can only get better.

There is much to commend the ambition. That young people should attend schools that are well designed, well resourced and generously staffed is laudable. In her subsequent speech, the minister acknowledged that no such school yet exists. She does, however, suggest that ICT has the potential to bring about the radical transformation of education in the same way the discovery of DNA revolutionised medicine or the invention of the internal combustion engine changed transport forever. She argues that:

> I think ICT is our DNA – it's our internal combustion engine. It is the trigger that can bring about a revolution in how we teach and how pupils learn, and that's why it's not just one more change – it's not just one more thing, it's not just one more Government announcement – it's not one more thing that fades out with time when teachers think that something better has come on the market. It's actually the thing that can change, and change for ever, how we teach children and how teachers do their job.

Technology, she suggests, will at last enable teachers to fulfil a long-held ambition:

> If we use ICT right it potentially ends the debate that every teacher has always, always wanted to teach children as individuals and not groups, but never had the tools to do the job. It empowers and enables us for the first time, the first generation of educationalists to be able to teach pupils as individuals at their own pace.

This ambition, just like the video, is predicated on the assumption that the core purpose of education is to impart knowledge skills to young people. Little mention is made of how students will relate to each other, what will be done for those who don't buy in to the vision, those who keep losing their swipe cards. Perhaps they do PSHE in the afternoon? And yet the minister, a former teacher herself, acknowledges that there is something vital that teachers will bring to such an institution:

> I think it's really important to say that, when we have this debate, we always start the debate by saying that nothing, nothing, nothing will ever, ever, ever replace the skills of teachers. It's not about not having teachers, or turning our back on their traditional skills, and that connection, that personal connection, between teacher and taught, the traditional teacher skills of coaxing, target-setting,

cajoling, encouraging, enthusing, comforting, celebrating, being joyous with, talking to parents, being a shoulder to cry on, all that carries on, and the real challenge we have as educationalists and as politicians, is how we mix, how we bring together those traditional skills of the teacher with the skills of other people who can work in schools.

In short, however grand the architecture and technology of 'the school of the future', it will have to open its doors to young human beings. They will continue to come from an extraordinary diversity of backgrounds, each with her own preoccupations, her own anxieties, her own experiences of how others behave towards her. What might happen when those worlds collide?

A dominant theme throughout this book has been the extent to which the voice of the student has impact not only on provision for PSHE and Citizenship, but also on a wide range of issues affecting students and their school. Earlier chapters have made reference to Article 12 of the UN Convention on the Rights of the Child which states that:

> 'The child who is capable of forming his or her own views (has) the right to express those views freely in all matters affecting the child.'

This statement raises some serious challenges. It must be the sincere ambition of anyone concerned with provision for PSHE, or indeed any aspect of education, that it will affect children profoundly. Why else do we bother? Yet making that right a reality in the daily lives of children may require some fundamental shifts in the thinking of teachers, school management teams, local and national policy makers. The current reality is that we are insistent – at times quite aggressively[3] – that children attend school every day. What they experience through that attendance, particularly the curriculum which informs their day-to-day experiences in the classroom, has been taken further and further from the control of individual schools. The structure and content of the National Curriculum was determined elsewhere: no one asked the students what they thought. More recently, national strategies have gone further than ever before in determining the daily detail of the curriculum. Only recently has the school inspection procedure been modified to take account formally of students' views – but only older students are thought capable of engaging in the process. The earlier chapter on the work of school councils, for instance, showed just how readily and seriously younger children will engage in the processes of a democratic school. But that chapter also highlighted the need for students' voices to make a genuine difference: they will be very quick to see through structures which *appear* to consult and take account of their views but which, in reality, give them little or no influence over the decisions that they regard as important. It is essential to recognise and understand these tensions: they are highly significant in determining the context within which any attempt to enhance PSHE operates. But in recognising them, understanding them, and remaining critical of the national contexts which contribute to them, we should not lose sight of the extent to which individual schools can and have developed structures and strategies that give their students a genuine voice. Enhancing PSHE, we suggest, should start from a consideration of the extent to which the student voice can and does have an impact.

A recurrent theme in many of the preceding chapters has been the extent to which the success of particular initiatives has been determined by the particular contexts in which they have taken place: all have needed to take full account of the 'big picture' of the school. We have argued that PSHE and Citizenship cannot simply be treated as 'extra subjects', given their tiny slice of the available teaching time, and left to an individual or small department to develop and teach 'schemes of work'. Practice in PSHE and Citizenship must be informed by, and will in turn inform, the much broader context of the institution in which young people live such a significant part of their lives. The members of staff who lead developments in PSHE can and should have a pivotal influence. And because we are dealing with matters which have a profound effect on young people and their development, matters of import which touch on the central purposes of education, we should expect them to be contested, at times very hotly. To represent the development of a curriculum for PSHE as straightforward and unproblematic is to run the risk of ignoring some of this contention, yet such contention is necessary and will be ultimately very productive in developing a school which reflects the views, aspirations and values of teachers, learners and the wider community.

The UN Charter specifies that it is 'the child who is capable of forming his or her own views' who has the right to express them. This too raises some difficult questions. How does one determine that a child has this capability? What responsibility do we have for developing such capability? Any parent will know only too well just how soon such capacity develops: how many have spent sleepless nights with a very young child who seems to have formed the very strong view that it is time to be fed? The capacity to form and express views is not a fixed point in a child's development, rather part of a process of personal, social and emotional growth. Enabling and encouraging such growth is a core purpose of PSHE. Enabling children to develop the capacity to form and express their own views demands serious consideration not just of the PSHE curriculum, but of the approaches that are taken to teaching and learning across the whole curriculum. About what matters will they be asked? Why should they care? The example with which we began Chapter 1 indicates that it may not be a simple matter of discussing issues that have a direct influence on children's lives, important though that remains. In that example, children were led to a deep understanding of some of the issues that surround archaeology so enabling them to form and express their own views. The content had to matter, to have a question of human significance at its very heart. Chapter 11 refers to the work of Parker *et al.* in developing a series of questions that provide a possible framework for thinking about citizenship issues from a local to a global level. Some of our own earlier work (Inman *et al.* 1998) takes a similar approach in placing questions of personal and social significance at the centre of the curriculum planning process. If children are to develop this vital capacity to form, express and contest views, they need a broad curriculum which is planned deliberately so that matters of personal and social significance arise regularly. In addition, teachers and learners must collaborate to develop a pedagogy that encourages and values the expression and discussion of individuals' views.

Thoughtful and deliberate planning across the whole curriculum, coupled with pedagogical approaches of the types described and exemplified throughout this book will do much, not just to enhance a school's provision for PSHE, but to develop a school culture where students' personal and social development is recognised as a central purpose. But such provision alone is not enough. We have argued throughout that there are elements of PSHE which require separate planned provision. The example in Chapter 2 illustrates how some elements of PSHE need separate provision. Though these elements may require careful liaison with other departments (for example the science department), they deal with matters that need dedicated time and space in the curriculum. Our central contention is that a discrete PSHE curriculum is necessary, but that it cannot be successful if whole school and whole curriculum matters are not also addressed.

As we have shown, some of this discrete provision may also benefit from the use of outside agencies and other providers. Whether the additional provision is a specific intervention to enable conflict resolution, or outside expertise brought in to develop drama in a primary school, issues of how these 'extras' relate to whole school provision and approach remain. It is vital that the outside providers establish a dialogue with resident staff at an early stage and that this dialogue is sustained throughout the project. Resident staff need to be clear about the purposes of the particular intervention: how it relates to whole school provision in general; how it relates to their plans for a particular group. It is conspicuous that some of the less successful work outlined in Chapter 8 occurred at a time when the class concerned was without a regular teacher, making it very difficult to establish a sustained dialogue between the school and the outside provider. In contrast, the most successful work involved a clear and purposeful collaboration between the class teacher, the headteacher and the outside provider – collaboration that led in turn to a clear vision and purpose that could be articulated and developed with the learners.

As we have already suggested, considerations about the personal and social development of young people and the subsequent planning of a PSHE and Citizenship curriculum are likely to lead to more fundamental questions about the curriculum as a whole. If, in exploring these issues in your own school, you raise concerns about the current structure and balance of the curriculum, it is worth knowing that you are not alone. *All Our Futures*, the report of the National Advisory Committee on Creative and Cultural Education (DfEE/DCMS 1999) recommended a radical overhaul of the scope and balance of the curriculum. Education at the beginning of the twenty-first century, it argues, faces a number of unprecedented challenges. The challenges are economic, technological, social and personal. Meeting these challenges, the report goes on to argue, requires fundamental rethinking and redefinition of the scope and purpose of education. While some of its more radical recommendations were not included in the review of the National Curriculum which led to *Curriculum 2000*, the idea that developing young people's creativity should be a central purpose of education has taken some hold.[4] Yet the report defines creativity as:

> Imaginative activity fashioned so as to produce outcomes that are both original and of value.
>
> (DfEE/DCMS 1999: 29)

The definition begs an important question: if we actively develop young people's creativity so that they produce a variety of outcomes, how will they know which are 'of value' and which are not? The challenges which the report outlines, and the recommendations for facing them, are *interrelated*. To imagine that we can take one aspect – creativity – and develop it independently of the report's other recommendations may be to miss the point. The four challenges outlined by the report, particularly when due account is taken of the 'social' and 'personal' challenges, demand just the kind of serious thought about a school's purpose and provision that we have been advocating. But the absence of the necessary vision in national policy-making need not preclude discussion and action at school level.

The Royal Society for the encouragement of Arts, Manufactures and Commerce (RSA) has also explored the kind of curriculum which is most likely to prepare young people for the nature and patterns of work they will experience in their adult lives. In *Redefining the Curriculum* (Bayliss *et al.* 2000) the authors propose a curriculum framework based on a number of 'competences'. The competences are in the areas of learning, managing information, managing, dealing with people and citizenship. This is clearly a very different way of seeking to define a curriculum from the subject centred model of the English National Curriculum. Not only is the model structured very differently, it is also important to recognise that the competences outlined are *interrelated*. The RSA model is not one which lends itself to immediate translation into a school management structure and student timetables: it is hard to imagine a school having a 'Head of Dealing with People' or students rushing to their next 'managing information' lesson. But that is not the intention. The authors suggest that the curriculum would continue to rely on 'traditional subject content' (Bayliss *et al.* 2000: 3), but this would be a 'medium through which individuals' competence portfolios would be developed'.

Ken Robinson (2001: 196–9) points out that any curriculum must serve two functions: epistemological and managerial. The epistemological function is to do with the organisation of knowledge. Robinson observes that the structure of the English National Curriculum was predicated on the misguided notion that there are ten subjects in the world. This epistemological breakthrough passed PSHE by and, as we have suggested, the later recognition that perhaps PSHE is a subject after all and that Citizenship is definitely one, albeit if only in the secondary phase, may not be helpful. The managerial function of a curriculum provides a structure which can form the basis for deployment of staff and resources. Once we have established that history and geography are different subjects, we know that they need different slots in the timetable, and probably different teachers in separate departments.

Robinson suggests that the managerial functions can often overtake the epistemological. We are left with a curriculum that is epistemologically outdated because it was designed to fit existing management structures, at least in secondary schools. Yet one of the commonest complaints that you will hear about the National Curriculum in primary schools is that it is *unmanageable* – a complaint that endures despite successive attempts to 'slim the curriculum down'.

Defining a curriculum is necessarily reductive. Condensing the sum of several years of daily school experience into a single volume can only be achieved by reducing it to what are seen to be its essential elements. From the original ten separate folders that appeared between 1989 and 1992, the National Curriculum has moved to its present form in which it can be collated into a single volume for Key Stages 1 and 2, and another for Key Stages 3 and 4. The principle is that the required skills, knowledge and understanding can be defined at a national level, and that schools can be left to design their own ways of implementing these. To do this they need to devise a 'scheme of work': detailed plans outlining how units of work will be developed to ensure continuity and progression through the separate subjects. Developing these schemes of work is hard going for individual teachers, especially if they happen to be one of only two or three teachers in a small primary school, each with a number of subjects to develop. Small wonder then, that when the Qualifications and Curriculum Authority developed model schemes of work, so many primary teachers welcomed them with open arms. Yet while they may have done something to alleviate teachers' heavy workload, these schemes have done little to tackle the problem of an overloaded primary curriculum. In addition, they have further embedded the notion of a subject-centred curriculum – history and geography must be different, they have different folders with separate units.

The QCA schemes of work, like the folders that accompany the National Strategies at Key Stages 1, 2 and 3, are predicated on the notion that knowledge, skills and understanding can be expressed as *objectives*. Clearly defined teaching objectives – in the QCA schemes they are referred to as learning objectives – are central to the process of defining and teaching a curriculum in which knowledge, skills and understanding build progressively one upon another. Most teachers are now very familiar with the idea that effective teaching starts with a clear definition of learning objectives, objectives which can be shared with learners at the start of the lesson and revisited at the end to check understanding. In 2002, most know that with an inspector in the room it would be unwise to do anything else. And there is much to commend this approach: it recognises the need for clarity of purpose in the classroom and acknowledges the need for the learner to be clear about what they are learning and how they are progressing. But to what extent is it appropriate for the kind of learning we have advocated and exemplified in PSHE?

Take a statement such as 'Pupils should be taught to recognise how their behaviour affects other people', from the Key Stage 1 non-statutory guidelines. It could be translated into the learner-friendly 'today we are going to learn . . .' form and off we go – a lesson in which children learn how their behaviour affects other people. And next week in PSHE & C, we'll be learning how to listen to other people. Devise enough of these lessons in a progressive order and lo, we have a scheme of work.

There are of course many such materials available from educational publishing houses. In one example of a 'Citizenship Resource File' (Watts *et al.* 2000), teachers of the Foundation Stage and Key Stage 1 are given a host of practical ideas for teaching Citizenship in their classrooms. There are clearly planned lessons with accompanying photocopiable resources for children. The attraction for busy teachers who feel uncertain about the inclusion of a new element in the curriculum is obvious.

One lesson plan (Watts *et al.* 2000: 54) in the section on 'Feeling and Relationships' deals with anger. It has a clear aim, a list of five learning outcomes, suggested resources, teaching and activities and suggestions for further work – all the right ingredients for good planning. The outlined lesson begins by listening to Stravinsky's *The Rite of Spring*, which is used to stimulate a discussion about feeling angry. The children then have the opportunity to compose their own 'angry music'. In the hands of a skilled and sensitive teacher such as the one in the 'West Ham' circle-time example in Chapter 6, these ideas could lead to some very valuable work in which children reflect deeply on the things that make them angry, the things that make others angry and the ways in which feeling angry might affect their own and others' behaviour. They may even begin to challenge the implied idea that anger is a 'bad' feeling. Are there not times when anger might lead to positive action? Anger, for example, about unfairness or injustice. Anger is a complex emotion, and a complex concept.

In materials such as these, there is a danger that concepts such as 'anger' or 'justice' will be treated in the abstract, singled out for discussion in a lesson or two. Page 55 deals with fear. Children are, of course, encouraged to relate their discussions to their own experience, but the question 'What makes you angry?' (Watts *et al.* 2000: 54) is still a tough one for a child of six. How quickly could *you* come up with answers?

One approach to dealing with the innate complexity of the ideas that lie at the heart of effective PSHE and Citizenship is to simplify them – think what 'justice' means in the simplest terms and define it. To this end the materials have a teacher's guide which includes a list of 'useful vocabulary'. It includes the following definitions:

Good   – morally sound, virtuous, honourable
Justice   – fairness, right or appropriate action, action according to the highest moral standards
Unjust   – not fair

(Watts *et al.* 2000: 78)

That anyone should imagine a teacher needing such a simple definition of justice is worrying enough; the idea that the concept of justice can be so reduced is even more alarming. Justice is an example of what Bernard Williams (1985) calls a 'thick concept'. Its vagueness in daily usage is not a weakness in our ability to define it, it is indicative of the extraordinary complexity of the concept. Joe Winston (1998) argues that if children are to begin to understand complex and 'thick' concepts such as justice, they need to encounter and explore them through forms that acknowledge their 'thickness' and complexity, particularly through stories:

. . . we may all agree that *courage* is a virtue; but what characterises it and how it will be expressed in different circumstances and contexts will vary according to individual perceptions shaped by personal, cultural and historical experience. Hence its *thickness* as a concept, its ability to embrace fact *and* value, and the role of stories in helping us to explore the depth and complexity of its thickness.

(Winston 1998: 23)

To take a 'thick' concept such as justice and reduce it to a definition of a few words is to render it all but meaningless. To do so in our classrooms would not only leave children with an inadequate grasp of the concept, their understanding of it would leave them helpless to know what to *do* and how to *act* in a given set of circumstances. Alisdair MacIntyre's observation is important here:

I can only answer the question 'What am I to do?' if I can answer the prior question 'Of what stories do I find myself a part?'

(MacIntyre 1981: 201)

The rights or wrongs of particular courses of action can only be understood within the thickness of the stories that gave rise to them. But it is not simply a matter of reading stories to children and discussing them, however valuable that might be.[5] Recognising the 'thickness' and complexity of the concepts that lie at the heart of effective PSHE and Citizenship should lead us towards a 'thickness' in both curriculum and pedagogy – a curriculum which acknowledges the essential 'messiness' of the ideas it explores with young people rather than simplifying them to a set of deceptively clear teaching objectives.

Certainly such an approach would place story at the heart of what we do; but beginning to develop such a curriculum and appropriate pedagogy will require a broad and embracing definition of the word story. When the social anthropologist Clifford Geertz boldly defines culture as 'the ensemble of stories we tell ourselves about ourselves' (Geertz 1975: 448), the definition should embrace all sorts of manifestations of the act of storytelling – from the television news to the soap opera to the night at the theatre. Indeed, just asking the question: 'What story does this tell us about ourselves?' can provoke insights into all sorts of areas of school life. Why do our students wear a uniform? Why do the children sit that way in assembly? All form part of our own particular ensemble of stories, and each tells us, and them, something of what we all value.

The example with which we opened Chapter 1 exhibits much of this 'thickness'. We have already alluded to its 'messiness' – the difficulty of specifying exactly where it fits in a subject based curriculum. Teachers and learners alike valued it as an experience of depth and richness for everyone involved. For all that, we can (and the teachers concerned did) identify clear teaching objectives. What mattered was that they didn't stop there – the development of children's ICT skills, their historical knowledge and understanding, their performance skills were all brought to bear on the *story* of the burial and discovery of Tutankhamun. It added what Margaret Donaldson has called 'human sense' (Donaldson 1978).

As we have already suggested, the issues at the heart of this book are much about pedagogy as they are about curriculum organisation – *what* we include in a PSHE and Citizenship curriculum is inextricably bound up with *how* we teach it. In Chapter 1, following on from the description of the work on Tutankhamun, we tried to draw up a list of *some* of the features which characterised the approach. But the list isn't the teaching: however hard we might try, and however useful we might feel such a list would be, it cannot be reduced to a few bullet points. Contributors from a diversity of school contexts have taken a range of curriculum content and teaching approaches, some of which may be directly applicable in your own school, some not. Each example though, offers an opportunity to reflect on the approach, to relate it to your own practice, and to inform your own discussion and debate. Whatever direction national policy may take, that discussion and debate – with students, with colleagues, with parents and the wider community – will continue to lead to the most effective action. Keep talking.

Notes

1. Estelle Morris, Secretary of State for Education, gave the opening address for the BETT conference on Wednesday 9 January 2002. At the time of writing the speech and video are available on the DfES website – www.dfes. gov.uk/speeches
2. Lara Croft is the central character from the 'Tomb Raider' series of computer games.
3. The recent case of the Banbury woman who was sent to prison for the non-attendance of her two children gave a harsh reminder of the legal position. See, for example, *The Guardian* 23 May 2002.
4. See the Qualifications and Curriculum Authority's work on developing creativity in the curriculum at http://www.qca.org.uk/onq/schools/creativity_curriculum.asp
5. We have written about the use of story, particularly in relation to value development in the Early Years, elsewhere (Tandy 1998).

References

Bayliss, V., Brown, J. and James, L. (2000) *Redefining the Curriculum*, London: The Royal Society for the encouragement of Arts, Manufactures & Commerce.

DfEE/DCMS (1999) *All Our Futures: Creativity, Culture and Education*. The Report of the National Advisory Committee on Creative and Cultural Education.

Donaldson, M. (1978) *Children's Minds*, London: Fontana.

Geertz, C. (1975) *The Interpretation of Cultures*, London: Hutchinson.

Inman, S., Buck, M. and Burke, H. (1998) *Assessing Personal and Social Development*, London: Falmer Press.

MacIntyre, A. (1981) *After Virtue: A Study in Moral Theory*, London: Duckworth.

Robinson, K. (2001) *Out of Our Minds: Learning to be Creative*, Oxford: Capstone.

Tandy, M. (1998) *Value Development in the Early Years: Approaches through Story*, in Inman, S., Buck, M. and Burke, H. (eds) *Asssessing Personal and Social Development*, London: Falmer Press.

Watts, D. (Project Editor) (2000) *Citizenship Resource Files Key Stage 1 and Early Years*, Leamington Spa: Language Centre Publications Limited.

Williams, B. (1985) *Ethics and the Limits of Philosophy*, London: Fontana/Collins.

Winston, J. (1998) *Drama, Narrative and Moral Education*, London: Falmer Press.

Index